Vue.js 2.x by Example

Example-driven guide to build web apps with Vue.js
for beginners

Mike Street

BIRMINGHAM - MUMBAI

Vue.js 2.x by Example

Copyright © 2017 Packt Publishing

First published: December 2017

Production reference: 1191217

Published by Packt Publishing Ltd.
Livery Place
35 Livery Street
Birmingham
B3 2PB, UK.

ISBN 978-1-78829-346-4

www.packtpub.com

Credits

Author
Mike Street

Reviewers
Bogdan Balc
Silva, Pablo Henrique P.

Commissioning Editor
Kunal Chaudhari

Acquisition Editor
Siddharth Mandal

Content Development Editor
Aditi Gour

Technical Editor
Sushmeeta Jena

Copy Editor
Safis Editing

Project Coordinator
Hardik Bhinde

Proofreader
Safis Editing

Indexer
Tejal Daruwale Soni

Graphics
Jason Monteiro

Production Coordinator
Aparna Bhagat

About the Author

Mike Street (aka mikestreety) is a frontend developer from Brighton, UK. Specializing in Gulp, SCSS, HTML, and Vue, he has been developing websites professionally since 2010. After making his first Vue app as an experimental side project, he's been hooked ever since. When not developing on the web, Mike likes to explore the Sussex countryside on his bike, start a new side-project without finishing the last, or heading to the cinema.

Acknowledgments

I would like to start by thanking my wife, Chilly, for everything she's had to put up with while I've been writing this book. From the tears after I forgot to press save, to the elation after I typed the last full stop. She has encouraged me to write on those days where I've wanted to walk away and had to tolerate those nights where I couldn't stop writing. Thank you.

I would also like to thank my family, friends, and the "Wilmy gang" for the support they showed during the whole book-writing process. Most of them didn't understand a single thing I was talking about when asking me about my progress. Despite this, they managed to feign enough enthusiasm to keep me motivated – even my Gran expressed interest.

I would like to thank the publishers for giving me the opportunity to write this book. Thank you for giving me this experience.

Lastly, I would like to thank my colleagues at Liquid Light for encouraging me to be the best frontend developer, productivity hipster, and writer I can be. Without any of these people, this book wouldn't be here.

For the Streets...

About the Reviewers

Bogdan Balc is a Team Lead with a passion for frontend technologies. He has worked with JavaScript for the past 10 years from the emergence of jQuery and Ajax to modern full-fledged MVC frameworks. When he is not fiddling with some new JavaScript challenge, he spends his time playing sports and games with friends, as well as watching sports and movies.

Nowadays, he channels most of his efforts into making we3interactive one of the most successful and creative startups in Cluj.

His passion with Vue.js pushed him to collaborate on two other awesome Vue.js books in the past: *Learning Vue.js* by Olga Filipova and *Vue.js 2 Cookbook* by Andrea Passaglia.

Silva, Pablo Henrique P. is a frontend developer, speaker, writer, and community leader focused on helping companies and individuals succeed with their frontend applications.

As a frontend developer, he has been using Vue.js since version 1.0 and kept continues to use it in several current projects. His current job as a Squad Leader at a Brazilian company gave him the opportunity to lead several developer teams and to see the benefits of Vue.js while creating products and services.

As a writer, he is curious, likes to solve problems and his style of writing follows the tl;dr; (too long; didn't read) style, meaning he tries to be as clear and goal-minded as possible. He uses this style because he believes developers (such as himself) should learn things quickly and not waste time reading some long articles that have only one or two paragraphs of true meaningful information.

Pablo Henrique frequently speaks about, and writes about frontend in general, but has given many presentations about Vue.js.

I would like to thank my entire family for supporting me while doing this job, especially my mother (Flávia Penha de Freitas Silva) and my father (Ézio Walter da Silva). I would like to thank my girlfriend too for having the patience and giving me insights while reviewing this book. Last but not least, I would like to thank Packt for this amazing opportunity.

www.PacktPub.com

For support files and downloads related to your book, please visit www.PacktPub.com. Did you know that Packt offers eBook versions of every book published, with PDF and ePub files available? You can upgrade to the eBook version at www.PacktPub.com and as a print book customer, you are entitled to a discount on the eBook copy. Get in touch with us at service@packtpub.com for more details.

At www.PacktPub.com, you can also read a collection of free technical articles, sign up for a range of free newsletters and receive exclusive discounts and offers on Packt books and eBooks.

https://www.packtpub.com/mapt

Get the most in-demand software skills with Mapt. Mapt gives you full access to all Packt books and video courses, as well as industry-leading tools to help you plan your personal development and advance your career.

Why subscribe?

- Fully searchable across every book published by Packt
- Copy and paste, print, and bookmark content
- On demand and accessible via a web browser

Customer Feedback

Thanks for purchasing this Packt book. At Packt, quality is at the heart of our editorial process. To help us improve, please leave us an honest review on this book's Amazon page at www.amazon.in/dp/1788293460.

If you'd like to join our team of regular reviewers, you can email us at customerreviews@packtpub.com. We award our regular reviewers with free eBooks and videos in exchange for their valuable feedback. Help us be relentless in improving our products!

Table of Contents

Preface

This book will cover the use of Vue.js 2. Vue can be used as both a frontend framework by including a JS file and also a backend framework with Node.js. The book was written using the frontend version of the framework—although it will be pointed out that it could easily be ported to using the node version if required, as the fundamentals of the framework remain the same in the two versions.

Vue is a framework that can be used for simple data display and creating full-blown web apps. This book will try and cover both ends of the spectrum while introducing plugins and add-ons to help with the creation of the bigger apps.

The use of Vue components will also be covered, including the benefits of using them over keeping all your data and methods contained within the main Vue instance. The book will also cover using the two most popular plugins for Vue: Vuex and Vue-Router. This book will not cover the process of styling the applications.

Vuex is a centralized state management pattern and library for Vue. It makes storing, manipulating, and accessing data a lot more manageable and is great for use with an app that requires a lot of data to be displayed. Vue-Router is used to handle navigation through the app, allowing different components to load depending on the URL.

Starting with a JSON dataset, the first part of the book will cover Vue objects and how to utilize each one. This will be covered by exploring different ways of displaying data from a JSON dataset. We will then move on to manipulating the data with filters and search and creating dynamic values.

Once complete, we will look at loading your data dynamically through an API—the example being the Dropbox API. Once the data is loaded, the book will walk through navigating through the folders while updating the URL and creating a download link for the files. We will then load in Vuex, and look at storing the data of each folder moving onto pre-caching the folders, making navigating through the app a lot quicker.

Lastly, we will look at creating an e-commerce frontend using the skills learned during previous projects while introducing new ones. Firstly, the products will be displayed in a list; using filters and search, you will be able to click on a product to find out more information and to add it to your basket. When ready, the "customer" will be able to view their basket and update items and quantities and finally check out.

What this book covers

Chapter 1, *Getting Started with Vue.js,* shows how to get started with Vue by including the JavaScript file. We then move onto initializing your first Vue instance and looking at the data object along with examining computed functions and properties and finally learning about Vue methods.

Chapter 2, *Displaying, Looping, Searching, and Filtering Data,* describes how to display lists and more complex data with Vue using `v-if`, `v-else` and `v-for`. It then looks at how to filter the lists using form elements, followed by applying conditional CSS classes based on the data.

Chapter 3, *Optimizing Our App and Using Components to Display Data,* is about optimizing our Vue.js code by reducing the repetition and logically organizing our code. Once complete, it looks at how to create Vue components and use them with Vue, how to use props and slots with components, and utilizing events to transfer data between components.

Chapter 4, *Getting a List of Files Using the Dropbox API,* presents loading and querying the Dropbox API and listing the directories and files from your Dropbox account. It then looks at adding a load state to your app along with using Vue animations.

Chapter 5, *Navigating through the File Tree and Loading Folders from the URL,* explains how to create a component for both files and folders, and add links to the folder component to update the directory listing. it also covers how to add a download button to the file component and create a breadcrumb component so the user can easily navigate back up the tree and dynamically update the browser URL, so if a folder is bookmarked or a link is shared, the correct folder loads.

Chapter 6, *Caching the Current Folder Structure Using Vuex,* shows how to get started with Vuex along with storing and retrieving data from the Vuex Store. It then looks at how to integrate Vuex with our Dropbox app, how to cache the current Dropbox folder's contents, and loading data from the store if required.

Chapter 7, *Pre-Caching Other Folders and Files for Faster Navigation,* describes the process fof pre-caching folders, storing the parent folder's contents, and how to cache the download links for the files.

Chapter 8, *Introducing Vue-Router and Loading URL-Based Components,* explores Vue-Router initialization and its options and how to create links with Vue-Router. It then looks at how to make dynamic routes to update the View based on the URL. From there, it describes how to use props with URLs, nest and name routes,and navigate programmatically.

Chapter 9, *Using Vue-Router Dynamic Routes to Load Data*, is about outlining our components and routes, loading a product CSV file and creating an individual product page with images and product variations.

Chapter 10, *Building an E-Commerce Store, Browsing Products,* describes how to create a homepage listing page with specific products, create a category page with a reusable component, create an ordering mechanism, create filters dynamically, and allow the user to filter the products.

Chapter 11, *Building an E-Commerce Store, Adding a Checkout,* is about building the functionality to allow the user to add and remove products to their basket, allow a user to check out and add an order confirmation page.

Chapter 12, *Using Vue Dev Tools and Testing Your SPA,* covers the usage of the Vue developer tools with the applications we've developed and has an overview of testing tools and applications.

What you need for this book

For this book, the reader will need the following:

- A text editor or IDE to write code. It can be as simple as Notepad or TextEdit, but one with syntax highlighting such as Sublime Text, Atom, or Visual Studio Code is recommended.
- A web browser.
- A Dropbox user account with files and folders.

Who this book is for

This book is for developers who are familiar with JavaScript but would like to explore the use of JavaScript MVVM frameworks for use with **Single Page Applications** (**SPA**s). They should be competent with HTML and familiar with CSS, so that they can to build and style the interfaces for the SPAs. This book takes the reader from initializing Vue and its basic functionality all the way to using advanced Vue plugins and techniques. The reader should be comfortable with JavaScript functions and variables and the use of ES6/ES2015 arrow functions.

Conventions

In this book, you will find a number of text styles that distinguish between different kinds of information. Here are some examples of these styles and an explanation of their meaning.

Code words in text, database table names, folder names, filenames, file extensions, pathnames, dummy URLs, user input, and Twitter handles are shown as follows: "Just assign the names of the layers you want to activate to the VK_INSTANCE_LAYERS environment variable."

A block of code is set as follows:

```
<div id="app">
  {{ calculateSalesTax(shirtPrice) }}
</div>
```

Any command-line input or output is written as follows:

```
app.salesTax = 20
```

New terms and **important words** are shown in bold. Words that you see on the screen, for example, in menus or dialog boxes, appear in the text like this: "Select **System info** from the **Administration** panel."

Warnings or important notes appear in a box like this.

Tips and tricks appear like this.

Reader feedback

Feedback from our readers is always welcome. Let us know what you think about this book-what you liked or disliked. Reader feedback is important for us as it helps us develop titles that you will really get the most out of.

To send us general feedback, simply e-mail feedback@packtpub.com, and mention the book's title on the subject of your message.

If there is a topic that you have expertise in and you are interested in either writing or contributing to a book, see our author guide at www.packtpub.com/authors.

Customer support

Now that you are the proud owner of a Packt book, we have a number of things to help you to get the most from your purchase.

Downloading the example code

You can download the example code files for this book from your account at http://www.packtpub.com. If you purchased this book elsewhere, you can visit http://www.packtpub.com/support and register to have the files e-mailed directly to you.

You can download the code files by following these steps:

1. Log in or register to our website using your e-mail address and password.
2. Hover the mouse pointer on the **SUPPORT** tab at the top.
3. Click on **Code Downloads & Errata**.
4. Enter the name of the book in the **Search** box.
5. Select the book for which you're looking to download the code files.
6. Choose from the drop-down menu where you purchased this book from.
7. Click on **Code Download**.

You can also download the code files by clicking on the **Code Files** button on the book's webpage at the Packt Publishing website. This page can be accessed by entering the book's name in the **Search** box. Please note that you need to be logged in to your Packt account.

Once the file is downloaded, please make sure that you unzip or extract the folder using the latest version of:

- WinRAR / 7-Zip for Windows
- Zipeg / iZip / UnRarX for Mac
- 7-Zip / PeaZip for Linux

The code bundle for the book is also hosted on GitHub at https://github.com/PacktPublishing/Vue.JS-2.5-by-Example. We also have other code bundles from our rich catalog of books and videos available at https://github.com/PacktPublishing/. Check them out!

Downloading the color images of this book

We also provide you with a PDF file that has color images of the screenshots/diagrams used in this book. The color images will help you better understand the changes in the output. You can download this file from `https://www.packtpub.com/sites/default/files/downloads/VueJS2.5+byExample_Color Images.pdf`.

Errata

Although we have taken every care to ensure the accuracy of our content, mistakes do happen. If you find a mistake in one of our books-maybe a mistake in the text or the code-we would be grateful if you could report this to us. By doing so, you can save other readers from frustration and help us improve subsequent versions of this book. If you find any errata, please report them by visiting `http://www.packtpub.com/submit-errata`, selecting your book, clicking on the **Errata Submission Form** link, and entering the details of your errata. Once your errata are verified, your submission will be accepted and the errata will be uploaded to our website or added to any list of existing errata under the Errata section of that title.

To view the previously submitted errata, go to `https://www.packtpub.com/books/content/support` and enter the name of the book in the search field. The required information will appear under the **Errata** section.

Piracy

Piracy of copyrighted material on the Internet is an ongoing problem across all media. At Packt, we take the protection of our copyright and licenses very seriously. If you come across any illegal copies of our works in any form on the Internet, please provide us with the location address or website name immediately so that we can pursue a remedy.

Please contact us at `copyright@packtpub.com` with a link to the suspected pirated material.

We appreciate your help in protecting our authors and our ability to bring you valuable content.

Questions

If you have a problem with any aspect of this book, you can contact us at `questions@packtpub.com`, and we will do our best to address the problem.

1
Getting Started with Vue.js

Vue (pronounced view) is a very powerful JavaScript library created for building interactive user interfaces. Despite having the ability to handle large single-page applications, Vue is also great for providing a framework for small, individual use cases. Its small file size means it can be integrated into existing ecosystems without adding too much bloat.

It was built to have a simple API, which makes it easier to get started in comparison with its rivals: React and Angular. Although it borrows some of the logic and methodologies from these libraries, it has identified a need for developers for a simpler library for building applications.

Unlike React or Angular, one of the benefits of Vue is the clean HTML output it produces. Other JavaScript libraries tend to leave the HTML scattered with extra attributes and classes in the code, whereas Vue removes these to produce clean, semantic output.

In the first part of this book, we are going to build an application that uses a JSON string to display data. We will then look at filtering and manipulating data, before moving on to building reusable components to reduce duplication in our code.

In this chapter, we will look at:

- How to get started with Vue by including the JavaScript file
- How to initialize your first Vue instance and look at the data object
- Examining computed functions and properties
- Learning about Vue methods

Creating the workspace

To use Vue, we first need to include the library in our HTML and initialize it. For the examples in the first section of this book, we are going to be building our application in a single HTML page. This means the JavaScript to initialize and control Vue will be placed at the bottom of our page. This will keep all our code contained, and means it will easily run on your computer. Open your favorite text editor and create a new HTML page. Use the following template as a starting point:

```html
<!DOCTYPE html>
<html>
  <head>
  <meta charset="utf-8">
  <title>Vue.js App</title>
  </head>
  <body>
  <div id="app">
    </div>
    <script src="https://unpkg.com/vue"></script>
    <script type="text/javascript">
      // JS Code here
    </script>
  </body>
</html>
```

The main HTML tags and structure should be familiar to you. Let's run over a few of the other aspects.

Application space

This is the container for your application and provides a canvas for Vue to work in. All the Vue code will be placed within this tag. The actual tag can be any HTML element - main, section, and so on. The ID of the element needs to be unique, but again, can be anything you wish. This allows you to have multiple Vue instances on one page or identify which Vue instance relates to which Vue code:

```html
<div id="app">
</div>
```

During the tutorials, this element with the ID will be referred to as the app space or view. It should be noted that all HTML and tags and code for your application should be placed within this container.

Although you can use most HTML tags for your application space, you cannot initialize Vue on the `<body>` or `<HTML>` tags - if you do so, Vue will throw a JavaScript error and will fail to initialize. You will have to use an element inside your body.

Vue library

For the examples in this book, we are going to be using a hosted version of Vue.js from a **CDN** (**Content Delivery Network**) unpkg. This ensures that we have the latest version of Vue in our application, and also means we do not need to create and host other JavaScript files. Unpkg is an independent site that hosts popular libraries. It enables you to quickly and easily add a JavaScript package to your HTML, without having to download and host the file yourself:

```
<script src="https://unpkg.com/vue"></script>
```

When deploying your code, it is a good practice to serve up your libraries from local files rather than relying on CDNs. This ensures that your implementation will work with the currently - saved version, should they release an update. It will also increase the speed of your application, as it will not need to request the file from another server.

The `script` block following the library include is where we are going to be writing all our JavaScript for our Vue application.

Initializing Vue and displaying the first message

Now that we have a template set up, we can initialize Vue and bind it to the HTML app space by using the following code:

```
const app = new Vue().$mount('#app');
```

This code creates a new instance of Vue and mounts it on the HTML element with the ID of `app`. If you save your file and open it up in a browser, you will notice nothing has happened. However, under the hood, this one line of code has linked the `div` with the `app` variable, which is an instance of a Vue application.

Vue itself has many objects and properties that we can now use to build our app. The first one you will encounter is the `el` property. Using an HTML ID, this property tells Vue which element it should bind to and where the app is going to be contained. This is the most common way of mounting your Vue instance and all Vue code should happen within this element:

```
const app = new Vue({
    el: '#app'
});
```

When the `el` property isn't specified in the instance, Vue initializes in an unmounted state—this allows any functions or methods you may have specified to run before mounting, to run and complete. You can then independently call the mounting function when ready. Behind the scenes, when using the `el` property, Vue is mounting the instance using a `$.mount` function. If you do want to wait, the `$mount` function can be called separately, for example:

```
const app = new Vue();

// When ready to mount app:
app.$mount('#app');
```

However, as we will not need to delay the execution of our mount timing throughout the book, we can use the `el` element with the Vue instance. Using the `el` property is also the most common way of mounting the Vue app.

Alongside the `el` value, Vue has a `data` object that contains any data we need to access the app or app space. Create a new data object within the Vue instance and assign a value to a property by doing the following:

```
const app = new Vue({
    el: '#app',

    data: {
        message: 'Hello!'
    }
});
```

Within the app space, we now have access to the `message` variable. To display data within the app, Vue uses the Mustache templating language to output data or variables. This is achieved by placing the variable name between double curly brackets `{{ variable }}`. Logic statements, such as `if` or `foreach`, get HTML attributes, which will be covered later in the chapter.

Within the app space, add the code to output the string:

```
<div id="app">
    {{ message }}
</div>
```

Save the file, open it up in your browser, and you should be presented with your
Hello! string.

 If you don't see any output, check the JavaScript console to see if there are
any errors. Ensure the remote JavaScript file is loading correctly, as some
browsers and operating systems require additional security steps before
allowing some remote files to be loaded when viewing pages locally on
your computer.

The data object can handle multiple keys and data types. Add some more values to the
data object and see what happens - make sure you add a comma after each value. Data
values are simple JavaScript and can handle basic math, too - try adding a new price key
and setting the value to 18 + 6 to see what happens. Alternatively, try adding a JavaScript
array and printing it out:

```
const app = new Vue({
    el: '#app',

    data: {
      message: 'Hello!',
      price: 18 + 6,
      details: ['one', 'two', 'three']
    }
});
```

In your app space, you can now output each of those values - {{ price }} and {{
details }} now output data - although the list may not be quite what you had expected.
We'll cover using and displaying lists in Chapter 2, *Displaying, Looping, Searching, and
Filtering Data*.

All the data in Vue is reactive and can be updated by either the user or the application. This
can be tested by opening up the browser's JavaScript console and updating the content
yourself. Try typing app.message = 'Goodbye!'; and pressing *Enter* - your app's
content will update. This is because you are referencing the property directly - the first app
refers to the const app variable that your app is initialized to in your JavaScript. The
period denotes a property within there, and the message refers to the data key. You could
also update app.details or price to anything you want!

Computed values

The `data` object in Vue is great for storing and retrieving data directly, however, there may be times where you want to manipulate the data before outputting it in your applications. We can do that using the `computed` object in Vue. Using this technique, we are able to start adhering to the **MVVM** (**Model-View-ViewModel**) methodology.

MVVM is a software architectural pattern where you separate out various parts of your application into distinct sections. The **Model** (or data) is your raw data input - be it from an API, database, or hardcoded data values. In the context of Vue, this is typically the `data` object we used earlier.

The **view** is the frontend of your application. This should just be used for outputting the data from the Model, and should not contain any logic or data manipulation, with the exception of some unavoidable `if` statements. For the Vue applications, this is all the code placed within the `<div id="app"></div>` tags.

The **ViewModel** is the bridge between the two. It allows you to manipulate the data from the Model before it is output by the view. Examples of this could range from changing a string to uppercase or prefixing a currency symbol, up to filtering out discounted products from a list or calculating the total value of a field across an array. In Vue, this is where the `computed` object comes in.

The computed object can have as many properties as required - however, they must be functions. These functions can utilize data already on the Vue instance and return a value, be it a string, number, or array that can then be used in the view.

The first step is to create a computed object within our Vue application. In this example, we are going to use a computed value to convert our string to lowercase, so set the value of `message` back to a string:

```
const app = new Vue({
    el: '#app',

  data: {
     message: 'Hello Vue!'
  },
    computed: {
  }
});
```

Don't forget to add a comma (,) after the closing curly bracket (}) of your data object so Vue knows to expect a new object.

The next step is to create a function inside the computed object. One of the hardest parts of development is naming things - make sure the name of your function is descriptive. As our application is quite small and our manipulation basic, we'll name it messageToLower:

```
const app = new Vue({
  el: '#app',
  data: {
    message: 'HelLO Vue!'
  },
  computed: {
    messageToLower() {
      return 'hello vue!';
    }
  }
});
```

In the preceding example, I've set it to return a hardcoded string, which is a lowercased version of the contents of the message variable. Computed functions can be used exactly as you would use a data key in the view. Update the view to output {{ messageToLower }} instead of {{ message }} and view the result in your browser.

There are a few issues with this code, however. Firstly, if the value of messageToLower was being hardcoded, we could have just added it to another data property. Secondly, if the value of message changes, the lowercase version will now be incorrect.

Within the Vue instance, we are able to access both data values and computed values using the this variable - we'll update the function to use the existing message value:

```
computed: {
  messageToLower() {
    return this.message.toLowerCase();
  }
}
```

The messageToLower function now references the existing message variable and, using a native JavaScript function, converts the string to lower case. Try updating the message variable in your application, or in the JavaScript console, to see it update.

Computed functions are not just limited to basic functionality - remember, they are designed to remove all logic and manipulations from the view. A more complex example might be the following:

```
const app = new Vue({
    el: '#app',
        data: {
        price: 25,
        currency: '$',
        salesTax: 16
    },
    computed: {
        cost() {
// Work out the price of the item including
        salesTax
            let itemCost = parseFloat(
                Math.round((this.salesTax / 100) *
                this.price) + this.price).toFixed(2);
            // Add text before displaying the currency and
            amount
            let output = 'This item costs ' +
            this.currency + itemCost;
            // Append to the output variable the price
                without salesTax
            output += ' (' + this.currency + this.price +
    ' excluding salesTax)';
            // Return the output value
                return output;
        }
    }
});
```

Although this might seem advanced at first glance, the code is taking a fixed price and calculating what it would be with sales tax added. The `price`, `salesTax`, and `currency` symbol are all stored as values on the data object and accessed within the `cost()` computed function. The view outputs `{{ cost }}`, which produces the following:

This item costs $29.00 ($25 excluding sales tax)

Computed functions will recalculate and update if any data is updated, by either the user or the application itself. This allows for our function to dynamically update based on the `price` and `salesTax` values. Try one of the following commands in the console in your browser:

```
app.salesTax = 20

app.price = 99.99
```

The paragraph and prices will update instantly. This is because computed functions are reactive to the `data` object and the rest of the application.

Methods and reusable functions

Within your Vue application, you may wish to calculate or manipulate data in a consistent or repetitive way or run tasks that require no output to your view.For example, if you wanted to calculate the sales tax on every price or retrieve some data from an API before assigning it to some variables.

Rather than creating computed functions for each time, we need to do this, Vue allows you to create functions or methods. These get declared in your application and can be accessed from anywhere - similar to the `data` or `computed` functions.

Add a method object to your Vue application and note the updates to the data object:

```
const app = new Vue({
  el: '#app',
  data: {
    shirtPrice: 25,
    hatPrice: 10,
    currency: '$',
    salesTax: 16
  },
  methods: {
  }
});
```

Within the `data` object, the `price` key has been replaced with two prices - `shirtPrice` and `hatPrice`. We'll create a method to calculate the sales tax for each of these prices.

Similar to creating a function for the computed object, create a method function title called `calculateSalesTax`. This function needs to accept a single parameter, which will be the `price`. Inside, we will use the code from the previous example to calculate the sales tax. Remember to replace `this.price` with just the parameter name: `price`, as shown here:

```
methods: {
    calculateSalesTax(price) {
      // Work out the price of the item including
      sales tax
      return parseFloat(
      Math.round((this.salesTax / 100) * price)
    + price).toFixed(2);
    }
}
```

Pressing save will not do anything to our application - we need to call the function. In your view, update the output to use the function and pass in the `shirtPrice` variable:

```
<div id="app">
   {{ calculateSalesTax(shirtPrice) }}
</div>
```

Save your documents and check the result in the browser - is it what you expected? The next task is to prepend the currency. We can do that by adding a second method that returns the parameter passed into the function with the currency at the beginning of the number:

```
methods: {
    calculateSalesTax(price) {
      // Work out the price of the item including
      sales tax
      return parseFloat(
        Math.round((this.salesTax / 100) * price) +
        price).toFixed(2);
    },
    addCurrency(price) {
      return this.currency + price;
    }
}
```

In our view, we then update our output to utilize both methods. Rather than assigning to a variable, we can pass the first function, `calculateSalesTax`, as the parameter for the second `addCurrency` function. This works because of the first method, `calculateSalesTax`, accepts the `shirtPrice` parameter and returns the new amount. Instead of saving this as a variable and passing the variable into the `addCurrency` method, we pass the result directly into this function, which is the calculated amount:

```
{{ addCurrency(calculateSalesTax(shirtPrice)) }}
```

However, it would start to get tiresome having to write these two functions every time we needed to output the price. From here, we have two options:

- We can create a third method, titled `cost()` - which accepts the price parameter and passes the input through the two functions
- Create a computed function, such as `shirtCost`, which uses `this.shirtPrice` instead of having a parameter passed in

We could, alternatively, create a method titled `shirtCost` that does the same as our computed function; however, it's better to practice to use computed in this case.

This is because `computed` functions are cached, whereas `method` functions are not. If you imagine our methods being a lot more complicated than they currently are, calling function after function repeatedly (for example, if we wanted to display the price in several locations) could have a performance impact. With computed functions, as long as the data does not change, you can call it as many times as you want, with the result being cached by the application. If the data does change, it only needs to recalculate once, and re-cache that result.

Make a computed function for both the `shirtPrice` and `hatPrice`, so that both variables can be used in the view. Don't forget that to call the functions internally you must use the `this` variable - for example, `this.addCurrency()`. Use the following HTML code as the template for your view:

```
<div id="app">
  <p>The shirt costs {{ shirtCost }}</p>
  <p>The hat costs {{ hatCost }}</p>
</div>
```

Have a go at creating the computed functions yourself before comparing against the following code. Don't forget that there are many ways to do things in development, so don't worry if your code works but doesn't match the following example:

```
const app = new Vue({
  el: '#app',
  data: {
    shirtPrice: 25,
    hatPrice: 10,

    currency: '$',
    salesTax: 16
  },
  computed: {
    shirtCost() {
      returnthis.addCurrency(this.calculateSalesTax(
        this.shirtPrice))
    },
    hatCost() {
    return this.addCurrency(this.calculateSalesTax(
    this.hatPrice))
    },
  },
  methods: {
    calculateSalesTax(price) {
      // Work out the price of the item including
      sales tax
      return parseFloat(
        Math.round((this.salesTax / 100) * price) +
        price).toFixed(2);
        },
        addCurrency(price) {
      return this.currency + price;
    }
  }
});
```

The result, although basic, should look like the following:

The shirt costs $29.00

The hat costs $12.00

Summary

In this chapter, we learned how to get started with the Vue JavaScript framework. We examined the `data`, `computed`, and `methods` objects within the Vue instance. We covered how to use each one within the framework and utilize each of its advantages.

2
Displaying, Looping, Searching, and Filtering Data

In Chapter 1, *Getting Started with Vue.js*, we covered the data, computed, and method objects within Vue and how to display static data values. In this chapter, were are going to cover:

- Displaying lists and more complex data with Vue using v-if, v-else, and v-for
- Filtering the lists using form elements
- Applying conditional CSS classes based on the data

The data we are going to be using is going to be randomly generated by the JSON generator service (http://www.json-generator.com/). This website allows us to get dummy data to practice with. The following template was used to generate the data we will be using. Copy the following into the left-hand side to generate data of the same format so the attributes match with the code examples, as follows:

```
[
  '{{repeat(5)}}',
  {
    index: '{{index()}}',
    guid: '{{guid()}}',
    isActive: '{{bool()}}',
    balance: '{{floating(1000, 4000, 2, "00.00")}}',
    name: '{{firstName()}} {{surname()}}',
    email: '{{email()}}',
    registered: '{{date(new Date(2014, 0, 1), new Date(), "YYYY-
    MM-ddThh:mm:ss")}}'
  }
]
```

Before we get into building our simple app and displaying our users, we'll cover some more of the features of Vue and the HTML-specific attributes available in your view. These range from dynamically rendering content to looping through arrays.

HTML declarations

Vue allows you to use HTML tags and attributes to control and alter the view of your application. This involves setting attributes dynamically, such as alt and href. It also allows you to render tags and components based on data in the application. These attributes begin with a v- and, as mentioned at the beginning of this book, get removed from the HTML on render. Before we start outputting and filtering our data, we'll run through a few of the common declarations.

v-html

The v-html directive allows you to output content without using the mustache-style curly bracket syntax. It can also be used if your output contains HTML tags – it will render the output as HTML instead of plain text. The value of the HTML attribute is that of the data key or computed function name:

View:

In your view app space, add the v-html attribute to an element:

```
<div id="app">
  <div v-html="message"></div>
</div>
```

JavaScript:

In the JavaScript, set the message variable to a string which contains some HTML elements:

```
const app = new Vue({
  el: '#app',

  data: {
    message: '<h1>Hello!</h1>'
  }
});
```

You should try and avoid adding HTML to your Vue instance, as it starts to mix up the View in the ViewModel and Model of our MVVM structure. There is also the danger you output an invalid HTML tag inside another. You should only use v-html with data you trust, because using it with an external API could be a security concern as it would allow the API to have control over your application. A potentially malicious API could use v-html to inject undesired content and HTML. Only use v-html with data you can fully trust.

Declarative rendering

Regular HTML attributes, such as the src of the <img> tag, can be dynamically populated with Vue using the v-bind: attribute. This allows you to populate any existing attribute with data from your Vue application. This might be an image source or element ID.

The bind option gets used by prepending the attribute you wish to populate. For example, if you wished to populate an image source with the value of a data key called imageSource, you would do the following:

View:

Create an img tag in your view app space, with a dynamic src attribute, using v-bind and a variable called imageSource.

```
<div id="app">
  <img v-bind:src="imageSource">
</div>
```

JavaScript:

Create a variable in your Vue JavaScript code called imageSource. Add the URL to the desired image:

```
const app = new Vue({
  el: '#app',

  data: {
    imageSource: 'http://via.placeholder.com/350x150'
  }
});
```

The v-bind: attribute can be shortened to just :, so, for example, v-bind:src would become :src.

Conditional rendering

Using custom HTML declarations, Vue allows you to render elements and contents conditionally based on data attributes or JavaScript declarations. These include v-if, for showing a container whether a declaration equates to true, and v-else, to show an alternative.

v-if

The most basic example of this would be the v-if directive – determining a value or function if the block should be displayed.

Create a Vue instance with a single div inside the view and a data key, isVisible, set to false.

View:

Start off with the view code as the following:

```
<div id="app">
  <div>Now you see me</div>
</div>
```

JavaScript:

In the JavaScript, initialize Vue and create an isVisible data property:

```
const app = new Vue({
  el: '#app',

  data: {
    isVisible: false
  }
});
```

Right now, your Vue app would be displaying the contents of your element. Now add the v-if directive to your HTML element with the value of isVisible:

```
<div id="app">
  <div v-if="isVisible">Now you see me</div>
</div>
```

Upon pressing save, your text should disappear. That is because the tag is being conditionally rendered based on the value, which is currently `false`. If you open up your JavaScript console and run the following code, your element should reappear:

```
app.isVisible = true
```

`v-if` doesn't just work with Boolean true/false values. You can check whether a data property is equal to a specific string:

```
<div v-if="selected == 'yes'">Now you see me</div>
```

For example, the preceding code checks whether a selected data property is equal to the value of `yes`. The `v-if` attribute accepts JavaScript operators, so can check not equals, bigger, or less than.

The danger here is that your logic starts to creep into your View away from your ViewModel. To combat this, the attribute also takes functions as a value. The method can be as complicated as required but ultimately must return a `true` if you wish to show the code and a `false` if not. Bear in mind that if the function returns anything other than a false value (such as `0` or `false`) then the result will be interpreted as true.

This would look something like this:

```
<div v-if="isSelected">Now you see me</div>
```

And your method could be as this:

```
isSelected() {
  return selected == 'yes';
}
```

If you don't wish to completely remove the element and only hide it, there is a more appropriate directive, `v-show`. This applies a CSS display property rather than manipulating the DOM – `v-show` is covered later in the chapter.

v-else

`v-else` allows you to render an alternative element based on the opposite of the `v-if` statement. If that results in `true`, the first element will be displayed; otherwise, the element containing `v-else` will.

The element with `v-else` needs to directly follow the one containing `v-if`; otherwise, your application will throw an error.

`v-else` has no value and is placed within the element tag.

```
<div id="app">
  <div v-if="isVisible">
    Now you see me
  </div>
  <div v-else>
    Now you don't
  </div>
</div>
```

Adding the preceding HTML to your app space will only show one of the `<div>` elements – toggling the value in your console as we did earlier will reveal the other container. You can also use `v-else-if` should you wish to chain your conditions. An example of `v-else-if` is as follows:

```
<div id="app">
  <div v-if="isVisible">
    Now you see me
  </div>
  <div v-else-if="otherVisible">
    You might see me
  </div>
  <div v-else>
    Now you don't
  </div>
</div>
```

You might see me will be displayed if the `isVisible` variable equates to `false`, but the `otherVisible` variable equates to `true`.

`v-else` should be used sparingly as can be ambiguous and might lead to false positive situation.

v-for and displaying our data

The next HTML declaration means we can start displaying our data and putting some of these attributes into practice. As our data is an array, we will need to loop through it to display each element. To do this, we will use the v-for directive.

Generate your JSON and assign it to a variable called people. During these examples, the generated JSON loop will be displayed in the code blocks as [...]. Your Vue app should look like the following:

```
const app = new Vue({
  el: '#app',

  data: {
    people: [...]
  }
});
```

We now need to start displaying each person's name in our View as a bulleted list. This is where the v-for directive comes in:

```
<div id="app">
  <ul>
    <li v-for="person in people">
      {{ person }}
    </li>
  </ul>
</div>
```

The v-for loops through the JSON list and for every entry temporarily assigns it the person variable. We can then output the value or attributes of the variable.

The v-for loop needs to be applied to the HTML element you want to be repeated, in this case, <li>. If you don't have a wrapping element or don't wish to use the HTML you can use the Vue <template> elements. These get removed at runtime while still creating a container for you to output the data with:

```
<div id="app">
  <ul>
    <template v-for="person in people">
      <li>
        {{ person }}
      </li>
    </template>
  </ul>
```

```
</div>
```

The template tag also hides the contents until the app has initialized, which may be handy if your network is slow or your JavaScript takes a while to fire.

Just leaving our view to output `{{ person }}` will create a long string of information, without any use to us. Update the output to target the `name` property of the `person` object:

```
<li v-for="person in people">
  {{ person.name }}
</li>
```

Viewing the result in the browser should reveal a list of the user's names. Update the HTML to list the users in a table showing their names, email addresses, and balance. Apply the `v-for` to the `<tr>` element:

```
<table>
  <tr v-for="person in people">
    <td>{{ person.name }}</td>
    <td>{{ person.email }}</td>
    <td>{{ person.balance }}</td>
    <td>{{ person.registered }}</td>
  </tr>
</table>
```

Add an extra cell to your table. This is going to display **Active** if they are active and **Inactive** if not, using the `isActive` property on the `person` object. This can be achieved in two ways – using the `v-if` directive or alternatively using a ternary `if`. Ternary ifs are in-line `if` statements that can be placed within the curly brackets of your View. We would use the `v-if` if we wanted to use HTML elements to apply some styling.

If we were using a ternary 'if', the cell would look like the following:

```
<td>{{ (person.isActive) ? 'Active' : 'Inactive' }}</td>
```

And if we opted for the `v-if` option with `v-else`, allowing us to use the HTML we wish, it would look like this:

```
<td>
  <span class="positive" v-if="person.isActive">Active</span>
  <span class="negative" v-else>Inactive</span>
</td>
```

This active element is a perfect example of where a Vue Component would be ideal – we'll cover that in `Chapter 3`, *Optimizing our App and Using Components to Display Data*. As an alternative that is more in keeping with our MVVM methodology, we could create a method, which returns the status text. This would tidy up our view and moves the logic to our app:

```
<td>{{ activeStatus(person) }}</td>
```

Our method would then carry out the same logic as our view was:

```
activeStatus(person) {
  return (person.isActive) ? 'Active' : 'Inactive';
}
```

Our table will now look like the following:

Morales Ochoa	moralesochoa@savvy.com	2570.32	2016-02-22T10:11:31	Active
Tyson Beard	tysonbeard@savvy.com	1892.1	2016-01-27T01:06:57	Active
Hawkins Gibbs	hawkinsgibbs@savvy.com	3423.69	2016-04-23T11:19:49	Inactive
Conley Boyle	conleyboyle@savvy.com	3277.41	2014-06-04T04:22:31	Active
Joy Mosley	joymosley@savvy.com	2180.15	2016-04-21T11:52:18	Active

Creating links using v-html

The next step is to link the email address so that it is clickable for users viewing the list of people. In this instance, we need to concatenate strings by adding a `mailto:` before the email address.

The first instinct is to do the following:

```
<a href="mailto:{{person.email}}">{{ person.email }}</a>
```

But Vue doesn't allow interpolation inside attributes. Instead, we must use the `v-bind` directive on the `href` attribute. This turns the attribute into a JavaScript variable, so any raw text must be written in quotes, and the concatenated with the desired variable:

```
<a v-bind:href="'mailto:' + person.email">{{ person.email }}</a>
```

Note the addition of `v-bind:`, the single quotes and concatenation + identifier.

Format balance

Before we move on to filtering the users, add a method to correctly format the balance, prepending a currency symbol defined in the data object and ensuring there are two numbers after the decimal point. We can adapt our method from Chapter 1, *Getting Started with Vue.js,* to achieve this. Our Vue application should now look like this:

```
const app = new Vue({
  el: '#app',

  data: {
    people: [...],
    currency: '$'
  },
  methods: {
    activeStatus(person) {
      return (person.isActive) ? 'Active' : 'Inactive';
    },
    formatBalance(balance) {
      return this.currency + balance.toFixed(2);
    }
  }
});
```

We can utilize this new method in our View:

```
<td>{{ formatBalance(person.balance) }}</td>
```

Format registered date

The registered date field in the data is computer friendly, which is not very human-friendly to read. Create a new method titled `formatDate` that takes one parameter — similar to the `formatBalance` method previously.

If you want full customization of the display of your date, there are several libraries available, such as `moment.js`, that give you much more flexibility over the output of any date and time-based data. For this method, we are going to use a native JavaScript function, to `LocaleString()`:

```
formatDate(date) {
    let registered = new Date(date);
    return registered.toLocaleString('en-US');
}
```

With the registered date, we pass it to the native `Date()` function so JavaScript knows to interpret the string as a date. Once stored in the registered variable, we return the object as a string with the `toLocaleString()` function. This function accepts a huge array of options (as outlined on MDN) to customize the output of your date. For now, we'll pass it the locale we wish to display and use the defaults for that location. We can now utilize our method in the view:

```
<td>{{ formatDate(person.registered) }}</td>
```

Each table row should now look like the following:

Morales Ochoa	moralesochoa@savvy.com	$2570.32	2/22/2016, 10:11:31 AM	Active

Filtering our data

With our data being listed out, we are now going to build filtering ability. This will allow a user to select a field to filter by and a text field to enter their query. The Vue application will then filter the rows as the user types. To do this, we are going to bind some form inputs to various values in the `data` object, create a new method, and use a new directive on the table rows; `v-show`.

Building the form

Start off by creating the HTML in your view. Create a `<select>` box with an `<option>` for each field you want to filter, an `<input>` for the query, and a pair of radio buttons – we'll use these to filter active and non-active users. Make sure the value attribute of each `<option>` reflects the key in the user data – this will save on code required and will make the purpose of the select box more obvious.

The data you are filtering by does not need to be displayed for our filtering to work, although a user experience consideration needs to come into play here. Would it make sense if a table row was being displayed without the data you're filtering it on?

Create the form that will be used for filtering:

```
<form>
  <label for="fiterField">
    Field:
    <select id="filterField">
      <option value="">Disable filters</option>
      <option value="isActive">Active user</option>
      <option value="name">Name</option>
      <option value="email">Email</option>
      <option value="balance">Balance</option>
      <option value="registered">Date registered</option>
    </select>
  </label>

  <label for="filterQuery">
    Query:
    <input type="text" id="filterQuery">
  </label>

  <span>
    Active:
    <label for="userStateActive">
      Yes:
      <input type="radio" value="true" id="userStateActive"
    selected>
    </label>
    <label for="userStateInactive">
      No:
      <input type="radio" value="false" id="userStateInactive">
    </label>
  </span>
</form>
```

This form includes a select box for selecting a field a filter by, an input box that would allow the user to enter a query to filter on, and a pair of radio buttons for when we wish to filter by active and non-active users. The imagined user flow is this: the user would select the field they wish to filter the data by and either enter their query or select the radio buttons. When the `isActive` (Active user) option is selected in the select box, the radio buttons will be displayed and the input box will be hidden. We have ensured the first radio button is selected by default to help.

The filtering inputs do not need to be included in a form to work; however, it is good practice to retain semantic HTML, even in a JavaScript application.

Binding the inputs

To bind inputs to a variable that can be accessed through your Vue instance requires an HTML attribute to be added to the fields and a corresponding key added to the data object. Create a variable in the data object for each of the fields so we can bind the form elements to them:

```
data: {
    people: [...],

    currency: '$',

    filterField: '',
    filterQuery: '',
    filterUserState: ''
}
```

The data object now has three additional keys: filterField, which will be used for storing the value of the dropdown; filterQuery, the placeholder for data entered into the textbox; and filterUserState, which allows us to store the radio button checkboxes.

Now there are data keys to utilize, we are able to bind form elements to them. Apply a v-model="" attribute to each form field, with the value of the data key.

Here's an example:

```
<input type="text" id="filterQuery" v-model="filterQuery">
```

Make sure the two radio buttons have exactly the same v-model="" attribute: this is so they can update the same value. To verify that it has worked, you can now output the data variables and get the value of the fields.

Try outputting filterField or filterQuery and changing the fields.

```
{{ filterField }}
```

One thing you may notice if you were to output the `filterUserState` variable is it appears to be in working, But, it is not getting the actual results desired. The output of the variable would be `true` and `false`as set in the value attributes.

On closer inspection, the values are actually strings, rather than a Boolean value. A Boolean value is a hard `true` or `false`, 1 or 0, which you can easily compare against, whereas a string would require exact checking on a hardcoded string. This can be verified by outputting the `typeof` variable that it is:

```
{{ typeof filterUserState }}
```

This can be resolved by binding the values of the radio buttons with the `v-bind:value` attribute. This attribute allows you to specify the value for Vue to interpret and can take Boolean, string, or object values. For now, we'll pass it `true` and `false`, as we were already doing with the standard value attribute, but Vue will know to interpret it as Boolean:

```
<span>
  Active:
  <label for="userStateActive">
    Yes:
    <input type="radio" v-bind:value="true" id="userStateActive"
   v-model="filterUserState" selected>
  </label>
  <label for="userStateInactive">
    No:
    <input type="radio" v-bind:value="false"
   id="userStateInactive" v-model="filterUserState">
  </label>
</span>
```

The next step is to show and hide the table rows based on these filters.

Showing and hiding Vue content

Along with `v-if` for showing and hiding content, you can also use the `v-show=""` directive. `v-show` is very similar to `v-if`; they both get added to the HTML wrapper and can both accept the same parameters, including a function.

The difference between the two is `v-if` alters the markup, removing and adding HTML elements as required, whereas `v-show` renders the element regardless, hiding and showing the element with inline CSS styles. `v-if` is much more suited to runtime renders or infrequent user interactivities as it could potentially be restructuring the whole page. `v-show` is favorable when lots of elements are quickly coming in and out of view, for example, when filtering!

When using `v-show` with a method, the function needs to return just a `true` or `false`. The function has no concept of where it is being used, so we need to pass in the current person being rendered to calculate if it should be shown.

Create a method on your Vue instance titled `filterRow()` and inside, set it to `return true`:

```
filterRow(person) {
    return true;
}
```

The function takes one parameter, which is the person will we pass in from though from the HTML. In your view, add the `v-show` attribute to the `<tr>` element with `filterRow` as the value while passing in the person object:

```
<table>
  <tr v-for="person in people" v-show="filterRow(person)">
    <td>{{ person.name }}</td>
    . . .
```

As a simple test, return the `isActive` value to the person. This should instantly filter out anyone who is inactive, as their value will return `false`:

```
filterRow(person) {
  return person.isActive;
}
```

Filtering our content

Now we have control over our people rows and some filter controls in our view, we need to make our filters work. We are already filtering by our isActive key, so the radio buttons will be the first to be wired up. We already have the value in a Boolean form for both the radio buttons values and the key we will be filtering by. For this filter to work, we need to compare the isActive key with the radio button's value.

- If the filterUserState value is true, show users where isActive is true
- If the filterUserState value is false, however, only show users where their isActive value is false as well

This can be written in one line by comparing the two variables:

```
filterRow(person) {
  return (this.filterUserState === person.isActive);
}
```

On page load, no users will be shown as the filterUserState key is set to neither true nor false. Clicking one of the radio buttons will reveal the corresponding users.

Let's make the filter work only if the active user option is selected in the dropdown:

```
filterRow(person) {
  let result = true;
  if(this.filterField === 'isActive') {
    result = this.filterUserState === person.isActive;
  }

  return result;
}
```

This code sets a variable to true as a default. We can then return the variable immediately and our row will show. Before returning, however, it checks the value of the select box and if is the desired value, will then filter by our radio buttons. As our select box is bound to the filterField value, as with the filterUserState variable, it updates while we interact with the app. Try selecting the **Active user** option in the select box and changing the radio buttons.

The next step is to use the input query box when the active user option is not selected. We also want our query to be a *fuzzy* search — for example, to match words containing the search query rather than matching exactly. We also want it to be case insensitive:

```
filterRow(person) {
  let result = true;

  if(this.filterField) {

    if(this.filterField === 'isActive') {
      result = this.filterUserState === person.isActive;
    } else {
    let query = this.filterQuery.toLowerCase(),
    field =  person[this.filterField].toString().toLowerCase();
    result = field.includes(query);
    }

  }

  return result;
}
```

There are a few things we had to add to this method in order to work. The first step is to check that our select field has a value to begin the filtering. As the first option in our select field has a `value=""`, this equates to `false`. If this is the case, the method returns the default of `true`.

If it does have a value, it then goes to our original `if` statement. This checks on the specific value to see whether it matches `isActive` – if it does, it runs the code we wrote previously. If not, we start our alternate filtering. A new variable of `query` is established, which takes the value of the input and converts it to lowercase.

The second variable is the data we are going to be filtering against. This uses the value of the select box, which is the field key on the person, to extract the value to filter with. This value is converted to a string (in the case of the date or balance), converted to lowercase and stored as the `field` variable. Lastly, we then use the `includes` function to check whether the field includes the query entered. If it does, we return `true` and the row is shown if; not, the row is hidden.

The next issue we can address is when filtering with numbers. It is not intuitive for the user to enter the exact balance of the user they are after — a much more natural way of searching is to find users with a balance under or over a certain amount, for example, `< 2000`.

The first step in doing this is to only apply this type of filtering when it is the `balance` field. We can approach this two ways – we can either check that the field name is `balance`, similar to how we check the `isActive` field, or we can check the type of data we are filtering on.

Checking against the field name is simpler. We can do an `else if()` in our method or even migrate to a `switch` statement for easier reading and expansion. The alternative of checking the field type, however, is more scalable. It means we can expand our dataset with more numeric fields without having to extend or change our code. It does mean, however, that there will be further `if` statements in our code.

What we will do first is alter our storing method, as we don't want to necessarily lowercase the field or query:

```
if(this.filterField === 'isActive') {
   result = this.filterUserState === person.isActive;
} else {

   let query = this.filterQuery,
       field = person[this.filterField];

}
```

The next step is to establish the type of data in the field variable. This can be established by, once again, using the `typeof` operator. This can be used in an `if` statement, to check whether the type of field is a number:

```
if(this.filterField === 'isActive') {
   result = this.filterUserState === person.isActive;
} else {

   let query = this.filterQuery,
       field = person[this.filterField];

   if(typeof field === 'number') {
     // Is a number
   } else {
     // Is not a number
     field = field.toLowerCase();
     result = field.includes(query.toLowerCase());
   }

}
```

Once our check is complete, we can default back to our original query code. It will use this if the select option *is not* isActive and the data were are filtering on *is not* a number. If this is the case, then it will lowercase the field and see if it includes what has been written in the query box when converted to lowercase as before.

The next stage is to actually compare our numbered data against what has been written in the query box. To do this, we are going to use the native JavaScript eval function.

The eval function can be a potentially dangerous function and should not be used in production code without some serious input sanitizing checks, plus, it is less performant than lengthier alternatives. It runs everything inside as native JavaScript and so can be open to abuse. However, as we are using this for a dummy application, with the focus being on Vue itself rather than creating a fully web-safe application, it is fine in this instance. You can read more about eval in 24 ways:

```
if(this.filterField === 'isActive') {
  result = this.filterUserState === person.isActive;
} else {

  let query = this.filterQuery,
      field = person[this.filterField];
  if(typeof field === 'number') {
    result = eval(field + query);
  } else {
    field = field.toLowerCase();
    result = field.includes(query.toLowerCase());
  }

}
```

This passes both the field and the query to the eval() function and passes the result (either true or false) to our result variable to determine the visibility of the row. The eval function literally evaluates the expression and determines if it is true or false. Here's an example:

```
eval(500 > 300); // true
eval(500 < 400); // false
eval(500 - 500); // false
```

In this example, the number 500 is our field, or in this specific example, balance. Anything that is after that is what is written by our user. Your filtering code is now ready to go. Try selecting the **balance** from the dropdown and filtering for users with a balance higher than 2000.

Before we move on, we need to add some error checking. If you have your JavaScript console open, you may have noticed an error when you typed the first greater or less than. This was because the `eval` function is unable to evaluate X > (where X is the balance). You may have also been tempted to type *$2000* with the currency and realized this doesn't work. This is because the currency is applied while rendering the view, whereas we are filtering the data before this is rendered.

In order to combat these two errors, we must remove any currency symbols typed in the query and test our `eval` function before relying on it to return the results. Remove the currency symbol with the native JavaScript `replace()` function. If it changes, uses the currency symbol stored in the app, rather than hardcoding the currently used one.

```
if(typeof field == 'number') {
  query = query.replace(this.currency, '');
  result = eval(field + query);
}
```

We now need to test the `eval` function so it does not throw an error with every key pressed. To do this, we use a `try...catch` statement:

```
if(typeof field == 'number') {
  query = query.replace(this.currency, '');
  try {
    result = eval(field + query);
  } catch(e) {}
}
```

As we don't want to output anything when an error is entered, we can leave the `catch` statement empty. We could put the `field.includes(query)` statement in here, so it falls back to the default functionality. Our full `filterRow()` method now looks like this:

```
filterRow(person) {
  let result = true;
  if(this.filterField) {

    if(this.filterField === 'isActive') {

      result = this.filterUserState === person.isActive;

    } else {

      let query = this.filterQuery,
    field = person[this.filterField];
      if(typeof field === 'number') {
        query = query.replace(this.currency, '');
```

```
        try {
          result = eval(field + query);
        } catch (e) {}

      } else {

        field = field.toLowerCase();
        result = field.includes(query.toLowerCase());

      }
    }
  }

  return result;

}
```

Filtering our filters

Now we have our filtering in place, we need to only show the radio buttons when the isActive option is selected in our dropdown. Using the knowledge we've learned, this should be relatively straightforward.

Create a new method that checks the select box value and returns true when **Active User** is selected in our dropdown:

```
isActiveFilterSelected() {
  return (this.filterField === 'isActive');
}
```

We can now use v-show for both the input and radio buttons, reversing the effect when on the query box:

```
<label for="filterQuery" v-show="!isActiveFilterSelected()">
  Query:
  <input type="text" id="filterQuery" v-model="filterQuery">
</label>
<span v-show="isActiveFilterSelected()">
  Active:
  <label for="userStateActive">
    Yes:
    <input type="radio" v-bind:value="true" id="userStateActive"
   v-model="filterUserState">
  </label>
  <label for="userStateInactive">
```

```
        No:
<input type="radio" v-bind:value="false" id="userStateInactive" v-
model="filterUserState">
  </label>
</span>
```

Take note of the exclamation point before the method call on the input field. This means not, and effectively reverses the result of the function, for example not true is the same as false and vice versa.

To improve user experience, we can also check that the filtering is active at all before showing either of the inputs. This can be added by including a secondary check in our v-show attribute:

```
<label for="filterQuery" v-show="this.filterField &&
!isActiveFilterSelected()">
  Query:
  <input type="text" id="filterQuery" v-model="filterQuery">
</label>
```

This now checks that `filterField` has a value and that the select box is not set to `isActive`. Make sure you add this to the radio buttons too.

A further user experience enhancement would be to ensure all the users don't disappear when the `isActive` option is chosen. This currently happens because the default is set to a string, which does not match with either the `true` or `false` values of the field. Before filtering in this field, we should check that the `filterUserState` variable is either `true` or `false`, that is a Boolean. We can do this by using `typeof` once more:

```
if(this.filterField === 'isActive') {
    result = (typeof this.filterUserState === 'boolean') ?
    (this.filterUserState === person.isActive) : true;
}
```

We are using a ternary operator to check that the result to filter on is `boolean`. If it is, then filter as we were; if it is not then simply show the row.

Changing CSS classes

As with any HTML attribute, Vue is able to manipulate CSS classes. As with everything in Vue, this can be done in a myriad of ways ranging from attributes on the object itself to utilizing methods. We'll start off adding a class if the user is active.

Binding a CSS class is similar to other attributes. The value takes an object that can calculate logic from within the view or be abstracted out into our Vue instance. This all depends on the complexity of the operation.

First, let's add a class to the cell containing the `isActive` variable if the user is active:

```
<td v-bind:class="{ active: person.isActive }">
   {{ activeStatus(person) }}
</td>
```

The class HTML attribute is first prepended by `v-bind:` to let Vue know it needs to process the attribute. The value is then an object, with the CSS class as the key and the condition as the value. This code toggles the `active` class on the table cell if the `person.isActive` variable equates to `true`. If we wanted to add an `inactive` class if the user was not active, we could add it to the object:

```
<td v-bind:class="{ active: person.isActive, inactive:
!person.isActive }">
   {{ activeStatus(person) }}
</td>
```

Here's we've used the exclamation point again to reverse the status. If you run this app, you should find the CSS classes applied as expected.

If we're just applying two classes based on one condition, a ternary `if` statement can be used inside of the class attribute:

```
<td v-bind:class="person.isActive ? 'active' : 'inactive'">
   {{ activeStatus(person) }}
</td>
```

Note the single quotes around the class names. Once again, however, logic has started to creep into our View and, should we wish to also use this class elsewhere, is not very scalable.

Create a new method on our Vue instance called `activeClass` and abstract the logic into that — not forgetting to pass the person object in:

```
activeClass(person) {
   return person.isActive ? 'active' : 'inactive';
}
```

We can now call that method in our view:

```
<td v-bind:class="activeClass(person)">
  {{ activeStatus(person) }}
</td>
```

I appreciate this is quite a simple execution; let's try a slightly more complex one. We want to add a conditional class to the balance cell depending on the value. If their balance is under $2000, we will add an error class. If it is between $2000 and $3000, a warning class will be applied and if it is over $3000 a success class will be added.

Along with the error, warning and success classes, a class of increasing will be added if the balance is over $500. For example, a balance of $2,600 will get both the warning, and increasing classes, whereas $2,400 would only receive the warning class.

As this contains several bits of logic, we will create a use a method in our instance. Create a balanceClass method and bind it to the class HTML attribute of the cell containing the balance. To begin with, we'll add the error, warning and success classes.

```
<td v-bind:class="balanceClass(person)">
  {{ formatBalance(person.balance) }}
</td>
```

In the method, we need to access the balance property of the person passed in and return the name of the class we wish to add. For now, we'll return a fixed result to verify that it's working:

```
balanceClass(person) {
  return 'warning';
}
```

We now need to evaluate our balance. As it's already a number, comparing it against our criteria won't involve any conversions:

```
balanceClass(person) {
  let balanceLevel = 'success';

  if(person.balance < 2000) {
    balanceLevel = 'error';
  } else if (person.balance < 3000) {
    balanceLevel = 'warning';
  }

  return balanceLevel;
}
```

In the preceding method, the class output gets set to success by default, as we only need to change the output if it is less than 3000. The first if checks whether the balance is below our first threshold – if it does, it sets the output to error. If not, it tries the second condition, which is to check whether the balance is below 3000. If successful, the class applied becomes warning. Lastly, it outputs the chosen class, which applies directly to the element.

We now need to consider how we can do the increasing class. To get it to output alongside the existing balanceLevel class, we need to convert the output from a single variable to an array. To verify that this works, hardcode the extra class to the output:

```
balanceClass(person) {
  let balanceLevel = 'success';
  if(person.balance < 2000) {
    balanceLevel = 'error';
  } else if (person.balance < 3000) {
    balanceLevel = 'warning';
  }
  return [balanceLevel, 'increasing'];
}
```

This adds the two classes to the element. Convert the string to a variable and set to false by default. Vue won't output anything for a false value passed in the array.

To work out if we need the increasing class, we need to do some calculations on the balance. As we want the increasing class if the balance is above 500 no matter what range it is in, we need to round the number and compare:

```
let increasing = false,
    balance = person.balance / 1000;

if(Math.round(balance) == Math.ceil(balance)) {
  increasing = 'increasing';
}
```

Initially, we set the increasing variable to false as a default. We also store a version of the balance divided by 1000. The means our balances turn out to be 2.45643 instead of 2456.42. From there, we compare the number after it has been rounded by JavaScript (For example 2.5 becomes 3, whereas 2.4 becomes 2) to the number that has been forced to round up (example 2.1 becomes 3, along with 2.9).

If the number output is the same, the `increasing` variable is set to the string of the class we want to set. We can then pass this variable along with the `balanceLevel` variable out as an array. The full method now looks like the following:

```
balanceClass(person) {
  let balanceLevel = 'success';

  if(person.balance < 2000) {
    balanceLevel = 'error';
  } else if (person.balance < 3000) {
    balanceLevel = 'warning';
  }

  let increasing = false,
      balance = person.balance / 1000;

  if(Math.round(balance) == Math.ceil(balance)) {
    increasing = 'increasing';
  }

  return [balanceLevel, increasing];
}
```

Filtering and custom classes

We now have a fully fledged user list/register that has filtering on selected fields and custom CSS classes depending on the criteria. To recap, this is what our view looks like now we have the filter in place:

```
<div id="app">
  <form>
    <label for="fiterField">
      Field:
      <select id="filterField" v-model="filterField">
        <option value="">Disable filters</option>
        <option value="isActive">Active user</option>
        <option value="name">Name</option>
        <option value="email">Email</option>
        <option value="balance">Balance</option>
        <option value="registered">Date registered</option>
      </select>
    </label>

    <label for="filterQuery" v-show="this.filterField &&
    !isActiveFilterSelected()">
```

```
        Query:
        <input type="text" id="filterQuery" v-model="filterQuery">
      </label>

      <span v-show="isActiveFilterSelected()">
     Active:
   <label for="userStateActive">
   Yes:
   <input type="radio" v-bind:value="true" id="userStateActive" v-
    model="filterUserState">
</label>
<label for="userStateInactive">
   No:
   <input type="radio" v-bind:value="false" id="userStateInactive"
v-model="filterUserState">
</label>
      </span>
    </form>

    <table>
      <tr v-for="person in people" v-show="filterRow(person)">
        <td>{{ person.name }}</td>
        <td>
    <a v-bind:href="'mailto:' + person.email">{{ person.email }}
      </a>
        </td>
        <td v-bind:class="balanceClass(person)">
          {{ formatBalance(person.balance) }}
        </td>
        <td>{{ formatDate(person.registered) }}</td>
        <td v-bind:class="activeClass(person)">
          {{ activeStatus(person) }}
        </td>
      </tr>
    </table>

  </div>
```

And the JavaScript for our Vue app should look something like this:

```
const app = new Vue({
  el: '#app',

  data: {
    people: [...],

    currency: '$',
```

```
          filterField: '',
          filterQuery: '',
          filterUserState: ''
      },
      methods: {
        activeStatus(person) {
          return (person.isActive) ? 'Active' : 'Inactive';
        },

        activeClass(person) {
          return person.isActive ? 'active' : 'inactive';
        },
        balanceClass(person) {
          let balanceLevel = 'success';

          if(person.balance < 2000) {
            balanceLevel = 'error';
          } else if (person.balance < 3000) {
            balanceLevel = 'warning';
          }

          let increasing = false,
        balance = person.balance / 1000;

          if(Math.round(balance) == Math.ceil(balance)) {
            increasing = 'increasing';
          }

          return [balanceLevel, increasing];
        },

        formatBalance(balance) {
          return this.currency + balance.toFixed(2);
        },
        formatDate(date) {
          let registered = new Date(date);
          return registered.toLocaleString('en-US');
        },

        filterRow(person) {
          let result = true;
          if(this.filterField) {

            if(this.filterField === 'isActive') {

            result = (typeof this.filterUserState === 'boolean') ?
            (this.filterUserState === person.isActive) : true;
          } else {
```

```
    let query = this.filterQuery,
        field = person[this.filterField];

    if(typeof field === 'number') {
      query.replace(this.currency, '');
      try {
        result = eval(field + query);
      } catch(e) {}
    } else {
      field = field.toLowerCase();
      result = field.includes(query.toLowerCase());
      }
    }
  }

    return result;
  },
  isActiveFilterSelected() {
    return (this.filterField === 'isActive');
  }
  }
});
```

With a small amount of CSS, our people filtering app now looks like the following:

Field:	Disable filters ⬍			
Morales Ochoa	moralesochoa@savvy.com	**$2570.32**	2/22/2016, 10:11:31 AM	Active
Tyson Beard	tysonbeard@savvy.com	**$1892.10**	1/27/2016, 1:06:57 AM	Active
Hawkins Gibbs	hawkinsgibbs@savvy.com	$3423.69	4/23/2016, 11:19:49 AM	Inactive
Conley Boyle	conleyboyle@savvy.com	$3277.41	6/4/2014, 4:22:31 AM	Active
Joy Mosley	joymosley@savvy.com	$2180.15	4/21/2016, 11:52:18 AM	Active

Summary

In this chapter, we looked at Vue HTML declarations, conditionally rendering our HTML and showing an alternative if required. We also put into practice what we learned about methods. Lastly, we built a filtering component for our table, allowing us to show active and inactive users, find users with specific names and emails, and filter out rows based on the balance.

Now we've got to a good point in our app, it's a good opportunity to take a look at our code to see if it can be optimized in any way. By optimizations, I mean reducing repetition, making the code simpler if possible, and abstracting logic out into smaller, readable, and reusable chunks.

In `Chapter 3`, *Optimizing Our App and Using Components to Display Data*, we will optimize our code and look at Vue components as a way of separating out logic into separate segments and sections.

3
Optimizing your App and Using Components to Display Data

In Chapter 2, *Displaying, Looping, Searching, and Filtering Data*, we got our Vue app displaying our people directory, we can use this opportunity to optimize our code and separate it out into components. This makes the code more manageable, easier to understand, and makes it easier for other developers to work out the flow of data (or you, when you come back and look at your code in a few months!).

This chapter is going to cover:

- Optimizing our Vue.js code by reducing the repetition, and logically organizing our code
- How to create Vue components and use them with Vue
- How to use props and slots with components
- Utilizing events to transfer data between components

Optimizing the code

As we wrote the code while we were figuring out the problem, there comes a point when you need to take a step back and look at your code to optimize it. This could include reducing the number of variables and methods or creating methods, to reduce repeating functionality. Our current Vue app looks like the following:

```
const app = new Vue({
  el: '#app',
  data: {
    people: [...],
```

```
        currency: '$',
        filterField: '',
        filterQuery: '',
        filterUserState: ''
    },
    methods: {
        activeStatus(person) {
            return (person.isActive) ? 'Active' :
            'Inactive';
        },
        activeClass(person) {
            return person.isActive ? 'active' :
            'inactive';
        },
        balanceClass(person) {
            let balanceLevel = 'success';
            if(person.balance < 2000) {
                balanceLevel = 'error';
            } else if (person.balance < 3000) {
                balanceLevel = 'warning';
            }
            let increasing = false,
            balance = person.balance / 1000;
            if(Math.round(balance) ==
             Math.ceil(balance)) {
                increasing = 'increasing';
            }
            return [balanceLevel, increasing];
        },
        formatBalance(balance) {
            return this.currency + balance.toFixed(2);
        },
        formatDate(date) {
            let registered = new Date(date);
            return registered.toLocaleString('en-US');
        },
        filterRow(person) {
            let result = true;
            if(this.filterField) {
                if(this.filterField === 'isActive') {
                    result = (typeof this.filterUserState
                     === 'boolean') ? (this.filterUserState
                     === person.isActive) : true;
                } else {
                    let query = this.filterQuery,
                        field = person[this.filterField];
                    if(typeof field === 'number') {
                        query.replace(this.currency, '');
```

```
        try {
            result = eval(field + query);
        } catch(e) {}
        } else {
            field = field.toLowerCase();
            result =
    field.includes(query.toLowerCase());
        }
      }
    }
    return result;
  },
  isActiveFilterSelected() {
    return (this.filterField === 'isActive');
  }
}
});
```

Looking at the preceding code, there are some improvements we can make. These include:

- Reducing the number of filter variables and grouping logically
- Combining the format functions
- Reducing the number of hard-coded variables and properties
- Re-ordering methods into a more logical order

We'll cover these points individually so we have a clean code base for building components with.

Reducing the number of filter variables and grouping logically

The filtering currently uses up three variables, `filterField`, `filterQuery`, and `filterUserState`. The only thing that currently links these variables is the name, rather than being in an object of their own to link them systematically. Doing this avoids any ambiguity as to whether they are related to the same component or just coincidentally the same. In the data object, create a new object titled `filter` and move each variable inside:

```
data: {
  people: [..],
  currency: '$',
  filter: {
```

```
        field: '',
        query: '',
        userState: '',
    }
}
```

To access the data, update any references of `filterField` to `this.filter.field`. Note the extra dot, denoting it is a key of the filter object. Don't forget to update `filterQuery` and `filterUserState` references as well. For example, the `isActiveFilterSelected` method would become:

```
isActiveFilterSelected() {
    return (this.filter.field === 'isActive');
}
```

You will also need to update the `v-model` and `v-show` attributes in your view—there are five occurrences of the various variables.

While updating the filtering variables, we can take this opportunity to remove one. With our current filtering, we can only have one filter active at a time. This means the `query` and `userState` variables are only being used at any one time, which gives us the opportunity to combine these two variables. To do so, we'll need to update the view and application code to cater for this.

Remove the `userState` variable from your filter data object and update any occurrence of `filter.userState` in your view to `filter.query`. Now do a *find and replace* in your Vue JavaScript code for `filter.userState`, again replacing it with `filter.query`.

Viewing your app in the browser, it will appear to initially work, being able to filter users by the field. However, if you filter by status, then switch to any other field, the query field won't show. This is because using the radio buttons sets the value to a Boolean which, when trying to convert to lowercase for the query field, fails to do so. To tackle this, we can convert whatever value is in the `filter.query` variable to a string using the native JavaScript `String()` function. This ensures that our filtering function can work with any filtering input:

```
if(this.filter.field === 'isActive') {
    result = (typeof this.filter.query ===
    'boolean') ? (this.filter.query ===
    person.isActive) : true;
      } else {
    let query = String(this.filter.query),
        field = person[this.filter.field];
        if(typeof field === 'number') {
```

```
      query.replace(this.currency, '');
      try {
        result = eval(field + query);
      } catch(e) {}
    } else {
      field = field.toLowerCase();
      result = field.includes(query.toLowerCase());
    }
```

Adding this to our code now ensures our query data is usable no matter what the value. The issue this now creates is when the user is switching between fields to filter. If you select the **Active user** and chose a radio button, the filtering works as expected, however, if you now switch to **Email**, or another field, the input box is prepopulated with either `true` or `false`. This instantly filters and will often return no results. This also occurs when switching between two text filtering fields, which is not the desired effect.

What we want is, whenever the select box is updated, the filter query should clear. Whether it is the radio buttons or input box, selecting a new field should reset the filter query, this ensures a new search can begin.

This is done by removing the link between the select box and the `filter.field` variable and creating our own method to handle the update. We then trigger the method when the select box is changed. This method will then clear the `query` variable and set the `field` variable to the select box value.

Remove the `v-model` attribute on the select box and add a new `v-on:change` attribute. We will pass a method name into this that will fire every time the select box is updated.

`v-on` is a new Vue binding that we've not encountered before. It allows you to bind actions from elements to Vue methods. For example, `v-on:click` is one that is used the most commonly - which allows you to bind a `click` function to the element. We'll cover more on this in the next section of the book.

Where v-bind can be abbreviated to just a colon, `v-on` can be shortened to an @ symbol, allowing you to use `@click=""`, for example:

```
<select v-on:change="changeFilter($event)"
  id="filterField">
  <option value="">Disable filters</option>
  <option value="isActive">Active user</option>
  <option value="name">Name</option>
  <option value="email">Email</option>
  <option value="balance">Balance</option>
  <option value="registered">Date
    registered</option>
```

```
</select>
```

This attribute is firing the `changeFilter` method on every update and passing it the `$event` data of the change. This default Vue event object contains a lot of information that we could utilize, but the `target.value` data is the key we are after.

Create a new method in your Vue instance that accepts the event parameter and updates both the `query` and `field` variables. The `query` variable needs to be cleared, so set it to an empty string, whereas the `field` variable can be set to the value of the select box:

```
changeFilter(event) {
  this.filter.query = '';
  this.filter.field = event.target.value;
}
```

Viewing your application now should clear whatever the filter query is, while still operating as expected.

Combining the format functions

Our next optimization will be to combine the `formatBalance` and `formatDate` methods in our Vue instance. This would then allow us to scale our format functions without bloating the code with several methods with similar functionality. There are two ways to approach a format style function—we can either auto-detect the format of the input or pass the desired format option in as a second option. Both have their pros and cons, but we'll walk through both.

Autodetection formatting

Autodetection of the variable type, when passed into a function, is great for cleaner code. In your view, you could invoke the function and pass the one parameter you wish to format. For example:

```
{{ format(person.balance) }}
```

The method would then contain a `switch` statement and format the variable based on the `typeof` value. A `switch` statement can evaluate a single expression and then execute different code based on the output. `Switch` statements can be very powerful as they allow clauses to be built up—utilizing several different bits of code based on the result. More can be read about `switch` statements on MDN.

`Switch` statements are a great alternative to `if` statements if you are comparing the same expression. You are also able to have several cases for one block of code and even include a default if none of the previous cases was met. As an example of one in use, our format method might look like:

```
format(variable) {
  switch (typeof variable) {
    case 'string':
    // Formatting if the variable is a string
    break;
    case 'number':
    // Number formatting
    break;
    default:
    // Default formatting
    break;
  }
}
```

The important thing to note is the `break;` lines. These finish each `switch` case. If a break was omitted, the code would carry on and execute the following case—which sometimes is the desired effect.

Autodetecting the variable type and formatting is a great way of simplifying your code. However, for our app, it is not a suitable solution as we are formatting the date, which when outputting the `typeof` results in a string, and would not be identifiable from other strings we may wish to format.

Passing in a second variable

The alternative to the preceding autodetection is to pass the second variable into the `format` function. This gives us greater flexibility and scalability should we wish to format other fields. With the second variable, we can either pass in a fixed string that matches a preselected list in our `switch` statement or we could pass in the field itself. An example of the fixed string approach in the view would be:

```
{{ format(person.balance, 'currency') }}
```

This would work perfectly and would be great if we had several different fields that all needed to be formatted like `balance` currently does, but there seems to be some slight repetition in using the `balance` key and `currency` format.

As a compromise, we are going to pass the `person` object as the first parameter, so we can access all the data, and the name of the field as the second parameter. We will then use this for both identifying the format method required and to return the specific data.

Creating the method

In your view, replace both the `formatDate` and `formatBalance` functions with a singular format one, passing in the `person` variable as the first parameter, and the field enclosed quotes as the second:

```
<td v-bind:class="balanceClass(person)">
  {{ format(person, 'balance') }}
</td>
<td>
  {{ format(person, 'registered') }}
</td>
```

Create a new format method inside your Vue instance, which accepts two parameters: `person` and `key`. As the first step, retrieve the field using the person object and the `key` variable:

```
format(person, key) {
  let field = person[key],
      output = field.toString().trim();
  return output;
}
```

We have also created a second variable inside the function titled `output`—this will be what is returned at the end of the function and is set to the `field` by default. This ensures that if our formatting key does not match the one passed in, the untouched field data is returned—we do, however, convert the field to a string and trim any whitespace from the variable. Running the app now will return the fields without any formatting.

Add a `switch` statement, setting the expression to be just the `key`. Add two cases to the `switch` statement—one being `balance` and the other `registered`. As we do not wish for anything to happen to our input when it does not match a case, there is no need for us to have a `default` statement:

```
format(person, key) {
  let field = person[key],
      output = field.toString().trim();

  switch(key) {
```

```
        case 'balance':
          break;
        case 'registered':
          break;
    }
    return output;
}
```

We now just need to copy the code from our original formatting functions into the individual cases:

```
format(person, key) {
    let field = person[key],
        output = field.toString().trim();
    switch(key) {
      case 'balance':
        output = this.currency + field.toFixed(2);
        break;
      case 'registered':
        let registered = new Date(field);
        output = registered.toLocaleString('en-US');
       break;
    }
    return output;
}
```

This format function is now a lot more flexible. We can add more `switch` cases should we need to cater for more fields (process the `name` field, for example) or we can add new cases to existing code. An example of this would be if our data contained a field that detailed the date on which the user `deactivated` their account, we could easily display it in the same format as registered:

```
case 'registered':
case 'deactivated':
  let registered = new Date(field);
  output = registered.toLocaleString('en-US');
  break;
```

Reducing the number of hard-coded variables and properties, and reducing redundancy

When looking at the Vue JavaScript, it is quickly evident that it can be optimized by introducing global variables and setting more local variables in the functions to make it more readable. We can also use existing functionality to stop repeating ourselves.

The first optimization is in our `filterRow()` method where we check whether `filter.field` is active. This is also repeated in the `isActiveFilterSelected` method we use to show and hide our radio buttons. Update the `if` statement to use this method instead, so the code is as follows:

```
...

if(this.filter.field === 'isActive') {
result = (typeof this.filter.query === 'boolean') ?
(this.filter.query === person.isActive) : true;
  } else {

...
```

The preceding code has the `this.filter.field === 'isActive'` code removed and replaced with the `isActiveFilterSelected()` method. It should now look like this:

```
...

if(this.isActiveFilterSelected()) {
result = (typeof this.filter.query === 'boolean') ?
 (this.filter.query === person.isActive) : true;
  } else {

...
```

While we're in the `filterRow` method, we can reduce the code by storing the `query` and `field` as variables at the start of the method. `result` is also not the right keyword for this, so let's change it to `visible`. First, create and store our two variables at the start and rename `result` to `visible`:

```
filterRow(person) {
   let visible = true,
       field = this.filter.field,
       query = this.filter.query;

...
```

Replace all instances in that function of the variables, for example, the first part of the method would look like this:

```
if(field) {
    if(this.isActiveFilterSelected()) {
        visible = (typeof query === 'boolean') ?
        (query === person.isActive) : true;
    } else {
    query = String(query),
    field = person[field];
```

Save your file and open the app in the browser to ensure your optimizations haven't broken the functionality.

The last stage is to reorder the methods into an order that makes sense to you. Feel free to add comments to separate out the different method types—for example, ones that relate to CSS classes or filtering. I have also removed the `activeStatus` method, as we are able to utilize our `format` method to *format* the output of this field. After the optimizations, the JavaScript code now looks like the following:

```
const app = new Vue({
  el: '#app',
   data: {
    people: [...],
    currency: '$',
    filter: {
       field: '',
       query: ''
    }
  },
  methods: {
    isActiveFilterSelected() {
      return (this.filter.field === 'isActive');
    },
    /**
     * CSS Classes
     */
    activeClass(person) {
        return person.isActive ? 'active' :
        'inactive';
    },
     balanceClass(person) {
      let balanceLevel = 'success';
      if(person.balance < 2000) {
        balanceLevel = 'error';
      } else if (person.balance < 3000) {
```

```
          balanceLevel = 'warning';
        }
          let increasing = false,
          balance = person.balance / 1000;
        if(Math.round(balance) ==
         Math.ceil(balance)) {
          increasing = 'increasing';
        }
        return [balanceLevel, increasing];
      },
      /**
       * Display
       */
      format(person, key) {
        let field = person[key],
        output = field.toString().trim();
        switch(key) {
          case 'balance':
            output = this.currency +
          field.toFixed(2);
            break;
          case 'registered':
      let registered = new Date(field);
      output = registered.toLocaleString('en-US');
      break;
    case 'isActive':
      output = (person.isActive) ? 'Active' :
      'Inactive';
        }
    return output;
      },
      /**
       * Filtering
       */
      changeFilter(event) {
        this.filter.query = '';
        this.filter.field = event.target.value;
      },
      filterRow(person) {
        let visible = true,
            field = this.filter.field,
            query = this.filter.query;
        if(field) {
          if(this.isActiveFilterSelected()) {
            visible = (typeof query === 'boolean') ?
            (query === person.isActive) : true;
          } else {
            query = String(query),
```

```
      field = person[field];
      if(typeof field === 'number') {
        query.replace(this.currency, '');
        try {
          visible = eval(field + query);
        } catch(e) {}
      } else {
        field = field.toLowerCase();
        visible =
        field.includes(query.toLowerCase());
      }
    }
  }
  return visible;
    }
  }
});
```

Creating Vue components

Now we're confident our code is cleaner, we can move on to making Vue components for the various parts of our app. Put aside your code for now and open a new document while you get to grips with components.

Vue components are extremely powerful and a great addition to any Vue app. They allow you to make packages of reusable code that include their own data, methods, and computed values.

For our app, we have the opportunity to create two components: one for each person and one for the filtering section of our app. I would encourage you to always look at breaking your app into components where possible—this helps group your code into related functions.

Components look like mini Vue instances as each one has its own data, methods, and computed objects—along with some component-specific options that we will cover shortly. Components are also extremely useful when it comes to creating an app with different pages and sections—this will be covered in Chapter 8, *Introducing Vue-Router and Loading URL-Based Components*.

When a component is registered, you create a custom HTML element to use in your view, for example:

```
<my-component></my-component>
```

When naming your component, you can use kebab-case (hyphens), PascalCase (no punctuation, but each word is capitalized) or camelCase (similar to Pascal but the first word is not capitalized). Vue components are not restricted by, or associated with, the W3C web components/custom element rules, but it is good practice to follow this convention of using kebab-case.

Creating and initializing your component

Vue components are registered using the `Vue.component(tagName, options)` syntax. Each component must have an associated tag name. The `Vue.component` registration **must** happen before you initialize your Vue instance. As a minimum, each component should have a `template` property—denoting what should be displayed when the component is used. Templates must always have a single wrapping element; this is so the custom HTML tag can be replaced with the parent container.

For example, you couldn't have the following as your template:

```
<div>Hello</div><div>Goodbye</div>
```

If you do pass a template of this format, Vue will throw an error in the browser's JavaScript console warning you.

Create a Vue component yourself, with a simple fixed template:

```
Vue.component('my-component', {
  template: '<div>hello</div>'
});

const app = new Vue({
  el: '#app',

  // App options
});
```

With this component declared, it would now give us a `<my-component></my-component>` HTML tag to use in our view.

You can also specify components on the Vue instance itself. This would be used if you had multiple Vue instances on one site and wished to contain a component to one instance. To do this, create your component as a simple object and assign the `tagName` within the `components` object of your Vue instance:

```
let Child = {
    template: '<div>hello</div>'
}

const app = new Vue({
    el: '#app',

    // App options

    components: {
        'my-component': Child
    }
});
```

For our app though, we are going to stick with the `Vue.component()` method of initializing our components.

Using your component

In your view, add your custom HTML element component:

```
<div id="app">
    <my-component></my-component>
</div>
```

Viewing this in the browser should replace the `<my-component>` HTML tag with a `<div>` and a **hello** message.

There may be some cases where a custom HTML tag won't be parsed and accepted - these cases tend to be in `<table>`, `<ol>`, `<ul>`, and `<select>` elements. If this is the case, you can use the `is=""` attribute on a standard HTML element:

```
<ol>
    <li is="my-component"></li>
</ol>
```

Using component data and methods

As Vue components are self-contained elements of your Vue app, they each have their own data and functions. This helps when re-using components on the same page, as the information is self-contained per instance of a component. `methods` and `computed` functions are declared the same as you would on the Vue app, however, the data key should be a function that returns an object.

The data object of a component must be a function. This is so that each component has its own self-contained data, rather than getting confused and sharing data between different instances of the same component. The function must still return an object as you would in your Vue app.

Create a new component called `balance`, add a `data` function and `computed` object to your component and an empty `<div>` to the `template` property for now:

```
Vue.component('balance', {
  template: '<div></div>',
  data() {
    return {
    }
  },
  computed: {
  }
});
```

Next, add a key/value pair to your `cost` data object with an integer and add the variable to your template. Add the `<balance></balance>` custom HTML element to your view and you should be presented with your integer:

```
Vue.component('balance', {
  template: '<div>{{ cost }}</div>',
  data() {
    return {
      cost: 1234
    }
  },
  computed: {
  }
});
```

As with our Vue instance in `Chapter 1`, *Getting Started with Vue.js*, add a function to the `computed` object that appends a currency symbol to the integer and ensures there are two decimal places. Don't forget to add the currency symbol to your data function.

Update the template to output the computed value instead of the raw cost:

```
Vue.component('balance', {
  template: '<div>{{ formattedCost }}</div>',
  data() {
    return {
      cost: 1234,
      currency: '$'
    }
  },
  computed: {
    formattedCost() {
    return this.currency + this.cost.toFixed(2);
    }
  }
});
```

This is a basic example of a component, however, it is quite restricted with the fixed `cost` on the component itself.

Passing data to your component – props

Having the balance as a component is great, but not very good if the balance is fixed. Components really come into their own when you add the ability to pass in arguments and properties via HTML attributes. In the Vue world, these are called **props**. Props can be either static or variable. In order for your component to expect these properties, you need to create an array on the component by using the `props` property.

An example of this would be if we wanted to make a `heading` component:

```
Vue.component('heading', {
  template: '<h1>{{ text }}</h1>',

  props: ['text']
});
```

The component would then be used in the view like so:

```
<heading text="Hello!"></heading>
```

With props, we don't need to define the `text` variable in the data object, as defining it in the props array automatically makes it available for use in the template. The props array can also take further options, allowing you to define the type of input expected, whether it is required or a default value to use if omitted.

Add a prop to the balance component so we can pass the cost as an HTML attribute. Your view should now look like this:

```
<balance cost="1234"></balance>
```

We can now add the cost prop to the component in the JavaScript, and remove the fixed value from our data function:

```
template: '<div>{{ formattedCost }}</div>',
props: ['cost'],
data() {
  return {
    currency: '$'
  }
},
```

Running this in our browser, however, will throw an error in our JavaScript console. This is because, natively, props being passed in are interpreted as strings. We can address this in two ways; we can either convert our prop to a number in our `formatCost ()` function or, alternatively, we can use the `v-bind:` HTML attribute to tell Vue to accept the input for what it is.

If you remember, we used this technique with our filters for the `true` and `false` values—allowing them to be used as Boolean instead of strings. Add `v-bind:` in front of your `cost` HTML attribute:

```
<balance v-bind:cost="15234"></balance>
```

There is an extra step we can do to ensure Vue knows what kind of input to expect and informs other users of your code as to what they should be passing to the component. This can be done in the component itself and, along with the format, allows you to specify default values along with whether the prop is required or not.

Convert your `props` array to an object, with `cost` as the key. If you are just defining the field type, you can use the Vue shorthand for declaring this by setting the value as the field type. These can be String, Number, Boolean, Function, Object, Array, or Symbol. As our cost attribute should be a number, add that as the key:

```
props: {
   cost: Number
},
```

It would be nice if, rather than throwing an error when nothing is defined, our component rendered $0.00. We can do this by setting the default to just 0. To define a default we need to convert our prop into an object itself - containing a `type` key that has the value of `Number`. We can then define another `default` key and set the value to 0:

```
props: {
  cost: {
     type: Number,
     default: 0
  }
},
```

Rendering the component in the browser should show whatever value is passed into the cost attribute—but removing this will render $0.00.

To recap, our component looks like :

```
Vue.component('balance', {
   template: '<div>{{ formattedCost }}</div>',

   props: {
     cost: {
        type: Number,
        default: 0
     }
   },

   data() {
     return {
        currency: '$'
     }
   },

   computed: {
     formattedCost() {
        return this.currency +
        this.cost.toFixed(2);
```

```
      }
    }
  });
```

We should be able to expand on this example when we make the person component of our listing app.

Passing data to your component – slots

There are times when you may need to pass chunks of HTML to your component that are not stored in a property or that you want to format before appearing in the component. Rather than trying to pre-format in a computed variable or similar, you can use slots with your component.

Slots are like placeholders and allow you to place content between the opening and closing tags of your component and determine where they are going to display.

A perfect example of this would be a modal window. These normally have several tags and often consist of a lot of HTML to copy and paste if you wish to use it in your application multiple times. Instead, you can create a modal-window component and pass your HTML with a slot.

Create a new component titled modal-window. This accepts one prop of visible, which accepts a Boolean value and is false by default. For the template, we'll use the HTML from the *Bootstrap modal* as a good example of how a component using slots can easily simplify your application. To ensure the component is styled, make sure you include the bootstrap *asset files* in your document:

```
Vue.component('modal-window', {
  template: `<div class="modal fade">
    <div class="modal-dialog" role="document">
      <div class="modal-content">
        <div class="modal-header">
          <button type="button" class="close"
          data-dismiss="modal" aria-label="Close">
          <span aria-hidden="true">&times;</span>
        </button>
      </div>
    <div class="modal-body">
    </div>
      <div class="modal-footer">
        <button type="button" class="btn btn-
        primary">Save changes</button>
```

```
        <button type="button" class="btn btn-
         secondary" data-dismiss="modal">Close
        </button>
        </div>
      </div>
    </div>
  </div>`,

  props: {
    visible: {
      type: Boolean,
      default: false
    }
  }
});
```

We will be using the visible prop to determine whether the modal window is open or not.
Add a v-show attribute to your outer container that accepts the visible variable:

```
Vue.component('modal-window', {
    template: `<div class="modal fade" v-
    show="visible">
      ...
    </div>`,

    props: {
      visible: {
        type: Boolean,
        default: false
      }
    }
});
```

Add your modal-window component to the app, specifying visible to be true for now,
so we can understand and see what is going on:

```
<modal-window :visible="true"></modal-window>
```

We now need to pass some data to our modal box. Add a heading and some paragraphs
between the two tags:

```
<modal-window :visible="true">
  <h1>Modal Title</h1>
  <p>Lorem ipsum dolor sit amet, consectetur
   adipiscing elit. Suspendisse ut rutrum ante, a
   ultrices felis. Quisque sodales diam non mi
   blandit dapibus. </p>
```

```
<p>Lorem ipsum dolor sit amet, consectetur
adipiscing elit. Suspendisse ut rutrum ante, a
ultrices felis. Quisque sodales diam non mi
blandit dapibus. </p>
</modal-window>
```

Pressing refresh in the browser won't do anything, as we need to tell the component what to do with the data. Inside your template, add a `<slot></slot>` HTML tag where you want your content to appear. Add it to the `div` with the `modal-body` class:

```
Vue.component('modal-window', {
  template: `<div class="modal fade" v-
show="visible">
    <div class="modal-dialog" role="document">
      <div class="modal-content">
        <div class="modal-header">
      <button type="button" class="close" data-
        dismiss="modal" aria-label="Close">
          <span aria-hidden="true">&times;</span>
        </button>
        </div>
        <div class="modal-body">
          <slot></slot>
        </div>
        <div class="modal-footer">
        <button type="button" class="btn btn-
      primary">Save changes</button>
        <button type="button" class="btn btn-
          secondary" data-
      dismiss="modal">Close</button>
      </div>
      </div>
  </div>
  </div>`,

  props: {
    visible: {
      type: Boolean,
      default: false
    }
  }
});
```

Viewing your app will now reveal the content you passed in inside the modal window. Already, the app is looking cleaner with this new component.

Viewing the Bootstrap HTML, we can see there is space for a header, body, and footer. We can identify these sections with named slots. This allows us to pass specific content to specific areas of our component.

Create two new `<slot>` tags in the header and footer of the modal window. Give these new ones a name attribute, but leave the existing one empty:

```
template: `<div class="modal fade" v-
show="visible">
  <div class="modal-dialog" role="document">
    <div class="modal-content">
      <div class="modal-header">
        <slot name="header"></slot>
        <button type="button" class="close" data-
          dismiss="modal" aria-label="Close">
          <span aria-hidden="true">&times;</span>
        </button>
      </div>
      <div class="modal-body">
        <slot></slot>
      </div>
      <div class="modal-footer">
        <slot name="footer"></slot>
        <button type="button" class="btn btn-
        primary">Save changes</button>
        <button type="button" class="btn btn-
        secondary" data-
        dismiss="modal">Close</button>
      </div>
    </div>
  </div>
</div>`,
```

In our app, we can now specify what content goes where by specifying a `slot` attribute in the HTML. This can either go on a specific tag or a container around several tags. Any HTML without a `slot` attribute will also default to your unnamed slot:

```
<modal-window :visible="true">
  <h1 slot="header">Modal Title</h1>
  <p>Lorem ipsum dolor sit amet, consectetur
  adipiscing elit. Suspendisse ut rutrum ante, a
  ultrices felis. Quisque sodales diam non mi
  blandit dapibus. </p>

  <p slot="footer">Lorem ipsum dolor sit amet,
  consectetur adipiscing elit. Suspendisse ut
  rutrum ante, a ultrices felis. Quisque sodales
```

```
      diam non mi blandit dapibus. </p>
</modal-window>
```

We can now specify and direct our content to specific places.

The last thing you can do with slots is specified a default value. For example, you may want to display the buttons in the footer most of the time, but want to have the ability to replace them if desired. With a `<slot>`, any content placed between the tags will be displayed unless overwritten when specifying the component in your app.

Create a new slot titled `buttons`, and place the buttons in the footer inside. Try replacing them with some other content.

The template becomes:

```
template: `<div class="modal fade" v-
show="visible">
  <div class="modal-dialog" role="document">
    <div class="modal-content">
      <div class="modal-header">
        <slot name="header"></slot>
        <button type="button" class="close" data-
        dismiss="modal" aria-label="Close">
          <span aria-hidden="true">&times;</span>
        </button>
      </div>
      <div class="modal-body">
        <slot></slot>
      </div>
      <div class="modal-footer">
        <slot name="footer"></slot>
        <slot name="buttons">
          <button type="button" class="btn btn-
          primary">Save changes</button>
          <button type="button" class="btn btn-
          secondary" data-
          dismiss="modal">Close</button>
        </slot>
      </div>
    </div>
  </div>
</div>`,
```

And the HTML:

```
<modal-window :visible="true">
<h1 slot="header">Modal Title</h1>
 <p>Lorem ipsum dolor sit amet, consectetur
 adipiscing elit. Suspendisse ut rutrum ante, a
 ultrices felis. Quisque sodales diam non mi blandit
 dapibus. </p>

  <p slot="footer">Lorem ipsum dolor sit amet,
  consectetur adipiscing elit. Suspendisse ut rutrum
  ante, a ultrices felis. Quisque sodales diam non mi
  blandit dapibus. </p>

 <div slot="buttons">
   <button type="button" class="btn btn-
   primary">Ok</button>
 </div>
</modal-window>
```

Although we won't be utilizing slots with our people listing app, it's good to be aware of the capabilities of a Vue component. If you wished to use a modal box like this, you can set the visibility to a variable that is false by default. You can then add a button with a click method that changes the variable from `false` to `true`—displaying the modal box.

Creating a repeatable component

The beauty of components is being able to use them multiple times in the same view. This gives you the ability to have one single "source of truth" for the layout of that data. We're going to make a repeatable component for our people list and a separate component for the filtering section.

Open your people listing code you created in the last couple of chapters and create a new component titled `team-member`. Don't forget to define the component before your Vue app is initialized. Add a `prop` to the component to allow the person object to be passed in. For validation purposes, only specify that it can be an `Object`:

```
Vue.component('team-member', {
  props: {
    person: Object
  }
});
```

We now need to integrate our template into the component, which is everything inside (and including) the `tr` in our View.

The template variable in the component just accepts a normal string without new lines, so we need to do one of the following:

- inline our HTML template—great for small templates but in this case will sacrifice readability
- add new lines with the + string concatenation—great for one or two lines, but would bloat our JavaScript
- create a template block—Vue gives us the option to use external templates that are defined in the view using the `text/x-template` syntax and an ID

As our template is quite big, we are going to choose the third option of declaring our template at the end of our view.

In your HTML, outside of your app, create a new script block and add a `type` and `ID` attribute:

```
<script type="text/x-template" id="team-member-
  template">
</script>
```

We can then move our person template into this block and remove the `v-for` attribute—we'll still use that in the app itself:

```
<script type="text/x-template" id="team-member-
template">
  <tr v-show="filterRow(person)">
    <td>
      {{ person.name }}
    </td>
    <td>
      <a v-bind:href="'mailto:' + person.email">{{
      person.email }}</a>
    </td>
    <td v-bind:class="balanceClass(person)">
      {{ format(person, 'balance') }}
    </td>
    <td>
      {{ format(person, 'registered') }}
    </td>
    <td v-bind:class="activeClass(person)">
      {{ format(person, 'isActive') }}
    </td>
```

```
    </tr>
  </script>
```

We now need to update the view to use the `team-member` component instead of the fixed code. To make our view cleaner and easier to understand, we are going to utilize the `<template>` HTML attribute mentioned earlier. Create a `<template>` tag and add the v-for loop we had before. To avoid confusion, update the loop to use `individual` as the variable for each person. They can be the same, but it makes the code easier to read if the variables, components, and props have different names. Update the `v-for` to be `v-for="individual in people"`:

```
<table>
  <template v-for="individual in people">
  </template>
</table>
```

Inside the `template` tags of your view, add a new instance of the `team-member` component, passing the `individual` variable to the `person` prop. Don't forget to add v-bind: to the person prop, otherwise, the component will interpret it as a fixed string with the value of the individual:

```
<table>
  <template v-for="individual in people">
    <team-member v-bind:person="individual"></team-member>
  </template>
</table>
```

We now need to update the component to use the template we have declared using the `template` property and the ID of the script block as the value:

```
Vue.component('team-member', {
  template: '#team-member-template',
  props: {
    person: Object
  }
});
```

Viewing the app in the browser will create several errors in the JavaScript console. This is because we are referencing several methods that are no longer available - as they are on the parent Vue instance, not on the component. If you want to verify that your component is working, change the code to only output the name of the person, and press refresh:

```
<script type="text/x-template" id="team-member-
  template">
<tr v-show="filterRow()">
  <td>
    {{ person.name }}
  </td>
</tr>
</script>
```

Creating component methods and computed functions

We now need to create the methods we had created on the Vue instance on the child component, so they are available to use. One thing we could do is cut and paste the methods from the parent into the child in the hope they would work; however, those methods rely on parent properties (such as filtering data) and we also have the opportunity to utilize `computed` properties, which cache the data and can speed up your app.

For now, remove the `v-show` attribute from the `tr` element—as this involves the filtering, and that will be covered once we have our rows displaying correctly. We'll step through the errors and resolve them one at a time to help you understand problem-solving with Vue.

CSS class functions

The first error we encounter when viewing the application in the browser is:

Property or method "balanceClass" is not defined

The first error is with regards to both the `balanceClass` and `activeClass` functions we use. Both of these functions add CSS classes based on the data of the person, which does not change once the component has been rendered.

Because of this, we are able to use the caching found in Vue. Move the methods across to the component but put them in a new `computed` object, instead of the `methods` one.

With components, a new instance is created every time it is called, so we can rely on the `person` object we passed in via a `prop` and no longer need to pass the `person` into the function. Remove the parameter from the function and the view—also update any reference to `person` *inside* the function to `this.person` to reference the object stored on the component:

```
computed: {
  /**
   * CSS Classes
   */
  activeClass() {
    return this.person.isActive ? 'active' :
'inactive';
  },
  balanceClass() {
    let balanceLevel = 'success';
    if(this.person.balance < 2000) {
      balanceLevel = 'error';
    } else if (this.person.balance < 3000) {
      balanceLevel = 'warning';
    }
    let increasing = false,
        balance = this.person.balance / 1000;
    if(Math.round(balance) == Math.ceil(balance)) {
      increasing = 'increasing';
    }

    return [balanceLevel, increasing];
  }
},
```

The part of our component template that utilizes this function should now look like:

```
<td v-bind:class="balanceClass">
    {{ format(person, 'balance') }}
</td>
```

Formatted value functions

When it comes to moving the `format()` function to the component for formatting our data, we are faced with two options. We can move it like-for-like and put it in the `methods` object, or we can take advantage of the Vue caching and conventions and create a `computed` function for each value.

We are building this app for scalability, so it's advisable to make computed functions for each value—it will also have the advantage of tidying up our template. Create three functions in the computed object titled `balance`, `dateRegistered`, and `status`. Copy the corresponding parts of the `format` function across to each one, updating the reference of `person` to `this.person` once more.

Where we were retrieving the field using a function parameter, you can now fix the value in each function. You will also need to add a data object with the currency symbol for the balance function—add this after the `props`:

```
data() {
  return {
    currency: '$'
  }
},
```

As the `team-member` component is the only place our currency symbol is used, we can remove it from the Vue app itself. We can also remove the format function from our parent Vue instance.

In total, our Vue `team-member` component should look like:

```
Vue.component('team-member', {
  template: '#team-member-template',
  props: {
    person: Object
  },
  data() {
    return {
      currency: '$'
    }
  },
  computed: {
    /**
     * CSS Classes
     */
    activeClass() {
      return this.person.isActive ? 'active' :
      'inactive';
    },
    balanceClass() {
      let balanceLevel = 'success';
      if(this.person.balance < 2000) {
        balanceLevel = 'error';
      } else if (this.person.balance < 3000) {
        balanceLevel = 'warning';
```

```
    }
  let increasing = false,
        balance = this.person.balance / 1000;
    if(Math.round(balance) == Math.ceil(balance))
    {
      increasing = 'increasing';
    }
    return [balanceLevel, increasing];
  },
  /**
   * Fields
   */
  balance() {
    return this.currency +
    this.person.balance.toFixed(2);
  },
  dateRegistered() {
    let registered = new
    Date(this.person.registered);
    return registered.toLocaleString('en-US');
  },
  status() {
    return (this.person.isActive) ? 'Active' :
    'Inactive';
  }
}
});
```

And our `team-member-template` should look fairly simple in comparison to what it did look like:

```
<script type="text/x-template" id="team-member-
template">
  <tr v-show="filterRow()">
    <td>
      {{ person.name }}
    </td>
    <td>
      <a v-bind:href="'mailto:' + person.email">{{
      person.email }}</a>
    </td>
    <td v-bind:class="balanceClass">
      {{ balance }}
    </td>
    <td>
      {{ dateRegistered }}
    </td>
```

```
      <td v-bind:class="activeClass">
        {{ status }}
      </td>
    </tr>
</script>
```

And lastly, our Vue instance should look significantly smaller:

```
const app = new Vue({
  el: '#app',
  data: {
    people: [...],
    filter: {
      field: '',
      query: ''
    }
  },
  methods: {
    isActiveFilterSelected() {
      return (this.filter.field === 'isActive');
    },
    /**
     * Filtering
     */
    filterRow(person) {
      let visible = true,
          field = this.filter.field,
          query = this.filter.query;
      if(field) {
        if(this.isActiveFilterSelected()) {
          visible = (typeof query === 'boolean') ?
            (query === person.isActive) : true;
        } else {
          query = String(query),
          field = person[field];
      if(typeof field === 'number') {
        query.replace(this.currency, '');
            try {
              visible = eval(field + query);
            } catch(e) {}
          } else {
            field = field.toLowerCase();
            visible =
            field.includes(query.toLowerCase())
          }
        }
      }
      return visible;
```

```
      }
    changeFilter(event) {
      this.filter.query = '';
      this.filter.field = event.target.value;
    }
  }
});
```

Viewing the app in the browser, we should be presented with our list of people with the correct classes added to the table cells and formatting added to the fields.

Making the filtering work again with props

Re-add the `v-show="filterRow()"` attribute to the containing `tr` element in your template. As our component has the person cached on each instance, we no longer need to pass the person object to the method. Refreshing the page will give you a new error in your JavaScript console:

```
Property or method "filterRow" is not defined on the instance but
referenced during render
```

This error is because our component has the `v-show` attribute, showing and hiding based on our filtering and properties, but not the corresponding `filterRow` function. As we don't use it for anything else, we can move the method from the Vue instance to the component, adding it to the `methods` component. Remove the person parameter and update the method to use `this.person`:

```
filterRow() {
  let visible = true,
      field = this.filter.field,
      query = this.filter.query;
      if(field) {
      if(this.isActiveFilterSelected()) {
      visible = (typeof query === 'boolean') ?
      (query === this.person.isActive) : true;
      } else {
      query = String(query),
      field = this.person[field];
      if(typeof field === 'number') {
        query.replace(this.currency, '');
        try {
          visible = eval(field + query);
        } catch(e) {}
        } else {
```

```
            field = field.toLowerCase();
            visible =
        field.includes(query.toLowerCase());
            }
        }
    }
    return visible;
}
```

The next error in the console is:

`Cannot read property 'field' of undefined`

The reason the filtering does not work is that the `filterRow` method is looking for `this.filter.field` and `this.filter.query` on the component, not the parent Vue instance where it belongs.

 As a quick fix, you can use `this.$parent` to reference data on the parent element—however, this is not recommended and should only be used in extreme circumstances or to quickly pass the data through.

To pass the data through to the component we are going to use another prop - similar to how we are passing the person into the component. Fortunately, we had grouped our filtering data already, so we are able to pass that one object instead of individual properties of `query` or `field`. Create a new prop on your component titled `filter` and ensure you only allow an `Object` to be passed through:

```
props: {
  person: Object,
  filter: Object
},
```

We can then add the prop to the `team-member` component, allowing us to pass the data:

```
<table>
  <template v-for="individual in people">
    <team-member v-bind:person="individual" v-
      bind:filter="filter"></team-member>
  </template>
</table>
```

In order for our filtering to work, we need to pass in one more property-
the isActiveFilterSelected() function. Create another prop, titled statusFilter,
allowing only a Boolean to be the value (as this is what the function equates to), and pass
the function through. Update the filterRow method to use this new value. Our
component now looks like:

```
Vue.component('team-member', {
  template: '#team-member-template',
  props: {
    person: Object,
    filter: Object,
    statusFilter: Boolean
  },
  data() {
    return {
      currency: '$'
    }
  },
  computed: {
    /**
     * CSS Classes
     */
    activeClass() {
      return this.person.isActive ? 'active' :
      'inactive';
      },
      balanceClass() {
      let balanceLevel = 'success';
  if(this.person.balance < 2000) {
   balanceLevel = 'error';
  } else if (this.person.balance < 3000) {
    balanceLevel = 'warning';
  }
    let increasing = false,
      balance = this.person.balance / 1000;
    if(Math.round(balance) == Math.ceil(balance)) {
      increasing = 'increasing';
  }
    return [balanceLevel, increasing];
  },
/**
* Fields
 */
balance() {
return this.currency +
this.person.balance.toFixed(2);
  },
```

```
dateRegistered() {
 let registered = new Date(this.registered);
  return registered.toLocaleString('en-US');
  },
  status() {
    return output = (this.person.isActive) ?
   'Active' : 'Inactive';
  }
 },
 methods: {
  filterRow() {
   let visible = true,
      field = this.filter.field,
      query = this.filter.query;
    if(field) {
     if(this.statusFilter) {
       visible = (typeof query === 'boolean') ?
       (query === this.person.isActive) : true;
     } else {
       query = String(query),
       field = this.person[field];
        if(typeof field === 'number') {
          query.replace(this.currency, '');
           try {
           visible = eval(field + query);
          } catch(e) {
      }
     } else {
      field = field.toLowerCase();
      visible = field.includes(query.toLowerCase());
       }
      }
     }
    return visible;
   }
  }
});
```

And the component within the View with the extra props now looks like the following. Note that the camel-cased prop becomes snake case (hyphenated) when used as an HTML attribute:

```
<template v-for="individual in people">
     <team-member v-bind:person="individual" v-
bind:filter="filter" v-bind:status-
     filter="isActiveFilterSelected()"></team-
     member>
```

```
</template>
```

Making the filters a component

We now need to make the filtering section its own component. This isn't strictly necessary in this scenario, but it's good practice and gives us more challenges.

The problem we face in making the filtering a component is a challenge of transferring filter data between the filtering component and the `team-member` component. Vue addresses this with custom events. These let you pass (or "emit") data to the parent or other components from the child component.

We are going to create a filtering component which, on filtering change, passes the data back to the parent Vue instance. This data is already passed through to the `team-member` component to filter.

Creating the component

As with the `team-member` component, declare a new `Vue.component()` in your JavaScript, referencing a template ID of `#filtering-template`. Create a new `<script>` template block in your view and give it the same ID. Replace the filtering form in the view with a `<filtering>` custom HTML template and put the form inside your `filtering-template` script block.

Your view should look like the following:

```
<div id="app">
  <filtering></filtering>
  <table>
    <template v-for="individual in people">
      <team-member v-bind:person="individual" v-
        bind:filter="filter" v-
        bind:statusfilter="isActiveFilterSelected()">            </team-
member>
    </template>
  </table>
</div>

<script type="text/x-template" id="filtering-
template">
  <form>
    <label for="fiterField">
```

```
        Field:
        <select v-on:change="changeFilter($event)"
 id="filterField">
          <option value="">Disable filters</option>
          <option value="isActive">Active user</option>
          <option value="name">Name</option>
          <option value="email">Email</option>
          <option value="balance">Balance</option>
          <option value="registered">Date
          registered</option>
        </select>
      </label>
      <label for="filterQuery" v-show="this.filter.field
      && !isActiveFilterSelected()">
        Query:
        <input type="text" id="filterQuery" v-
        model="filter.query">
      </label>
      <span v-show="isActiveFilterSelected()">
        Active:
      <label for="userStateActive">
        Yes:
          <input type="radio" v-bind:value="true"
 id="userStateActive" v-model="filter.query">
        </label>
        <label for="userStateInactive">
        No:
    <input type="radio" v-bind:value="false"
    id="userStateInactive" v-model="filter.query">
      </label>
    </span>
  </form>
</script>
<script type="text/x-template" id="team-member-
template">
// Team member template
</script>
```

And you should have the following in your JavaScript:

```
Vue.component('filtering', {
  template: '#filtering-template'
});
```

Resolving JavaScript errors

As with the `team-member` component, you are going to experience some errors in your JavaScript console. These can be resolved by copying the `filter` data object and both the `changeFilter` and `isActiveFilterSelected` methods from the parent instance. We'll leave them in both the component and parent instance for now, but we'll remove the duplication later:

```
Vue.component('filtering', {
  template: '#filtering-template',
  data() {
    return {
      filter: {
        field: '',
        query: ''
      }
    }
  },
  methods: {
    isActiveFilterSelected() {
      return (this.filter.field === 'isActive');
    },
    changeFilter(event) {
      this.filter.query = '';
      this.filter.field = event.target.value;
    }
  }
});
```

Running the app will show both the filters and person listing, but the filters won't update the people list as they are not communicating yet.

Using custom events to change the filter field

With custom events, you can pass data back up to the parent instances using the `$on` and `$emit` functions. For this app, we are going to store the filtering data on the parent Vue instance and update it from the component. The `team-member` component can then read the data from the Vue instance and filter accordingly.

The first step is to utilize the filter object on the parent Vue instance. Remove the `data` object from your component and pass in the parent one via a prop - just as we did with the `team-member` component:

```
<filtering v-bind:filter="filter"></filtering>
```

We are now going to modify the `changeFilter` function to emit the event data so the parent instance, so it can update the `filter` object.

Remove the existing `changeFilter` method from the `filtering` component and create a new one called `change-filter-field`. Within this method, we just need to `$emit` the name of the field selected in the drop-down menu. The `$emit` function takes two parameters: a key and the value. Emit a key of `change-filter-field` and pass the `event.target.value` as the data. When using variables with multiple words (For example, `changeFilterField`), ensure these are hyphenated for the event name (the first parameter of the `$emit` function) and the HTML attribute:

```
changeFilterField(event) {
   this.$emit('change-filter-field',
event.target.value);
}
```

In order to then pass the data to the changeFilter method on our parent Vue instance, we need to add a new prop to our `<filtering>` element. This uses `v-on` and binds to the custom event name. It then has the parent method name as the attribute value. Add the attribute to your element:

```
<filtering v-bind:filter="filter" v-on:change-filter-
field="changeFilter"></filtering>
```

This attribute preceding tells Vue to trigger the `changeFilter` method when a `change-filter-field` event is emitted. We can then tweak our method to accept the parameter as the value:

```
changeFilter(field) {
   this.filter.query = '';
   this.filter.field = field;
}
```

This then clears the filters and updates the field value, which then ripples down to our components via props.

Updating the filter query

To emit the query field, we are going to use a new Vue key that we have not used before, called watch. The watch function tracks a data property and can run methods based on the output. The other thing it is able to do is to emit events. As both, our text field and radio buttons are set to update the field.query variable, we will create a new watch function on this.

Create a new watch object after the methods on your component:

```
watch: {
  'filter.query': function() {
  }
}
```

The key is the variable you wish to watch. As ours contains a dot, it needs to be wrapped in quotes. Within this function, create a new $emit event of change-filter-query that outputs the value of filter.query:

```
watch: {
    'filter.query': function() {
    this.$emit('change-filter-query',
    this.filter.query)
    }
}
```

We now need to bind this method and custom event to the component in the view, so it is able to pass the data to the parent instance. Set the value of the attribute to changeQuery—we'll make a method to handle this:

```
<filtering v-bind:filter="filter" v-on:change-
filter-field="changeFilter" v-on:change-filter-
query="changeQuery"></filtering>
```

On the parent Vue instance, make a new method, titled changeQuery, that simply updates the filter.query value based on the input:

```
changeQuery(query) {
   this.filter.query = query;
}
```

Our filtering is now working again. Both updating the select box and the input box (or radio buttons) will now update our person list. Our Vue instance is significantly smaller and our templates and methods are contained with separate components.

The last step is to avoid the repetition of the `isActiveFilterSelected()` method, as this is only used once on the `team-member` component, but several times on the `filtering` component. Remove the method from the parent Vue instance, the prop from the `team-member` HTML element, and replace the `statusFilter` variable in the `filterRow` method within the `team-member` component with the contents of the function being passed through.

The final JavaScript now looks like:

```
Vue.component('team-member', {
  template: '#team-member-template',
  props: {
    person: Object,
    filter: Object
  },
  data() {
    return {
      currency: '$'
    }
  },
  computed: {
    /**
     * CSS Classes
     */
    activeClass() {
      return this.person.isActive ? 'active' :
'inactive';
    },
    balanceClass() {
      let balanceLevel = 'success';
      if(this.person.balance < 2000) {
        balanceLevel = 'error';
      } else if (this.person.balance < 3000) {
        balanceLevel = 'warning';
      }
      let increasing = false,
        balance = this.person.balance / 1000;
      if(Math.round(balance) == Math.ceil(balance))         {
        increasing = 'increasing';
      }
      return [balanceLevel, increasing];
    },
    /**
     * Fields
     */
    balance() {
```

```
        return this.currency +
      this.person.balance.toFixed(2);
      },
      dateRegistered() {
        let registered = new Date(this.registered);
        return registered.toLocaleString('en-US');
      },
      status() {
        return output = (this.person.isActive) ?
       'Active' : 'Inactive';
      }
    },
     methods: {
     filterRow() {
       let visible = true,
       field = this.filter.field,
       query = this.filter.query;
       if(field) {
         if(this.filter.field === 'isActive') {
         visible = (typeof query === 'boolean') ?
        (query === this.person.isActive) : true;
          } else {
            query = String(query),
            field = this.person[field];
            if(typeof field === 'number') {
              query.replace(this.currency, '');
           try {
           visible = eval(field + query);
         } catch(e) {}
       } else {
         field = field.toLowerCase();
         visible = field.includes(query.toLowerCase());
           }
        }
      }
        return visible;
      }
      }
     });
Vue.component('filtering', {
template: '#filtering-template',
  props: {
  filter: Object
},
  methods: {
  isActiveFilterSelected() {
   return (this.filter.field === 'isActive');
  },
```

```
       changeFilterField(event) {
        this.filedField = '';
      this.$emit('change-filter-field',
       event.target.value);
         },
        },
       watch: {
  'filter.query': function() {
     this.$emit('change-filter-query', this.filter.query)
          }
         }
       });
      const app = new Vue({
        el: '#app',

        data: {
          people: [...],
          filter: {
            field: '',
            query: ''
          }
        },
        methods: {
          changeFilter(field) {
            this.filter.query = '';
            this.filter.field = field;
          },
          changeQuery(query) {
            this.filter.query = query;
          }
        }
      });
```

And the view is now:

```
    <div id="app">
      <filtering v-bind:filter="filter" v-on:change-
        filter-field="changeFilter" v-on:change-filter-
        query="changeQuery"></filtering>
     <table>
       <template v-for="individual in people">
        <team-member v-bind:person="individual" v-
        bind:filter="filter"></team-member>
       </template>
      </table>
   </div>
  <script type="text/x-template" id="filtering-
    template">
```

```
<form>
<label for="fiterField">
 Field:
<select v-on:change="changeFilterField($event)"
  id="filterField">
 <option value="">Disable filters</option>
 <option value="isActive">Active user</option>
 <option value="name">Name</option>
 <option value="email">Email</option>
 <option value="balance">Balance</option>
 <option value="registered">Date
   registered</option>
 </select>
 </label>
 <label for="filterQuery" v-
  show="this.filter.field &&
  !isActiveFilterSelected()">
 Query:
<input type="text" id="filterQuery" v-
 model="filter.query">
 </label>
 <span v-show="isActiveFilterSelected()">
  Active:
   <label for="userStateActive">
     Yes:
    <input type="radio" v-bind:value="true"
   id="userStateActive" v-model="filter.query">
   </label>
   <label for="userStateInactive">
    No:
    <input type="radio" v-bind:value="false"
id="userStateInactive" v-model="filter.query">
    </label>
   </span>
  </form>
 </script>
 <script type="text/x-template" id="team-member-
 template">
   <tr v-show="filterRow()">
     <td>
       {{ person.name }}
     </td>
     <td>
       <a v-bind:href="'mailto:' + person.email">{{
person.email }}</a>
     </td>
     <td v-bind:class="balanceClass">
       {{ balance }}
```

```
      </td>
      <td>
        {{ dateRegistered }}
      </td>
      <td v-bind:class="activeClass">
        {{ status }}
      </td>
    </tr>
</script>
```

Summary

Over the last three chapters, you have learned how to initialize a new Vue instance, what the meaning behind computed, method, and data objects are, and how to list out data from an object and manipulate it to be displayed correctly. You have also learned how to make components and what benefits there are to keeping your code clean and optimized.

In the next section of the book, we are going to introduce Vuex, something which helps us store and manipulate stored data better.

4

Getting a List of Files Using the Dropbox API

Over the next few chapters, we are going to be building a Vue-based Dropbox browser. This app will take your Dropbox API key and allow you to navigate to folders and download files. You will learn about interacting with an API within a Vue app, the Vue life cycle hooks, including the `created()` method, and finally we will introduce a library called `Vuex` to handle the caching and state of the app. The app will have shareable URLs and retrieve the contents of the folder passed in via the # URL parameter.

This kind of app would be useful if you wanted to give users access to the contents of your Dropbox without giving out a username and password. Be warned, however, a tech-savvy user could find your API key in the code and abuse it, so don't publish this code to the World Wide Web.

This chapter is going to cover:

- Loading and querying the Dropbox API
- Listing the directories and files from your Dropbox account
- Adding a loading state to your app
- Using Vue animations

You will need a Dropbox account to follow these next few chapters. If you don't have one, sign up and add a few dummy files and folders. The contents of the Dropbox don't matter, but having folders to navigate through will help with understanding the code.

Getting started—loading the libraries

Create a new HTML page for your app to run in. Create the HTML structure required for a web page and include your app view wrapper:

```
<!DOCTYPE html>
<html>
<head>
  <title>Dropbox App</title>
</head>
<body>
  <div id="app">
  </div>
</body>
</html>
```

It's called `#app` here, but call it whatever you want - just remember to update the JavaScript.

As our app code is going to get quite chunky, make a separate JavaScript file and include it at the bottom of the document. You will also need to include Vue and the Dropbox API SDK.

As with before, you can either reference the remote files or download a local copy of the library files. Download a local copy for both speed and compatibility reasons. Include your three JavaScript files at the bottom of your HTML file:

```
<script src="js/vue.js"></script>
<script src="js/dropbox.js"></script>
<script src="js/app.js"></script>
```

Create your `app.js` and initialize a new Vue instance, using the `el` tag to mount the instance onto the ID in your view.

```
new Vue({
    el: '#app'
});
```

Creating a Dropbox app and initializing the SDK

Before we interact with the Vue instance, we need to connect to the Dropbox API through the SDK. This is done via an API key that is generated by Dropbox itself to keep track of what is connecting to your account and where Dropbox requires you to make a custom Dropbox app.

Head to the Dropbox developers area and select **Create your app**. Choose **Dropbox API** and select either a restricted folder *or* full access. This depends on your needs, but for testing, choose **Full Dropbox**. Give your app a name and click the button **Create app**.

Generate an access token to your app. To do so, when viewing the app details page, click the **Generate** button under the **Generated access token**. This will give you a long string of numbers and letters - copy and paste that into your editor and store it as a variable at the top of your JavaScript. In this book, the API key will be referred to as XXXX:

```
/**
 * API Access Token
 */
let accessToken = 'XXXX';
```

Now that we have our API key, we can access the files and folders from our Dropbox. Initialize the API and pass in your `accessToken` variable to the `accessToken` property of the Dropbox API:

```
/**
 * Dropbox Client
 * @type {Dropbox}
 */
const dbx = new Dropbox({
  accessToken: accessToken
});
```

We now have access to Dropbox via the `dbx` variable. We can verify our connection to Dropbox is working by connecting and outputting the contents of the root path:

```
dbx.filesListFolder({path: ''})
    .then(response => {
      console.log(response.entries);
    })
    .catch(error => {
      console.log(error);
    });
```

This code uses JavaScript promises, which are a way of adding actions to code without requiring callback functions. If you are unfamiliar with promises, check out this blog post from Google (`https://developers.google.com/web/fundamentals/primers/promises`).

Take a note of the first line, particularly the `path` variable. This lets us pass in a folder path to list the files and folders within that directory. For example, if you had a folder called `images` in your Dropbox, you could change the parameter value to `/images` and the file list returned would be the files and folders within that directory.

Open your JavaScript console and check the output; you should get an array containing several objects - one for each file or folder in the root of your Dropbox.

Displaying your data and using Vue to get it

Now that we can retrieve our data using the Dropbox API, it's time to retrieve it within our Vue instance and display in our view. This app is going to be entirely built using components so we can take advantage of the compartmentalized data and methods. It will also mean the code is modular and shareable, should you want to integrate into other apps.

We are also going to take advantage of the native Vue `created()` function - we'll cover it when it gets triggered in a bit.

Create the component

First off, create your custom HTML element, `<dropbox-viewer>`, in your View. Create a `<script>` template block at the bottom of the page for our HTML layout:

```
<div id="app">
  <dropbox-viewer></dropbox-viewer>
</div>
<script type="text/x-template" id="dropbox-viewer-
  template">
   <h1>Dropbox</h1>
</script>
```

Initialize your component in your `app.js` file, pointing it to the template ID:

```
Vue.component('dropbox-viewer', {
   template: '#dropbox-viewer-template'
});
```

Viewing the app in the browser should show the heading from the template. The next step is to integrate the Dropbox API into the component.

Retrieve the Dropbox data

Create a new method called `dropbox`. In there, move the code that calls the Dropbox class and returns the instance. This will now give us access to the Dropbox API through the component by calling `this.dropbox()`:

```
Vue.component('dropbox-viewer', {
  template: '#dropbox-viewer-template',
  methods: {
    dropbox() {
      return new Dropbox({
        accessToken: this.accessToken
      });
    }
  }
});
```

We are also going to integrate our API key into the component. Create a data function that returns an object containing your access token. Update the Dropbox method to use the local version of the key:

```
Vue.component('dropbox-viewer', {
  template: '#dropbox-viewer-template',
  data() {
    return {
      accessToken: 'XXXX'
    }
  },
  methods: {
    dropbox() {
      return new Dropbox({
        accessToken: this.accessToken
      });
    }
  }
});
```

We now need to add the ability for the component to get the directory list. For this, we are going to create another method that takes a single parameter—the path. This will give us the ability later to request the structure of a different path or folder if required.

Use the code provided earlier - changing the dbx variable to `this.dropbox()`:

```
getFolderStructure(path) {
  this.dropbox().filesListFolder({path: path})
  .then(response => {
    console.log(response.entries);
  })
  .catch(error => {
    console.log(error);
  });
}
```

Update the Dropbox `filesListFolder` function to accept the path parameter passed in, rather than a fixed value. Running this app in the browser will show the Dropbox heading, but won't retrieve any folders because the methods have not been called yet.

The Vue life cycle hooks

This is where the `created()` function comes in. The `created()` function gets called once the Vue instance has initialized the data and methods, but has yet to mount the instance on the HTML component. There are several other functions available at various points in the life cycle; more about these can be read at Alligator.io. The life cycle is as follows:

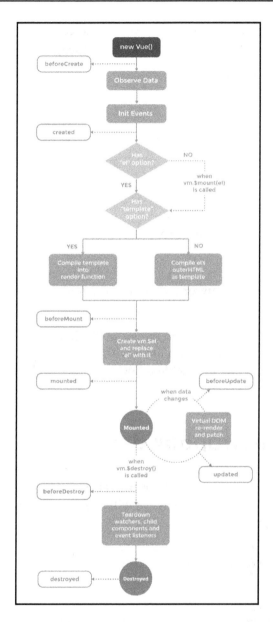

Using the created() function gives us access to the methods and data while being able to start our retrieval process as Vue is mounting the app. The time between these various stages is split-second, but every moment counts when it comes to performance and creating a quick app. There is no point waiting for the app to be fully mounted before processing data if we can start the task early.

Create the `created()` function on your component and call the `getFolderStructure` method, passing in an empty string for the path to get the root of your Dropbox:

```
Vue.component('dropbox-viewer', {
  template: '#dropbox-viewer-template',
  data() {
    return {
      accessToken: 'XXXX'
    }
  },
  methods: {
    ...
  },
  created() {
    this.getFolderStructure('');
  }
});
```

Running the app now in your browser will output the folder list to your console, which should give the same result as before.

We now need to display our list of files in the view. To do this, we are going to create an empty array in our component and populate it with the result of our Dropbox query. This has the advantage of giving Vue a variable to loop through in the view, even before it has any content.

Displaying the Dropbox data

Create a new property in your data object titled `structure`, and assign this to an empty array. In the response function of the folder retrieval, assign `response.entries` to `this.structure`. Leave `console.log` as we will need to inspect the entries to work out what to output in our template:

```
Vue.component('dropbox-viewer', {
  template: '#dropbox-viewer-template',
  data() {
    return {
      accessToken: 'XXXX',
      structure: []
    }
  },
  methods: {
    dropbox() {
      return new Dropbox({
```

```
          accessToken: this.accessToken
        });
      },
      getFolderStructure(path) {
        this.dropbox().filesListFolder({path: path})
        .then(response => {
          console.log(response.entries);
          this.structure = response.entries;
        })
        .catch(error => {
          console.log(error);
        });
      }
    },
    created() {
      this.getFolderStructure('');
    }
  });
```

We can now update our view to display the folders and files from your Dropbox. As the structure array is available in our view, create a `<ul>` with a repeatable `<li>` looping through the structure.

As we are now adding a second element, Vue requires templates to have one containing the element, wrap your heading and list in a `<div>`:

```
<script type="text/x-template" id="dropbox-viewer-
  template">
  <div>
    <h1>Dropbox</h1>
    <ul>
      <li v-for="entry in structure">
      </li>
    </ul>
  </div>
</script>
```

Viewing the app in the browser will show a number of empty bullet points when the array appears in the JavaScript console. To work out what fields and properties you can display, expand the array in the JavaScript console and then further for each object. You should notice that each object has a collection of similar properties and a few that vary between folders and files.

The first property, `.tag`, helps us identify whether the item is a file or a folder. Both types then have the following properties in common:

- `id`: A unique identifier to Dropbox
- `name`: The name of the file or folder, irrespective of where the item is
- `path_display`: The full path of the item with the case matching that of the files and folders
- `path_lower`: Same as `path_display` but all lowercase

Items with a `.tag` of a file also contain several more fields for us to display:

- `client_modified`: This is the date when the file was added to Dropbox.
- `content_hash`: A hash of the file, used for identifying whether it is different from a local or remote copy. More can be read about this on the Dropbox website.
- `rev`: A unique identifier of the version of the file.
- `server_modified`: The last time the file was modified on Dropbox.
- `size`: The size of the file in bytes.

To begin with, we are going to display the name of the item and the size, if present. Update the list item to show these properties:

```
<li v-for="entry in structure">
  <strong>{{ entry.name }}</strong>
  <span v-if="entry.size"> - {{ entry.size }}</span>
</li>
```

More file meta information

To make our file and folder view a bit more useful, we can add more rich content and metadata to files such as images. These details are available by enabling the `include_media_info` option in the Dropbox API.

Head back to your `getFolderStructure` method and add the parameter after `path`. Here are some new lines of readability:

```
getFolderStructure(path) {
  this.dropbox().filesListFolder({
    path: path,
    include_media_info: true
  })
  .then(response => {
```

```
        console.log(response.entries);
        this.structure = response.entries;
      })
      .catch(error => {
        console.log(error);
      });
    }
```

Inspecting the results from this new API call will reveal the `media_info` key for videos and images. Expanding this will reveal several more pieces of information about the file, for example, dimensions. If you want to add these, you will need to check that the `media_info` object exists before displaying the information:

```
<li>
  <strong>{{ f.name }}</strong>
  <span v-if="f.size"> - {{ bytesToSize(f.size) }}
  </span> -
  <span v-if="f.media_info">
    [
    {{ f.media_info.metadata.dimensions.width }}px x
    {{ f.media_info.metadata.dimensions.height }}px
    ]
  </span>
</li>
```

Try updating the path when retrieving the data from Dropbox. For example, if you have a folder called `images`, change the `this.getFolderStructure` parameter to `/images`. If you're not sure what the path is, analyze the data in the JavaScript console and copy the value of the `path_lower` attribute of a folder, for example:

```
created() {
  this.getFolderStructure('/images');
}
```

Formatting the file sizes

With the file size being output in plain bytes it can be quite hard for a user to decipher. To combat this, we can add a formatting method to output a file size which is more user-friendly, for example displaying *1kb* instead of *1024*.

First, create a new key on the data object that contains an array of units called `byteSizes`:

```
data() {
  return {
    accessToken: 'XXXX',
```

```
        structure: [],
        byteSizes: ['Bytes', 'KB', 'MB', 'GB', 'TB']
    }
}
```

This is what will get appended to the figure, so feel free to make these properties either lowercase or full words, for example, *megabyte*.

Next, add a new method, `bytesToSize`, to your component. This will take one parameter of `bytes` and output a formatted string with the unit at the end:

```
bytesToSize(bytes) {
  // Set a default
  let output = '0 Byte';
  // If the bytes are bigger than 0
  if (bytes > 0) {
    // Divide by 1024 and make an int
    let i = parseInt(Math.floor(Math.log(bytes) /
    Math.log(1024)));
    // Round to 2 decimal places and select the
      appropriate unit from the array
    output = Math.round(bytes / Math.pow(1024, i),
      2) + ' ' + this.byteSizes[i];
    }
    return output
  }
```

We can now utilize this method in our view:

```
<li v-for="entry in structure">
  <strong>{{ entry.name }}</strong>
  <span v-if="entry.size"> - {{
  bytesToSize(entry.size) }}</span>
</li>
```

Adding a loading screen

The last step of this chapter is to make a loading screen for our app. This will tell the user the app is loading, should the Dropbox API be running slowly (or you have a lot of data to show!).

The theory behind this loading screen is fairly basic. We will set a loading variable to `true` by default that then gets set to `false` once the data has loaded. Based on the result of this variable, we will utilize view attributes to show, and then hide, an element with the loading text or animation in and also reveal the loaded data list.

Create a new key in the data object titled `isLoading`. Set this variable to `true` by default:

```
data() {
  return {
    accessToken: 'XXXX',
    structure: [],
    byteSizes: ['Bytes', 'KB', 'MB', 'GB', 'TB'],
    isLoading: true
  }
}
```

Within the `getFolderStructure` method on your component, set the `isLoading` variable to `false`. This should happen within the promise after you have set the structure:

```
getFolderStructure(path) {
  this.dropbox().filesListFolder({
    path: path,
    include_media_info: true
  })
  .then(response => {
    console.log(response.entries);
    this.structure = response.entries;
    this.isLoading = false;
  })
  .catch(error => {
    console.log(error);
  });
}
```

We can now utilize this variable in our view to show and hide a loading container.

Create a new `<div>` before the unordered list containing some loading text. Feel free to add a CSS animation or an animated gif—anything to let the user know the app is retrieving data:

```
<h1>Dropbox</h1>
<div>Loading...</div>
<ul>
...
```

We now need to only show the loading div if the app is loading and the list once the data has loaded. As this is just one change to the DOM, we can use the v-if directive. To give you the freedom of rearranging the HTML, add the attribute to both instead of using v-else.

To show or hide, we just need to check the status of the isLoading variable. We can prepend an exclamation mark to the list to only show if the app is not loading:

```
<div>
  <h1>Dropbox</h1>
  <div v-if="isLoading">Loading...</div>
   <ul v-if="!isLoading">
    <li v-for="entry in structure">
      <strong>{{ entry.name }}</strong>
      <span v-if="entry.size">- {{
      bytesToSize(entry.size) }}</span>
    </li>
  </ul>
</div>
```

Our app should now show the loading container once mounted, and then it should show the list once the app data has been gathered. To recap, our complete component code now looks like this:

```
Vue.component('dropbox-viewer', {
  template: '#dropbox-viewer-template',
  data() {
    return {
      accessToken: 'XXXX',
      structure: [],
      byteSizes: ['Bytes', 'KB', 'MB', 'GB', 'TB'],
      isLoading: true
    }
  },
  methods: {
    dropbox() {
      return new Dropbox({
        accessToken: this.accessToken
      });
    },
    getFolderStructure(path) {
      this.dropbox().filesListFolder({
        path: path,
        include_media_info: true
      })
      .then(response => {
```

```
            console.log(response.entries);
            this.structure = response.entries;
            this.isLoading = false;
        })
        .catch(error => {
          console.log(error);
        });
    },
    bytesToSize(bytes) {
      // Set a default
      let output = '0 Byte';
      // If the bytes are bigger than 0
      if (bytes > 0) {
        // Divide by 1024 and make an int
        let i = parseInt(Math.floor(Math.log(bytes)
        / Math.log(1024)));
        // Round to 2 decimal places and select the
          appropriate unit from the array
        output = Math.round(bytes / Math.pow(1024,
        i), 2) + ' ' + this.byteSizes[i];
      }
     return output
    }
  },
  created() {
    this.getFolderStructure('');
  }
});
```

Animating between states

As a nice enhancement for the user, we can add some transitions between components and states. Helpfully, Vue includes some built-in transition effects. Working with CSS, these transitions allow you to add fades, swipes, and other CSS animations easily when DOM elements are being inserted. More information about transitions can be found in the Vue documentation.

The first step is to add the Vue custom HTML <transition> element. Wrap both your loading and list with separate transition elements and give it an attribute of name and a value of fade:

```
<script type="text/x-template" id="dropbox-viewer-
  template">
  <div>
```

```
<h1>Dropbox</h1>
<transition name="fade">
  <div v-if="isLoading">Loading...</div>
</transition>
<transition name="fade">
  <ul v-if="!isLoading">
    <li v-for="entry in structure">
      <strong>{{ entry.name }}</strong>
      <span v-if="entry.size">- {{
      bytesToSize(entry.size) }}</span>
    </li>
  </ul>
</transition>
  </div>
</script>
```

Now add the following CSS to either the head of your document or a separate style sheet if you already have one:

```
.fade-enter-active,
.fade-leave-active {
  transition: opacity .5s
}
.fade-enter,
.fade-leave-to {
  opacity: 0
}
```

With the transition element, Vue adds and removes various CSS classes based on the state and time of the transition. All of these begin with the name passed in via the attribute and are appended with the current stage of transition:

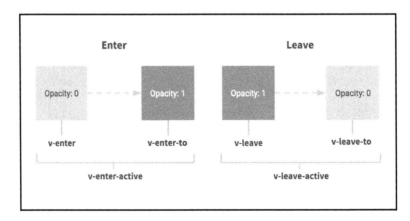

Try the app in your browser, you should notice the loading container fading out and the file list fading in. Although in this basic example, the list jumps up once the fading has completed, it's an example to help you understand using transitions in Vue.

Summary

In this chapter, we learned how to make a Dropbox viewer, which is a single-page application that lists out files and folders from our Dropbox account and allows us to show different folder contents by updating the code. We have learned how to add a basic loading state to our apps and use the Vue animations for navigation.

In Chapter 5, *Navigating through the File Tree and Loading Folders from the URL*, we are going to navigate through our app folders and add download links to our files.

5
Navigating through the File Tree and Loading Folders from the URL

In `Chapter 4`, *Getting a List of Files Using the Dropbox API,* we created an app that listed the file and folder contents of a specified Dropbox folder. We now need to make our app easy to navigate. This means the user will be able to click the folder names to navigate into and list the contents of, and also give the user the ability to download the file.

Before you proceed, ensure you have the Vue and Dropbox JavaScript files included in your HTML.

In this chapter, we are going to be:

- Creating a component for both files and folders
- Adding links to the folder component to update the directory listing
- Adding a download button to the file component
- Creating a breadcrumb component, so the user can easily navigate back up the tree
- Dynamically updating the browser URL, so if a folder is bookmarked or a link shared, the correct folder loads

Separating out files and folders

Before we create the components, we need to separate our files and folders in our structure, so we can easily identify and display our different types. Thanks to the `.tag` attribute on each item, we can split up our folders and files.

First, we need to update our `structure` data property to be an object containing both the `files` and the `folders` array:

```
data() {
  return {
    accessToken: 'XXXX',
    structure: {
      files: [],
      folders: []
    },
    byteSizes: ['Bytes', 'KB', 'MB', 'GB', 'TB'],
    isLoading: true
  }
}
```

This gives us the ability to append our files and folders to different arrays, meaning we can display them differently in our view.

The next step is to populate these arrays with the data of the current folder. All the following code takes place in the first `then()` function of the `getFolderStructure` method.

Create a JavaScript loop to cycle through the entries and check the `.tag` property of the item. If it is equal to `folder`, append it to the `structure.folder` array, otherwise, add it to the `structure.files` array:

```
getFolderStructure(path) {
  this.dropbox().filesListFolder({
    path: path,
    include_media_info: true
  })
  .then(response => {
    for (let entry of response.entries) {
      // Check ".tag" prop for type
      if(entry['.tag'] === 'folder') {
        this.structure.folders.push(entry);
      } else {
        this.structure.files.push(entry);
      }
```

```
  }
  this.isLoading = false;
})
.catch(error => {
  console.log(error);
});
},
```

This code loops through the entries, as we were in the view and checks the `.tag` attribute. As the attribute itself begins with a `.`, we are unable to use the object style notation to access the property like we would, for example, do for the name - `entry.name`. We then append the entry to either the `files` or `folders` array using JavaScript push, depending on the type.

To display this new data, we need to update the view to loop through both types of array. This is a perfect use case for using the `<template>` tag as we want to append both arrays to the same unordered list.

Update the view to list the two arrays separately. We can remove the size option from the folder display section, as it will never feature a `size` property:

```
<ul v-if="!isLoading">
  <template v-for="entry in structure.folders">
    <li>
      <strong>{{entry.name }}</strong>
    </li>
  </template>
  <template v-for="entry in structure.files">
<li>
  <strong>{{ entry.name }}</strong>
  <span v-if="entry.size">- {{ bytesToSize(entry.size)        }}</span>
    </li>
  </template>
</ul>
```

This now gives us the opportunity to create components for both types.

Making file and folder components

With our data types separated out, we can create individual components to compartmentalize the data and methods. Create a `folder` component that accepts a single property, allowing the `folder` object variable to be passed through. As the template is so small, there is no need for a view or `<script>` block-based template; instead, we can pass it in as a string on the component:

```
Vue.component('folder', {
  template: '<li><strong>{{ f.name }}</strong>
  </li>',
  props: {
    f: Object
  },
});
```

To make our code smaller and less repetitive, the prop is called `f`. This tidies up the view and lets the component name determine the display type without repeating the word `folder` several times.

Update the view to use the folder component, and pass in the `entry` variable to the `f` property:

```
<template v-for="entry in structure.folders">
  <folder :f="entry"></folder>
</template>
```

Repeat the process with files by creating a `file` component. When creating the `file` component, we can move both the `bytesToSize` method and `byteSizes` data property from the parent `dropbox-viewer` component as it would only ever be used when displaying files:

```
Vue.component('file', {
  template: '<li><strong>{{ f.name }}</strong><span      v-
if="f.size"> - {{ bytesToSize(f.size) }}</span>          </li>',
  props: {
    f: Object
  },
  data() {
    return {
      byteSizes: ['Bytes', 'KB', 'MB', 'GB', 'TB']
    }
  },
  methods: {
    bytesToSize(bytes) {
```

```
// Set a default
let output = '0 Byte';
// If the bytes are bigger than 0
if (bytes > 0) {
  // Divide by 1024 and make an int
  let i = parseInt(Math.floor(Math.log(bytes)
  / Math.log(1024)));
  // Round to 2 decimal places and select the
appropriate unit from the array
  output = Math.round(bytes / Math.pow(1024, i),
  2) + ' ' + this.byteSizes[i];
  }
  return output
  }
 }
});
```

Once again, we can use `f` for the prop name to reduce repetition (and the file size of our app). Update the view once again to use this new component:

```
<template v-for="entry in structure.files">
  <file :f="entry"></file>
</template>
```

Linking folders and updating the structure

Now that we have our folders and files separated, we can transform our folder names into links. These links will then update the structure to show the contents of the selected folder. For this, we are going to use the `path_lower` property in each folder to build the link target.

Create a dynamic link to each folder `name`, linking to the folder's `path_lower`. As we are getting more familiar with Vue, the `v-bind` property has been shortened to just the colon notation:

```
Vue.component('folder', {
  template: '<li><strong><a :href="f.path_lower">{{
  f.name }}</a></strong></li>',
  props: {
    f: Object
  },
});
```

We now need to add a `click` listener for this link. When clicked, we need to trigger the `getFolderStructure` method on the `dropbox-viewer` component. Although the click method will use the `f` variable on each instance to get the data, it's good practice to have the `href` attribute set to the folder URL.

Using what we learned in the early chapters of the book, create a method on the `folder` component that, when triggered, emits the folder path to the parent component. The `dropbox-viewer` component also needs a new method to update the structure with the given parameter when fired.

Create the new method on the `folder` component and add the `click` event to the folder link. As with the `v-bind` directive, we are now using the shorthand notation for `v-on`, represented by an @ symbol:

```
Vue.component('folder', {
  template: '<li><strong><a
@click.prevent="navigate()" :href="f.path_lower">{{
f.name }}</a></strong></li>',
  props: {
    f: Object
  },
  methods: {
    navigate() {
      this.$emit('path', this.f.path_lower);
    }
  }
});
```

Along with defining the `click` event, an event modifier has also been added. Using `.prevent` after the click event adds `preventDefault` to the link action, this stops the link from actually going to the specified URL and instead lets the `click` method handle everything. More event modifiers and details about them can be found in the Vue documentation.

When clicked, the navigate method is fired, which emits the folder's lower path using the `path` variable.

Now that we have our `click` handler and the variable being emitted, we need to update the view to trigger a method on the parent `dropbox-viewer` component:

```
<template v-for="entry in structure.folders">
  <folder :f="entry" @path="updateStructure">
  </folder>
</template>
```

Create a new method on the Dropbox component with the same name as the value of the v-on attribute, in this case `updateStructure`. This method will have one parameter, which is the path we emitted earlier. From here, we can trigger our original `getFolderStructure` method using the path variable:

```
updateStructure(path) {
   this.getFolderStructure(path);
}
```

Viewing our app in the browser should now list the folders and links and, when clicked, show the contents of the new folder.

When doing so, however, there are a couple of issues that are raised. Firstly, the files and folders are appended to the existing list rather than replacing it. Secondly, there is no feedback to the user that the app is loading the next folder.

The first issue can be resolved by clearing the folder and file arrays before appending the new structure. The second can be addressed by utilizing the loading screen we used at the beginning of the app - this will give the user some feedback.

To address the first issue, create a new `structure` object inside the success promise function for the `getFolderStructure` method. This object should replicate that of the `structure` object in the `data` object. This should set blank arrays for both files and folders. Update the `for` loop to use the local structure arrays rather than the component ones. Lastly, update the component `structure` object with the new version, including the updated files and folders:

```
getFolderStructure(path) {
  this.dropbox().filesListFolder({
    path: path,
    include_media_info: true
  })
  .then(response => {
    const structure = {
      folders: [],
      files: []
    }
    for (let entry of response.entries) {
      // Check ".tag" prop for type
      if(entry['.tag'] == 'folder') {
        structure.folders.push(entry);
      } else {
        structure.files.push(entry);
      }
    }
```

```
      this.structure = structure;
      this.isLoading = false;
    })
    .catch(error => {
      console.log(error);
    });
  }
```

As this method gets called when the app gets mounted and creates its own version of the structure object, there is no need to declare the arrays in the `data` function. Update the data object to just initialize the `structure` property as an object:

```
data() {
  return {
    accessToken: 'XXXX',
    structure: {},
    isLoading: true
  }
}
```

Running the app now will render the file list, which will be cleared and updated when a new folder is clicked into. To give the user some feedback and let them know the app is working, let's toggle the loading screen after each click.

Before we do this, however, let's fully understand where the delay comes from and where is best to trigger the loading screen.

The click on the link is instantaneous, which triggers the navigate method on the folder component, which in turn fires the `updateStructure` method on the Dropbox component. The delay comes when the app gets to the `filesListFolder` function on the Dropbox instance, inside the `getFolderStructure` method. As we may want to fire the `getFolderStucture` method at a later date without triggering the loading screen, set the `isLoading` variable to `true` inside the `updateStructure` method:

```
updateStructure(path) {
  this.isLoading = true;
  this.getFolderStructure(path);
}
```

With the animations in place, the app fades between both the loading screen and folder structure when navigating through folders.

Creating a breadcrumb from the current path

When navigating through folders or a nested structure of any kind, it's always nice to have a breadcrumb available so the user knows where they are, how far they've gone, and also so they can get back to a previous folder easily. We are going to make a component for the breadcrumb as it is going to feature various properties, computed functions, and methods.

The breadcrumb component is going to list each folder depth as a link to a folder icon. Clicking the link will take the user directly to that folder - even if it is several layers up. To achieve this, we will need to have a list of links we can loop through, each with two properties - one being the full path to the folder and the other just being the folder name.

For example, if we had the folder structure of `/images/holiday/summer/iphone`, we would want to be able to click on `Holiday` and for the app to navigate to `/images/holiday`.

Create your breadcrumb component — for now, add an empty `<div>` to the template property:

```
Vue.component('breadcrumb', {
  template: '<div></div>'
});
```

Add the component to your view. We're going to want the breadcrumb to fade in and out with the structure list, so we need to tweak the HTML to wrap both the list and breadcrumb component in a container that has the `v-if` declaration:

```
<transition name="fade">
  <div v-if="!isLoading">
    <breadcrumb></breadcrumb>
    <ul>
      <template v-for="entry in structure.folders">
        <folder :f="entry" @path="updateStructure">
</folder>
      </template>
      <template v-for="entry in structure.files">
        <file :f="entry"></file>
      </template>
    </ul>
  </div>
</transition>
```

We now need to make a variable available to us that stores the current folder path. We can then manipulate this variable within the breadcrumb component. This will be stored and updated on the Dropbox component and passed down to the breadcrumb component.

Create a new property called `path` on the `dropbox-viewer` component:

```
data() {
  return {
    accessToken: 'XXXXX',
    structure: {},
    isLoading: true,
    path: ''
  }
}
```

We now need to ensure this path gets updated whenever the structure is retrieved from the Dropbox API. Do this within the `getFolderStructure` method, just before the `isLoading` variable is disabled. This ensures it only gets updated once the structure has been loaded, but before the files and folders are displayed:

```
getFolderStructure(path) {
  this.dropbox().filesListFolder({
    path: path,
    include_media_info: true
  })
  .then(response => {
    const structure = {
      folders: [],
      files: []
    }
    for (let entry of response.entries) {
      // Check ".tag" prop for type
      if(entry['.tag'] == 'folder') {
        structure.folders.push(entry);
      } else {
        structure.files.push(entry);
      }
    }
    this.path = path;
    this.structure = structure;
    this.isLoading = false;
  })
  .catch(error => {
    console.log(error);
  });
},
```

Now that we have a variable populated with the current path, we can pass it through to the breadcrumb component as a prop. Add a new attribute to the breadcrumb with the path variable as the value:

```
<breadcrumb :p="path"></breadcrumb>
```

Update the component to accept the prop as a string:

```
Vue.component('breadcrumb', {
    template: '<div></div>',
    props: {
        p: String
    }
});
```

The p attribute now contains the full path of where we are (for example /images/holiday/summer). We want to break up this string so we can identify the folder name and build the breadcrumb for the component to render.

Create a computed object on the component and create a new function titled folders(). This is going to create the breadcrumb array for us to loop through in the template:

```
computed: {
    folders() {
    }
}
```

We now need to set up some variables for us to use. Create a new, empty array called output. This is where we are going to build up our breadcrumb. We also need an empty variable titled slug as a string. The slug variable refers to a part of a URL and its use was made popular by WordPress. The last variable is the path created as an array. As we know, each folder is separated by a /, we can use this to explode or split the string into various parts:

```
computed: {
    folders() {
        let output = [],
            slug = '',
            parts = this.p.split('/');
    }
}
```

If we were to look at the parts variable for our Summer folder, it would look like the following:

```
['images', 'holiday', 'summer']
```

We can now loop through the array to create the breadcrumb. Each breadcrumb item is going to be an object with the name of the individual folder, for example, `holiday` or `summer`, and the `slug`, which would be `/images/holiday` for the former and `/images/holiday/summer` for the latter.

Each object will be constructed and then added to the `output` array. We can then return the output for our template to use:

```
folders() {
  let output = [],
      slug = '',
      parts = this.p.split('/');
  for (let item of parts) {
    slug += item;
    output.push({'name': item, 'path': slug});
    slug += '/';
  }
  return output;
}
```

This loop creates our breadcrumb by taking the following steps. For this example, we'll assume we are in the `/images/holiday` folder:

1. `parts` will now be an array containing three items, `['', 'images', holiday']`. If the string you split on begins with the item you're splitting, an empty item will be made as the first item.
2. At the beginning of the loop, the first slug variable will be equal to `''`, as it is the first item.
3. The `output` array will have a new item appended to it with the object of `{'name': '', 'path': ''}`.
4. The `slug` variable then has a `/` added to the end.
5. Looping through the next item, the `slug` variable gets the name of the item (`images`) added to it.
6. `output` now has a new object added, with the value of `{'name': 'images', 'path': '/images'}`.
7. For the last item, another `/` is added along with the next name, `holiday`.
8. `output` gets the last object added, the value being `{'name': 'holiday', 'path': '/images/holiday'}` - note the path is building up whereas the name remains the singular folder name.

We now have our breadcrumb output array that we can loop through in the view.

 The reason we add the slash after we've appended to the output array is that the API states that to get the root of the Dropbox we pass in an empty string, whereas all other paths must begin with a /.

The next step is to output the breadcrumb into our view. As this template is small, we are going to use the multiline JavaScript notation. Loop through the items within the `folders` computed variable, outputting a link for each of the items. Don't forget to keep a containing element around all the links:

```
template: '<div>' +
  '<span v-for="f in folders">' +
    '<a :href="f.path">{{ f.name }}</a>' +
  '</span>' +
'</div>'
```

Rendering this app in the browser should reveal a breadcrumb - albeit a bit squished together and missing a home link (as the first item didn't have a name). Head back to the `folders` function and add an `if` statement - checking whether the item has a name and, if it doesn't, adding a hard-coded value:

```
folders() {
  let output = [],
    slug = '',
    parts = this.p.split('/');
  console.log(parts);
  for (let item of parts) {
    slug += item;
    output.push({'name': item || 'home', 'path':
      slug});
    slug += '/';
  }
  return output;
}
```

The other option is to add the `if` statement in the template itself:

```
template: '<div>' +
  '<span v-for="f in folders">' +
    '<a :href="f.path">{{ f.name || 'Home' }}</a>' +
  '</span>' +
'</div>'
```

If we wanted to display a divider between the folder names, such as a slash or chevron, this can be easily added. However, a slight hurdle arises when we want to display the separator between the links, but not at the beginning or end. To resolve this, we are going to utilize the index keyword available when doing a loop. We are then going to compare this against the length of the array and operate a v-if declaration on an element.

When looping through an array, Vue allows you to utilize another variable. This, by default, is the index (the position of the item in the array); however, the index may be set to a value if your array is constructed in a key/value fashion. If this is the case, you can still access the index by adding a third variable. As our array is a simple list, we can easily use this variable:

```
template: '<div>' +
  '<span v-for="(f, i) in folders">' +
    '<a :href="f.path">{{ f.name || 'Home' }}</a>' +
    '<span v-if="i !== (folders.length - 1)"> »
      </span>' +
  '</span>' +
'</div>',
```

Update the f variable to a pair of brackets containing an f and an i, comma separated. The f variable is the current folder in the loop, while the i variable that has been created is the index of the item. Bear in mind that the array indexes start at 0 instead of 1.

The separator we've added is contained in a span tag with a v-if attribute, the contents of which could look confusing. This is confusing the current index with the length of the folders array (how many items it has) minus 1. The – 1 is because of the index starting at 0 and not 1, as you would expect. If the numbers do not match, then the span element is displayed.

The last thing we need to do is make our breadcrumb navigate to the selected folder. We can do this by adapting the navigate function we wrote for the folder component. However, because our whole component is the breadcrumb and not each individual link, we need to alter it so it accepts a parameter.

Start off by adding the click event to the link, passing in the folder object:

```
template: '<div>' +
  '<span v-for="(f, i) in folders">' +
    '<a @click.prevent="navigate(f)"
      :href="f.path">
      {{ f.name || 'Home' }}</a>' +
    '<i v-if="i !== (folders.length - 1)"> &raquo;
      </i>' +
```

```
'</span>' +
'</div>',
```

Next, create the `navigate` method on your breadcrumb component, making sure you accept the `folder` parameter and emit the path:

```
methods: {
  navigate(folder) {
    this.$emit('path', folder.path);
  }
}
```

The last step is to trigger the parent method when the path gets emitted. For this, we can utilize the same `updateStructure` method on the `dropbox-viewer` component:

```
<breadcrumb :p="path" @path="updateStructure">
</breadcrumb>
```

We now have a fully operational breadcrumb that allows the user to navigate down the folder structure using the folder links and back up via breadcrumb links.

Our full breadcrumb component looks like is:

```
Vue.component('breadcrumb', {
  template: '<div>' +
    '<span v-for="(f, i) in folders">' +
      '<a @click.prevent="navigate(f)"
        :href="f.path">{{
        f.name || 'Home' }}</a>' +
        '<i v-if="i !== (folders.length - 1)"> »
        </i>' + '</span>' +
      '</div>',

    props: {
  p: String
},

computed: {
  folders() {
    let output = [],
        slug = '',
        parts = this.p.split('/');
    console.log(parts);
    for (let item of parts) {
      slug += item;
      output.push({'name': item || 'home', 'path':
      slug});
```

```
            slug += '/';
        }
        return output;
      }
    },

    methods: {
      navigate(folder) {
        this.$emit('path', folder.path);
      }
    }
  });
```

Adding the ability to download files

Now that our users can navigate through the folder structure, we need to add the ability to download the files. Unfortunately, this isn't as simple as accessing a link attribute on the file. To get the download link, we have to query the Dropbox API for each file.

We will query the API on the creation of the file component, this will asynchronously get the download link and show it once available. Before we can do this, we need to make the Dropbox instance available to the file component.

Add a new attribute to the file component in the view, and pass the Dropbox method through as the value:

```
<file :d="dropbox()" :f="entry"></file>
```

Add the d variable to the props object of your component accepting an Object:

```
props: {
  f: Object,
  d: Object
},
```

We are now going to add a data attribute of link. This should be set to false by default, so we can hide the link, and we'll populate it with the download link once the API has returned with the value.

Add the created() function to the file component, and inside add the API call:

```
created() {
  this.d.filesGetTemporaryLink({path:
    this.f.path_lower}).then(data => {
    this.link = data.link;
```

```
     });
   }
```

This API method accepts an object, similar to the `filesListFolder` function. We're passing the path of the current file. Once the data is returned, we can set the component's `link` attribute to the download link.

We can now add a download link to the template of the component. Add a `v-if` to only show the `<a>` once the download link has been retrieved:

```
template: '<li><strong>{{ f.name }}</strong><span v-
if="f.size"> - {{ bytesToSize(f.size) }}</span><span
v-if="link"> - <a :href="link">Download</a></span>
</li>'
```

Browsing through the files, we can now see a download link appearing next to each file, the speed of which will depend on your internet connection and the API speed.

The full file component, with the download link added, now looks like:

```
Vue.component('file', {
  template: '<li><strong>{{ f.name }}</strong><span v-
  if="f.size"> - {{ bytesToSize(f.size) }}</span><span
  v-if="link"> - <a :href="link">Download</a></span>
  </li>',
  props: {
    f: Object,
    d: Object
    },
data() {
  return {
    byteSizes: ['Bytes', 'KB', 'MB', 'GB', 'TB'],
    link: false
    }
},
 methods: {
  bytesToSize(bytes) {
    // Set a default
    let output = '0 Byte';
    // If the bytes are bigger than 0
    if (bytes > 0) {
      // Divide by 1024 and make an int
      let i = parseInt(Math.floor(Math.log(bytes) /
        Math.log(1024)));
      // Round to 2 decimal places and select the
      appropriate unit from the array
      output = Math.round(bytes / Math.pow(1024, i), 2)
```

```
      + ' ' + this.byteSizes[i];
    }
    return output
    }
  },
  created() {
  this.d.filesGetTemporaryLink({path:
   this.f.path_lower}).then(data => {
    this.link = data.link;
    });
  },
});
```

Updating the URL hash and using it to navigate through the folders

With our Dropbox web app now fully navigable via both the structure list and breadcrumb, we can now add and update the browser URL for quick folder access and sharing. We can do this in two ways: we can either update the hash, for example, `www.domain.com/#/images/holiday/summer`, or we can redirect all the paths to the single page and handle the routing without the hash in the URL.

For this app, we will use the # method in the URL. We'll cover the URL routing technique in the third section of the book when we introduce `vue-router`.

Before we get the app to show the corresponding folder of the URL, we first need to get the URL to update when navigating to a new folder. We can do this using the native `window.location.hash` JavaScript object. We want to update the URL as soon as the user clicks a link, rather than waiting for the data to load to update.

As the `getFolderStructure` method gets fired whenever we update the structure, add the code to the top of this function. This would mean the URL gets updated and then the Dropbox API is called to update the structure:

```
getFolderStructure(path) {
  window.location.hash = path;

  this.dropbox().filesListFolder({
    path: path,
    include_media_info: true
  })
  .then(response => {
```

```
        const structure = {
          folders: [],
          files: []
        }
      for (let entry of response.entries) {
        // Check ".tag" prop for type
          if(entry['.tag'] == 'folder') {
            structure.folders.push(entry);
          } else {
            structure.files.push(entry);
          }
      }
      this.path = path;
      this.structure = structure;
      this.isLoading = false;
    })
      .catch(error => {
        console.log(error);
    });
  }
```

As you navigate through your app, it should be updating the URL to include the current folder path.

However, what you will find when you press refresh with a folder; is that the URL resets to just having a hash with no folder afterward as it is being reset by the empty path passed in via the method in the created() function.

We can remedy this by passing in the current hash to the getFolderStructure within the created function, however, there will be a few checks and error catching we will need to do if we do this.

First, when calling window.location.hash, you also get the hash returned as part of the string, so we will need to remove that. Second, we need to handle the instance of an incorrect URL, should the user enter an incorrect path or the folder gets moved. Lastly, we need to let the user use the back and forward buttons (or keyboard shortcuts) in their browsers.

Showing the folder based on the URL

When our app mounts, it already calls a function to request the structure for the base folder. We wrote this function to allow the path to be passed in and, within the `created()` function, we have fixed the value to be the root folder of `' '`. This gives us the flexibility to adapt this function to pass in the hash from the URL, instead of a fixed string.

Update the function to accept the hash of the URL and, if it doesn't have one, the original fixed string:

```
created() {
    let hash = window.location.hash.substring(1);
    this.getFolderStructure(hash || '');
}
```

Create a new variable called `hash` and assign `window.location.hash` to it. Becuase the variable starts with #, which is not needed for our app, use the `substring` function to remove the first character from the string. We can then use a logical operator to use either the hash variable, or if that equates to nothing, the original fixed string.

You should now be able to still navigate through your app with the URL updating. If you press refresh at any time or copy and paste the URL into a different browser window, the folder you were in should load.

Displaying an error message

With our app accepting URLs, we need to handle a case where someone is entering a URL and makes a mistake, or a folder is shared that has since been moved.

As this error is an edge case, we are going to hijack the `isLoading` parameter if there is an error in loading the data. In the `getFolderStructure` function, we have a `catch` function returned as a promise that gets fired if there is an error with the API call. In this function, set the `isLoading` variable to `'error'`:

```
getFolderStructure(path) {
    window.location.hash = path;
    this.dropbox().filesListFolder({
        path: path,
        include_media_info: true
    })
    .then(response => {
        const structure = {
            folders: [],
```

```
      files: []
    }
    for (let entry of response.entries) {
      // Check ".tag" prop for type
      if(entry['.tag'] == 'folder') {
        structure.folders.push(entry);
      } else {
        structure.files.push(entry);
      }
    }
    this.path = path;
    this.structure = structure;
    this.isLoading = false;
  })
  .catch(error => {
    this.isLoading = 'error';
    console.log(error);
  });
}
```

The `console.log` has been left in, should we need to diagnose a problem beyond a wrong file path. Although the API can throw several different errors, we are going to assume for this app that the error is due to a wrong path. If you wanted to cater for other errors in the app, you can identify the error type by its `status_code` attribute. More details on this can be found in the Dropbox API documentation.

Update your view to handle this new `isLoading` variable property. When set to error, the `isLoading` variable is still "true," so within your loading element, add a new `v-if` to check whether the loading variable is set to `error`:

```
<transition name="fade">
  <div v-if="isLoading">
    <div v-if="isLoading === 'error'">
      <p>There seems to be an issue with the URL entered.
      </p>
      <p><a href="">Go home</a></p>
    </div>
    <div v-else>
      Loading...
    </div>
  </div>
</transition>
```

This is set to display the first element of the `isLoading` variable is set to `error`; otherwise, show the loading text. In the error text, a link is included to send the user back to the current URL without any URL hash. This will "reset" them back to the top of the document tree so they can navigate back down. An improvement could be to break the current URL down and suggest the same URL with the last folder removed.

Verify the error code is loading by adding a nonexistent path to the end of your URL and ensuring the error message is displayed. Bear in mind your user may experience a false positive on this error message in the sense that if the Dropbox API throws any kind of error, this message will be displayed.

Using the back and forward buttons in your browser

To use the back and forward buttons in our browser, we are going to need to update our code significantly. Currently, when the user clicks on a folder from either the structure or breadcrumb, we prevent the default behavior of the browser by using `.prevent` on our `click` handlers. We then immediately update the URL before we process the folder.

However, if we allow the app to update the URL using native behavior, we can then watch for a hash URL update and use this to retrieve our new structure. Using this methodology, the back and forward buttons would work without any further intervention, as they would be updating the URL hash.

This would also improve the readability of our app, and reduce code weight as we would be able to remove the `navigate` methods and `click` handlers on the links.

Removing unneeded code

The first step, before we add more code, is to remove the unnecessary code from our components. Starting with the breadcrumb, remove the `navigate` method from the component and the `@click.prevent` attribute from the link in the template.

We also need to update the `slug` of each of the items to prepend a # - this ensures the app doesn't try and navigate to a brand new page when clicked. As we are looping through our breadcrumb items in the folders `computed` function, add a hash to each `slug` when pushing the object to the `output` array:

```
Vue.component('breadcrumb', {
  template: '<div>' +
    '<span v-for="(f, i) in folders">' +
      '<a :href="f.path">{{ f.name || 'Home' }}</a>' +
      '<i v-if="i !== (folders.length - 1)"> &raquo;
      </i>' + '</span>' +
    '</div>',
  props: {
    p: String
  },
  computed: {
    folders() {
      let output = [],
        slug = '',
        parts = this.p.split('/');
      for (let item of parts) {
        slug += item;
        output.push({'name': item || 'home', 'path':
        '#' + slug});
        slug += '/';
      }
      return output;
    }
  }
});
```

We can also remove the `v-on` declaration on the breadcrumb component in the `dropbox-viewer-template`. It should only have the path being passed in as a prop:

```
<breadcrumb :p="path"></breadcrumb>
```

We can now repeat the same pattern for the folder component. Remove the `@click.prevent` declaration from the link and delete the `navigate` method.

As we are not looping through or editing the folder object before displaying it, we can prepend the # in the template. As we are telling Vue the `href` is bound to a JavaScript object (with the colon), we need to encapsulate the hash in quotes and concatenate it with the folder path using the JavaScript + notation.

We are already inside both single and double quotes, so we need to inform JavaScript we *literally* mean a single quote and this is done by using a backslash in front of the single quote character:

```
Vue.component('folder', {
  template: '<li><strong><a :href="\'#\' +
  f.path_lower">{{ f.name }}</a></strong></li>',
  props: {
    f: Object
  }
});
```

We can also remove the @path attribute from the <folder> component in the view:

```
<template v-for="entry in structure.folders">
  <folder :f="entry"></folder>
</template>
```

Already our code is looking cleaner, less cluttered, and smaller in file size. Viewing the app in the browser will render the structure of the folder you are in; however, clicking links will update the URL but not change what is displayed.

Updating the structure with a URL change and setting Vue data outside of the instance

Now that we have our URL updating correctly, we can get the new structure whenever the hash changes. This can be done natively with JavaScript with the onhashchange function.

We are going to create a function that fires whenever the hash of the URL updates, which, in turn, will update a path variable on the parent Vue instance. This variable will be passed to the child dropbox-viewer component as a prop. This component will be watching for a change in the variable and, upon update, it will retrieve the new structure.

To begin with, update the parent Vue instance to have a data object with a path key - set to the empty string property. We are also going to assign our Vue instance to a constant variable of app—this allows us to set data and call methods outside of the instance:

```
const app = new Vue({
  el: '#app',

  data: {
    path: ''
  }
});
```

The next step is to update this data property every time the URL gets updated. This is done using `window.onhashchange`, which is a native JavaScript function that fires every time the hash changes in the URL.

Copy and paste the hash modifier from the `created` function on the Dropbox component, and use that to modify the hash and store the value on the Vue instance. If the hash doesn't exist, we will pass an empty string to the path variable:

```
window.onhashchange = () => {
  let hash = window.location.hash.substring(1);
  app.path = (hash || '');
}
```

We now need to pass this path variable through to the Dropbox component. Add a prop of p with the `path` variable as the value in your view:

```
<div id="app">
 <dropbox-viewer :p="path"></dropbox-viewer>
</div>
```

Add the `props` object to the Dropbox component to accept a string:

```
props: {
  p: String
},
```

We are now going to add a watch function to the `dropbox-viewer` component. This function will watch the p prop and, when updated, call the `updateStructure()` method with the modified path:

```
watch: {
  p() {
    this.updateStructure(this.p);
  }
}
```

Heading back to the browser we should now be able to navigate through our Dropbox structure, as before, using both the folder links and breadcrumb as navigation. We should now be able to use the back and forward browser buttons, plus any keyboard shortcuts, to also navigate back through the folders.

Before we head to `Chapter 6`, *Caching the Current Folder Structure Using Vuex,* and introduce folder caching to our app using `vuex`, there are a few optimizations we can make to our Dropbox component.

First, in the `getFolderStructure` function, we can remove the first line where the URL hash gets set to the path. This is because the URL has already been updated when the link is used. Remove this line from your code:

```
window.location.hash = path;
```

Second, there is now repetition in the Dropbox component with the `this.path` variable and the `p` prop. Eliminating this requires some slight reworking, as you are not allowed to modify a prop directly as you are with the path; however, it needs to be kept in sync so the breadcrumb can be correctly rendered.

Remove the `path` property from the data object in the Dropbox component, and also delete the `this.path = path` line from the `getFolderStructure` function.

Next, update the prop to be equal to `path`, not `p`. This will also require the `watch` function to be updated to watch the `path` variable and not `p()`.

Update the created method to just use `this.path` as the parameter to the function. The Dropbox component should now look like this:

```
Vue.component('dropbox-viewer', {
  template: '#dropbox-viewer-template',
  props: {
   path: String
  },
  data() {
    return {
      accessToken: 'XXXX',
      structure: {},
      isLoading: true
    }
  },
  methods: {
    dropbox() {
      return new Dropbox({
        accessToken: this.accessToken
      });
    },
    getFolderStructure(path) {
      this.dropbox().filesListFolder({
        path: path,
        include_media_info: true
      })
        .then(response => {
        const structure = {
          folders: [],
```

```
          files: []
        }
      for (let entry of response.entries) {
        // Check ".tag" prop for type
        if(entry['.tag'] == 'folder') {
          structure.folders.push(entry);
        } else {
        }
      }
      this.structure = structure;
      this.isLoading = false;
    })
      .catch(error => {
        this.isLoading = 'error';
        console.log(error);
      });
    },
    updateStructure(path) {
      this.isLoading = true;
      this.getFolderStructure(path);
    }
  },
  created() {
    this.getFolderStructure(this.path);
  },
    watch: {
    path() {
      this.updateStructure(this.path);
    }
  },
});
```

Update the view to accept the prop as path:

```
<dropbox-viewer :path="path"></dropbox-viewer>
```

We now need to ensure the parent Vue instance has the correct path on both page load and hash change. To avoid repetition, we are going to extend our Vue instance with both a method and a created function.

Keep the path variable set to an empty string. Create a new method titled updateHash() that removes the first character from the window hash and then sets the path variable either to the hash or an empty string. Next, create a created() function that runs the updateHash method.

The `Vue` instance now looks like this:

```
const app = new Vue({
  el: '#app',

  data: {
    path: ''
  },
  methods: {
    updateHash() {
      let hash = window.location.hash.substring(1);
      this.path = (hash || '');
    }
  },
  created() {
    this.updateHash()
  }
});
```

Lastly, to remove repetition, we can fire the `updateHash` method when the hash changes in the address bar:

```
window.onhashchange = () => {
  app.updateHash();
}
```

Final Code

With our code now complete your view and JavaScript file should look like the following. Firstly, the view should look like this:

```
<div id="app">
  <dropbox-viewer :path="path"></dropbox-viewer>
</div>
<script type="text/x-template" id="dropbox-viewer-
  template">
<div>
  <h1>Dropbox</h1>
  <transition name="fade">
    <div v-if="isLoading">
      <div v-if="isLoading == 'error'">
        <p>There seems to be an issue with the URL
        entered.</p>
        <p><a href="">Go home</a></p>
      </div>
```

```
      <div v-else>
        Loading...
      </div>
    </div>
  </transition>
  <transition name="fade">
    <div v-if="!isLoading">
      <breadcrumb :p="path"></breadcrumb>
      <ul>
        <template v-for="entry in structure.folders">
         <folder :f="entry"></folder>
        </template>
        <template v-for="entry in structure.files">
          <file :d="dropbox()" :f="entry"></file>
        </template>
      </ul>
    </div>
  </transition>
 </div>
</script>
```

The accompanying JavaScript app should look like this:

```
Vue.component('breadcrumb', {
    template: '<div>' +
    '<span v-for="(f, i) in folders">' +
    '<a :href="f.path">{{ f.name || 'Home' }}</a>' +
     '<i v-if="i !== (folders.length - 1)"> &raquo;
      </i>' + '</span>' +
    '</div>',
  props: {
  p: String
  },
  computed: {
    folders() {
      let output = [],
        slug = '',
        parts = this.p.split('/');
      for (let item of parts) {
        slug += item;
          output.push({'name': item || 'home', 'path':
          '#' + slug});
        slug += '/';
      }
      return output;
    }
  }
});
```

```
Vue.component('folder', {
    template: '<li><strong><a :href="\'#\' +
    f.path_lower">{{ f.name }}</a></strong></li>',
   props: {
    f: Object
    }
});
Vue.component('file', {
    template: '<li><strong>{{ f.name }}</strong><span
    v-if="f.size"> - {{ bytesToSize(f.size) }}</span>
    <span v-if="link"> - <a :href="link">Download</a>
    </span></li>',
    props: {
    f: Object,
    d: Object
    },
  data() {
   return {
    byteSizes: ['Bytes', 'KB', 'MB', 'GB', 'TB'],
    link: false
    }
   },
  methods: {
    bytesToSize(bytes) {
     // Set a default
     let output = '0 Byte';
     // If the bytes are bigger than 0
      if (bytes > 0) {
       // Divide by 1024 and make an int
       let i = parseInt(Math.floor(Math.log(bytes) /
       Math.log(1024)));
      // Round to 2 decimal places and select the
        appropriate unit from the array
       output = Math.round(bytes / Math.pow(1024, i), 2)
       + ' ' + this.byteSizes[i];
     }
     return output
    }
  },
  created() {
    this.d.filesGetTemporaryLink({path:
    this.f.path_lower}).then(data => {
      this.link = data.link;
    });
    },
  });
  Vue.component('dropbox-viewer', {
```

```
  template: '#dropbox-viewer-template',
props: {
  path: String
 },
data() {
  return {
  accessToken: 'XXXX',
  structure: {},
  isLoading: true
 }
},
methods: {
 dropbox() {
    return new Dropbox({
      accessToken: this.accessToken
    });
  },
getFolderStructure(path) {
 this.dropbox().filesListFolder({
    path: path,
    include_media_info: true
  })
  .then(response => {
    const structure = {
      folders: [],
      files: []
    }
    for (let entry of response.entries) {
      // Check ".tag" prop for type
      if(entry['.tag'] == 'folder') {
        structure.folders.push(entry);
      } else {
        structure.files.push(entry);
      }
    }
    this.structure = structure;
    this.isLoading = false;
  })
  .catch(error => {
   this.isLoading = 'error';
   console.log(error);
  });
 },
updateStructure(path) {
  this.isLoading = true;
  this.getFolderStructure(path);
 }
},
```

```
    created() {
     this.getFolderStructure(this.path);
    },
   watch: {
     path() {
        this.updateStructure(this.path);
      }
     },
  });
    const app = new Vue({
     el: '#app',

     data: {
     path: ''
     },
   methods: {
    updateHash() {
       let hash = window.location.hash.substring(1);
       this.path = (hash || '');
     }
   },
    created() {
     this.updateHash()
     }
  });
  window.onhashchange = () => {
  app.updateHash();
 }
```

Summary

We now have a fully functioning Dropbox viewer app featuring navigation for folders and download links for files. We can use either the folder links or breadcrumb for navigation and use the back and/or forward buttons. We can also share or bookmark a link and load the contents of that folder.

In Chapter 6, *Caching the Current Folder Structure Using Vuex,* we are going to speed up the navigation process by caching the current folder contents using Vuex.

6
Caching the Current Folder Structure Using Vuex

In this chapter, we are going to introduce an official Vue plugin called Vuex. Vuex is a state management pattern and library that allows you to have a centralized store for all your Vue components, irrelevant of whether they are child components or a Vue instance. It gives us a centralized, simple way of keeping our data in sync across the whole app.

This chapter is going to cover:

- Getting started with Vuex
- Storing and retrieving data from the Vuex store
- Integrating Vuex with our Dropbox app
- Caching the current Dropbox folder contents and loading data from the store if required

Instead of requiring custom events and the $emit functions on every component, and trying to keep components and child components up to date, every part of your Vue app can update the central store, and others can react and update their data and state based on that information. It also gives us a common place to store data so, rather than trying to decide whether it is more semantic to place the data object on the component, a parent component, or the Vue instance, we can use the Vuex store.

Vuex is also integrated into the Vue dev tools—something that is covered in the last chapter of this book, Chapter 12, *Using Vue Dev Tools and Testing Your SPA*. With the integration of the library, it makes debugging and viewing the current and past states of the store easy. The dev tools reflect state changes, or data updates, and allow you to inspect each part of the store.

As mentioned, Vuex is a state management pattern, which is the source of truth for your Vue app. For example, keeping track of a shopping basket or logged in user is vital for some apps and could wreak havoc if this data got out of sync between components. It is also impossible to pass data between child components without using the parent to handle the exchange. Vuex removes this complication by handling the storage, mutation, and actions on the data.

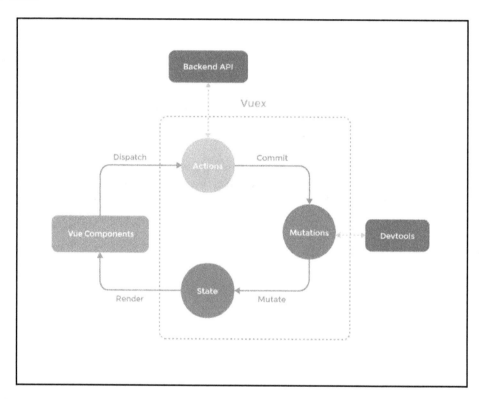

When initially using Vuex, it may seem quite verbose and like overkill for what is required; however, this is a great example of getting to grips with the library. More information about Vuex can be found in their documentation.

For our Dropbox app, the Vuex store can be utilized to store the folder structure, file list, and download links. This means if a user visits the same folder more than once, the API will not need to be queried as all the information is stored already. This will speed up the navigation of the folders.

Including and initializing Vuex

The Vuex library is included the same way as Vue itself. You can either use a hosted version by using the previously mentioned unpkg service (`https://unpkg.com/vuex`) or you can download the JavaScript library from their `https://github.com/vuejs/vuex`.

Add a new `<script>` block to the bottom of your HTML file. Ensure the Vuex library is included after your `vue.js` library but before your application JavaScript:

```
<script type="text/javascript" src="js/vue.js"></script>
<script type="text/javascript" src="js/vuex.js"></script>
<script type="text/javascript" src="js/dropbox.js"></script>
<script type="text/javascript" src="js/app.js"></script>
```

 If you are deploying an app with several JavaScript files, it is worth investigating whether it is more efficient to combine and compress them into one file or configure your server to use HTTP/2 push.

With the library included, we can initialize and include the store within our app. Create a new variable called a `store` and initialize the `Vuex.Store` class, assigning it to the variable:

```
const store = new Vuex.Store({
});
```

With the Vuex store initialized, we can now utilize its functionality with the `store` variable. Using `store`, we can access the data within and alter that data with mutations. With an independent `store`, many Vue instances could update the same `store`; this may be desired in some instances, but, it could be an undesirable side effect in others.

To circumvent this, we can associate a store with a specific Vue instance. This is done by passing the `store` variable to our Vue class. Doing this also injects the `store` instance into all our child components. Although not strictly required for our app, it's good practice to get into the habit of associating the store with the app:

```
const app = new Vue({
  el: '#app',

  store,
  data: {
    path: ''
  },
  methods: {
    updateHash() {
```

```
        let hash = window.location.hash.substring(1);
        this.path = (hash || '');
    }
  },
  created() {
    this.updateHash()
  }
});
```

With the `store` variable added, we can now access the `store` in our components using the `this.$store` variable.

Utilizing the store

To help us get to grips with how to use the store, let's move the `path` variable that is currently stored on the parent Vue instance. Before we start writing and moving code, there are a few phrases and words that are different when using the Vuex store and we should familiarize ourselves with them:

- `state`: This is the store's equivalent of the data object; the raw data is stored within this object.
- `getters`: These are the Vuex equivalent of computed values; the function of the `store` that may process the raw state value before returning it for use in a component.
- `mutations`: Vuex doesn't allow modification of the state object directly outside of the `store` and this must be done via a mutation handler; these are functions on the `store` that then allow the state to be updated. They always take `state` as the first parameter.

These objects belong directly in the `store`. Updating the `store`, however, is not as simple as calling `store.mutationName()`. Instead, we must call the method by using a new `commit()` function. This function accepts two parameters: the name of the mutation and the data being passed to it.

Although initially difficult to understand, the verbose nature of the Vuex store allows for powerful capabilities. An example of the store in action, adapting the original example from `Chapter 1`, *Getting Started with Vue.js*, is as follows:

```
const store = new Vuex.Store({
  state: {
    message: 'HelLO Vue!'
```

```
    },

    getters: {
      message: state => {
        return state.message.toLowerCase();
      }
    },

    mutations: {
      updateMessage(state, msg) {
        state.message = msg;
      }
    }
  });
```

The preceding `store` example includes the `state` object, which is our raw data store; a `getters` object, which includes our processing of the state; and finally, a `mutations` object, which allows us to update the message. Notice how both the `message` getter and the `updateMessage` mutation have the store's state as the first parameter.

To use this `store`, you could do the following:

```
  new Vue({
    el: '#app',

    store,
    computed: {
      message() {
        return this.$store.state.message
      },
      formatted() {
        return this.$store.getters.message
      }
    }
  });
```

Retrieving the message

In the `{{ message }}` computed function, we have retrieved the raw, unprocessed message from the state object and used the following path:

```
  this.$store.state.message
```

This is literally accessing the `store`, then the state object, followed by the message object key.

In a similar vein, the `{{ formatted }}` computed value uses the getter from the `store`, which lowercases the string. This is retrieved by accessing the `getters` object instead:

```
this.$store.getters.message
```

Updating the message

To update the message, you need to call the `commit` function. This accepts the method name as the first parameter with the payload, or data, being the second. The payload can be either a simple variable, an array, or an object if several variables need to be passed.

The `updateMessage` mutation in the `store` accepts a single parameter and sets the message to equal that, so to update our message the code would be:

```
store.commit('updateMessage', 'VUEX Store');
```

This can be run anywhere in the app and will automatically update the previous values used, as they all rely on the same `store`.

Returning our message getter now would return **VUEX Store**, as we've updated the state. With that in mind, let's update our app to use a path variable in the `store`, rather than the Vue instance.

Using the Vuex store for the folder path

The first step in using the Vue store for our global Dropbox path variable is to move the data object from the Vue instance to the `Store`, and rename it to `state`:

```
const store = new Vuex.Store({
  state: {
    path: ''
  }
});
```

We also need to create a mutation to allow the path to be updated from the hash of the URL. Add a `mutations` object to the store and move the `updateHash` function from the Vue instance—don't forget to update the function to accept the store as the first parameter. Also, change the method so it updates `state.path` rather than `this.path`:

```
const store = new Vuex.Store({
  state: {
    path: ''
  },
  mutations: {
    updateHash(state) {
      let hash = window.location.hash.substring(1);
      state.path = (hash || '');
    }
  }
});
```

By moving the path variable and mutation to the store, it makes the Vue instance significantly smaller, with both the `methods` and `data` objects being removed:

```
const app = new Vue({
  el: '#app',

  store,
  created() {
    this.updateHash()
  }
});
```

We now need to update our app to use the path variable from the `store`, instead of on the Vue instance. We also need to ensure we call the `store` `mutation` function to update the path variable instead of the method on the Vue instance.

Updating the path methods to use store commits

Start with the Vue instance, changing `this.Updatehash` to `store.commit('updateHash')` instead. Don't forget to also update the method in the `onhashchange` function. The second function should reference the `store` object on our Vue instance, rather than the `store` directly. This is done by accessing the Vue instance variable, `app`, and then referencing the Vuex store in this instance.

When referring to the Vuex store on a Vue instance, it is saved under the variable as `$store`, regardless of the variable name it was initially declared against:

```
const app = new Vue({
  el: '#app',

  store,
  created() {
    store.commit('updateHash');
  }
});
window.onhashchange = () => {
  app.$store.commit('updateHash');
}
```

Using the path variable

We now need to update the components to use the path from the `store`, rather than one passed down through components. Both `breadcrumb` and `dropbox-viewer` need to be updated to accept this new variable. We can also remove unneccesary props from the components.

Updating the breadcrumb component

From the HTML, remove the `:p` prop, leaving a simple breadcrumb HTML tag:

```
<breadcrumb></breadcrumb>
```

Next, remove the `props` object from the component in the JavaScript file. The `parts` variable will also need to be updated to use `this.$store.state.path`, instead of `this.p`:

```
Vue.component('breadcrumb', {
  template: '<div>' +
    '<span v-for="(f, i) in folders">' +
      '<a :href="f.path">[F] {{ f.name }}</a>' +
      '<i v-if="i !== (folders.length - 1)"> &raquo; </i>' +
    '</span>' +
  '</div>',

  computed: {
    folders() {
      let output = [],
```

```
        slug = '',
        parts = this.$store.state.path.split('/');
      for (let item of parts) {
        slug += item;
        output.push({'name': item || 'home', 'path': '#' + slug});
        slug += '/';
      }
      return output;
    }
  }
});
```

Updating the dropbox-viewer component to work with Vuex

As with the `breadcrumb` component, the first step is to remove the HTML prop from the view. This should simplify the view of your app even more and you should be left with a handful of HTML tags:

```
<div id="app">
  <dropbox-viewer></dropbox-viewer>
</div>
```

The next step is to clean up the JavaScript, removing any unnecessary function parameters. Remove the `props` object from the `dropbox-viewer` component. Next, update the `filesListFolder` Dropbox method located inside `getFolderStructure` to use the store path, instead of using the path variable:

```
this.dropbox().filesListFolder({
  path: this.$store.state.path,
  include_media_info: true
})
```

As this method is now using the `store`, instead of a function parameter, we can remove the variable from the method declaration itself, along with removing it from the `updateStructure` method and from whenever these two functions get called. For example:

```
updateStructure(path) {
  this.isLoading = true;
  this.getFolderStructure(path);
}
```

This would become the following:

```
updateStructure() {
  this.isLoading = true;
  this.getFolderStructure();
}
```

We do, however, still need to store the path as a variable on this component. This is due to our `watch` method, which calls the `updateStructure` function. To do this, we need to store our path as a computed value, rather than a fixed variable. This is so it can dynamically update when the `store` updates, rather than a fixed value when the component gets initialized.

Create a computed object on the `dropbox-viewer` component with a method called `path`—this should just return the `store` path:

```
computed: {
  path() {
    return this.$store.state.path
  }
}
```

We now have it as a local variable, so the Dropbox `filesListFolder` method can be updated to once again use `this.path`.

The newly-updated `dropbox-viewer` component should look like the following. Viewing the app in your browser, it should appear as though nothing has changed—however, the inner workings of the app are now reliant on the new Vuex store, rather than a variable stored on the Vue instance:

```
Vue.component('dropbox-viewer', {
  template: '#dropbox-viewer-template',
  data() {
    return {
      accessToken: 'XXXX',
      structure: {},
      isLoading: true
    }
  },
  computed: {
    path() {
      return this.$store.state.path
    }
  },
  methods: {
    dropbox() {
```

```
      return new Dropbox({
        accessToken: this.accessToken
      });
    },
    getFolderStructure() {
      this.dropbox().filesListFolder({
        path: this.path,
        include_media_info: true
      })
      .then(response => {
        const structure = {
          folders: [],
          files: []
        }
        for (let entry of response.entries) {
          // Check ".tag" prop for type
          if(entry['.tag'] == 'folder') {
            structure.folders.push(entry);
          } else {
            structure.files.push(entry);
          }
        }
        this.structure = structure;
        this.isLoading = false;
      })
      .catch(error => {
        this.isLoading = 'error';
        console.log(error);
      });
    },
    updateStructure() {
      this.isLoading = true;
      this.getFolderStructure();
    }
  },
  created() {
    this.getFolderStructure();
  },
  watch: {
    path() {
      this.updateStructure();
    }
  },
});
```

Caching the folder contents

Now that we have Vuex in our app and are utilizing it for the path, we can begin to look at storing the contents of the currently-displayed folder so that if the user returns to the same place, the API does not need to be queried to retrieve the results. We are going to do this by storing the object returned by the API the Vuex store.

When the folder gets requested, the app will check whether the data exists in the store. If it does, the API call will be omitted and the data loaded from the storage. If it doesn't exist, the API will be queried and the results saved in the Vuex store.

The first step is to separate out the data processing into its own method. This is because the files and folders are going to need to be split regardless of whether the data comes from the store or API.

Create a new method in the `dropbox-viewer` component titled `createFolderStructure()` and move the code from inside the `then()` function, following the Dropbox `filesListFolder` method. Call the new method inside this function instead.

Your two methods should now look like the following, and your app should still be working as it was before:

```
createFolderStructure(response) {
    const structure = {
        folders: [],
        files: []
    }

    for (let entry of response.entries) {
        // Check ".tag" prop for type
        if(entry['.tag'] == 'folder') {
            structure.folders.push(entry);
        } else {
            structure.files.push(entry);
        }
    }
    this.structure = structure;
    this.isLoading = false;
},

getFolderStructure() {
    this.dropbox().filesListFolder({
        path: this.path,
        include_media_info: true
```

```
  })
  .then(this.createFolderStructure)
  .catch(error => {
    this.isLoading = 'error';
    console.log(error);
  });
}
```

Using promises, we can use `createFolderStructure` as the action for the API call.

The next step is to store the data we are processing. To do this, we are going to take advantage of the ability to pass an object to the `commit` function of the `store` and use the path as the key in the storage object. Rather than nest the file structures, we are going to store the information in a flat structure. For example, after we've navigated through a few folders, our store would look like this:

```
structure: {
  'images': [{...}],
  'images-holiday': [{...}],
  'images-holiday-summer': [{...}]
}
```

There will be several transformations made to the path to make it object key-friendly. It will be lowercased and any punctuation will be removed. We will also replace all spaces and slashes with hyphens.

To begin, create an empty object in the Vuex store state object titled `structure`; this is where we are going to store the data:

```
state: {
  path: '',
  structure: {}
}
```

We now need to create a new `mutation`, to allow us to store the data as we load it. Create a new function inside the `mutations` object. Call it `structure`; it needs to accept the `state` as a parameter, plus a `payload` variable which will be an object passed in:

```
structure(state, payload) {
}
```

The path object will consist of a `path` variable, plus the `data` returned from the API. For example:

```
{
  path: 'images-holiday',
  data: [{...}]
}
```

With this object being passed in, we can use the path as the key and the data as the value. Store the data with a key of the path inside the mutation:

```
structure(state, payload) {
  state.structure[payload.path] = payload.data;
}
```

We can now commit this data at the end of our new `createFolderStructure` method in our component:

```
createFolderStructure(response) {
  const structure = {
    folders: [],
    files: []
  }

  for (let entry of response.entries) {
    // Check ".tag" prop for type
    if(entry['.tag'] == 'folder') {
      structure.folders.push(entry);
    } else {
      structure.files.push(entry);
    }
  }
  this.structure = structure;
  this.isLoading = false;

  this.$store.commit('structure', {
    path: this.path,
    data: response
  });
}
```

This will now store each folder's data when navigating through the app. This can be verified by adding a `console.log(state.structure)` inside the structure mutation.

Although this works as is, it would be good practice to sanitize the path when using it as the key in an object. To do this, we are going to remove any punctuation, replace any spaces and slashes with hyphens, and change the path to lowercase.

Create a new computed function called `slug` on the `dropbox-viewer` component. The term slug is often used for sanitized URLs and originates from newspapers and how editors used to reference stories. This function will run several JavaScript `replace` methods to create a safe object key:

```
slug() {
  return this.path.toLowerCase()
    .replace(/^\/|\/$/g, '')
    .replace(/ /g,'-')
    .replace(/\//g,'-')
    .replace(/[-]+/g, '-')
    .replace(/[^\w-]+/g,'');
}
```

The slug function carries out the following operations. An example path of `/images/iPhone/mom's Birthday - 40th` would be affected in the following way:

- Convert the string to lowercase: `/images/iphone/mom's birthday - 40th`
- Remove any slashes at the beginning and end of the path: `images/iphone/mom birthday - 40th`
- Replace any spaces with hyphens: `images/iphone/mom-birthday---40th`
- Replace any slashes with hyphens: `images-iphone-mom-birthday---40th`
- Replace any multiple hyphens with just a singular hyphen: `images-iphone-mom-birthday-40th`
- Finally, remove any punctuation: `images-iphone-moms-birthday-40th`

With the slug now created, we can use this as the key when storing the data:

```
this.$store.commit('structure', {
  path: this.slug,
  data: response
});
```

With our folder contents now being cached in the Vuex store, we can add a check to see whether the data exists in the store and if it does, load it from there.

Loading data from the store if it exists

Loading our data from the store requires a couple of changes to our code. The first step is to check whether the structure exists in the `store` and if it does, load it. The second step is to only commit the data to storage if it is new data—calling the existing `createFolderStructure` method will update the structure but also re-commit the data to storage. Although not detrimental to the user as it currently stands, unnecessarily writing data to the `store` could cause issues when your app grows. This will also help us when we come to precaching the folders and files.

Loading the data from the store

As a `store` is a JavaScript object and our `slug` variable is a consistent computed value on our component, we can check whether the object key exists with an `if` statement:

```
if(this.$store.state.structure[this.slug]) {
  // The data exists
}
```

This gives us the flexibility to load the data from the `store` if it exists, using the `createFolderStructure` method and, if not, trigger the Dropbox API call.

Update the `getFolderStructure` method to include the `if` statement and add the method call if the data exists:

```
getFolderStructure() {
  if(this.$store.state.structure[this.slug]) {
    this.createFolderStructure(this.$store.state.structure[this.slug]);
  } else {
    this.dropbox().filesListFolder({
      path: this.path,
      include_media_info: true
    })
    .then(this.createFolderStructure)
    .catch(error => {
      this.isLoading = 'error';
      console.log(error);
    });
  }
}
```

The path to the data is quite long and can make our code unreadable. To make it easier to understand, assign the data to a variable, which allows us to check whether it exists and returns the data with cleaner, smaller, and less repeatable code. It also means we only have to update one line if the path to our data changes:

```
getFolderStructure() {
  let data = this.$store.state.structure[this.slug];
  if(data) {
    this.createFolderStructure(data);
  } else {
    this.dropbox().filesListFolder({
      path: this.path,
      include_media_info: true
    })
    .then(this.createFolderStructure)
    .catch(error => {
      this.isLoading = 'error';
      console.log(error);
    });
  }
}
```

Only storing new data

As mentioned earlier, the current `createFolderStructure` method both displays the structure and caches the response in the `store`, thus re-saving the structure even when the data is loaded from the cache.

Create a new method that the Dropbox API will fire once the data has loaded. Call it `createStructureAndSave`. This should accept the response variable as its only parameter:

```
createStructureAndSave(response) {
}
```

We can now move the `store commit` function from the `createFolderStructure` method into this new one, along with a call to fire the existing method with the data:

```
createStructureAndSave(response) {
  this.createFolderStructure(response)
  this.$store.commit('structure', {
    path: this.slug,
    data: response
  });
}
```

Lastly, update the Dropbox API function to call this method:

```
getFolderStructure() {
  let data = this.$store.state.structure[this.slug];
  if(data) {
    this.createFolderStructure(data);
  } else {
    this.dropbox().filesListFolder({
      path: this.path,
      include_media_info: true
    })
    .then(this.createStructureAndSave)
    .catch(error => {
      this.isLoading = 'error';
      console.log(error);
    });
  }

},
```

Open your app in the browser and navigate through the folders. When you navigate back up using the breadcrumb, the response should be a lot quicker—as it is now loading from the cache you've created instead of querying the API every time.

In Chapter 7, *Pre-Caching Other Folders and Files for Faster Navigation,* we will be looking at precaching the folders to try and preempt where the user is heading next. We will also look at caching the download links for the files.

Our full app JavaScript should now look like:

```
Vue.component('breadcrumb', {
  template: '<div>' +
    '<span v-for="(f, i) in folders">' +
      '<a :href="f.path">[F] {{ f.name }}</a>' +
      '<i v-if="i !== (folders.length - 1)"> &raquo; </i>' +
    '</span>' +
  '</div>',
  computed: {
    folders() {
      let output = [],
        slug = '',
        parts = this.$store.state.path.split('/');
      for (let item of parts) {
        slug += item;
        output.push({'name': item || 'home', 'path': '#' + slug});
        slug += '/';
      }
```

```
      return output;
    }
  }
});
Vue.component('folder', {
  template: '<li><strong><a :href="\'#\' + f.path_lower">{{ f.name
}}</a></strong></li>',
  props: {
    f: Object
  }
});
Vue.component('file', {
  template: '<li><strong>{{ f.name }}</strong><span v-if="f.size"> - {{
bytesToSize(f.size) }}</span> - <a v-if="link"
:href="link">Download</a></li>',
  props: {
    f: Object,
    d: Object
  },
  data() {
    return {
      byteSizes: ['Bytes', 'KB', 'MB', 'GB', 'TB'],
      link: false
    }
  },
  methods: {
    bytesToSize(bytes) {
      // Set a default
      let output = '0 Byte';
      // If the bytes are bigger than 0
      if (bytes > 0) {
        // Divide by 1024 and make an int
        let i = parseInt(Math.floor(Math.log(bytes) / Math.log(1024)));
        // Round to 2 decimal places and select the appropriate unit from
the array
        output = Math.round(bytes / Math.pow(1024, i), 2) + ' ' +
this.byteSizes[i];
      }
      return output
    }
  },
  created() {
    this.d.filesGetTemporaryLink({path: this.f.path_lower}).then(data => {
      this.link = data.link;
    });
  },
});
Vue.component('dropbox-viewer', {
```

```
template: '#dropbox-viewer-template',
data() {
  return {
    accessToken: 'XXXX',
    structure: {},
    isLoading: true
  }
},
computed: {
  path() {
    return this.$store.state.path
  },
  slug() {
    return this.path.toLowerCase()
      .replace(/^\/|\/$/g, '')
      .replace(/ /g,'-')
      .replace(/\//g,'-')
      .replace(/[-]+/g, '-')
      .replace(/[^\w-]+/g,'');
  }
},
methods: {
  dropbox() {
    return new Dropbox({
      accessToken: this.accessToken
    });
  },

  createFolderStructure(response) {

    const structure = {
      folders: [],
      files: []
    }

    for (let entry of response.entries) {
      // Check ".tag" prop for type
      if(entry['.tag'] == 'folder') {
        structure.folders.push(entry);
      } else {
        structure.files.push(entry);
      }
    }
    this.structure = structure;
    this.isLoading = false;

  },
```

```
      createStructureAndSave(response) {
        this.createFolderStructure(response)
        this.$store.commit('structure', {
          path: this.slug,
          data: response
        });
      },

      getFolderStructure() {
        let data = this.$store.state.structure[this.slug];
        if(data) {
          this.createFolderStructure(data);
        } else {
          this.dropbox().filesListFolder({
            path: this.path,
            include_media_info: true
          })
          .then(this.createStructureAndSave)
          .catch(error => {
            this.isLoading = 'error';
            console.log(error);
          });
        }

      },
      updateStructure() {
        this.isLoading = true;
        this.getFolderStructure();
      }
    },
    created() {
      this.getFolderStructure();
    },
    watch: {
      path() {
        this.updateStructure();
      }
    },
});

const store = new Vuex.Store({
    state: {
      path: '',
      structure: {}
    },
    mutations: {
      updateHash(state) {
        let hash = window.location.hash.substring(1);
```

```
      state.path = (hash || '');
    },
    structure(state, payload) {
      state.structure[payload.path] = payload.data;
    }
  }
});
const app = new Vue({
  el: '#app',

  store,
  created() {
    store.commit('updateHash');
  }
});
window.onhashchange = () => {
  app.$store.commit('updateHash');
}
```

Summary

After this chapter, your app should now be integrated with Vuex and be caching the contents of the Dropbox folders. The Dropbox folder path should also be utilizing the store to make the app more efficient. We are also querying the API only when we need to.

In Chapter 7, *Pre-Caching Other Folders and Files for Faster Navigation,* we will look at precaching the folders—actively querying the API in advance to speed up the app navigation and usability.

7
Pre-Caching Other Folders and Files for Faster Navigation

In this chapter, the last of this section, we are going to look at speeding up our Dropbox file explorer further by introducing, even more, caching to the app. So far, we have built an app that can query the Dropbox API, and return files and folders. From there, we added folder navigation, including updating the URL for link sharing and being able to use the back and forward buttons. With that in place, in Chapter 6, *Caching the Current Folder Structure Using Vuex*, we introduced Vuex for storing the current folder path and the contents of the folders we had visited.

This chapter is going to look at:

- Pre-caching not only the folder the user is currently in but also the child folders. This will be done by looping through the folders in the current display and checking if they have been cached yet. If not, we can gather the data from the API.
- Storing the parent folder's contents, should the user have entered via a direct URL. This will be done by utilizing the breadcrumb path to traverse up the tree.
- Cache the download links for the files. This currently requires an API for every file encountered, regardless of whether the folder has been cached by our code or not.

With these improvements, we can ensure the app only contacts the API once for every item, rather than the countless times it was originally doing.

Caching subfolders

With both the subfolder and parent folder caching, we won't necessarily be writing new code, but reorganizing and repurposing the existing code into a more modular system, so that each part can be called separately.

The following flowchart should help you visualize the steps required to cache the current folder and subfolders:

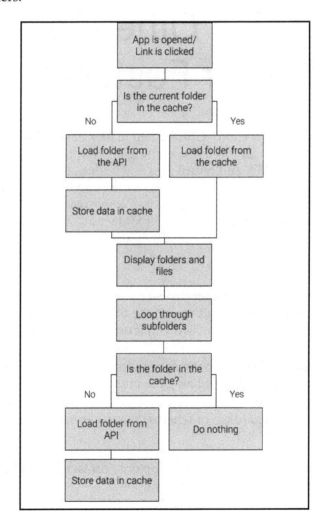

When looking at the flowchart, you can immediately see some duplication in events required for the app. At two points the app needs to decide whether a folder exists in the cache and, if it does not, query the API to get the data and store the result. Although it appears only twice on the flowchart, this functionality is required several times, once for every folder in the current location.

We will also need to separate out our displaying logic from our querying and storing logic, as we may need to load from the API and store, without updating the view.

Planning app methods

With the previous section in mind, we can take the opportunity to revise and refactor the methods on our `dropbox-viewer` app, ensuring each action has its own method. This would allow us to call each action as and when we want to. Before we head into the code, let's plan out the methods we need to create based on the preceding flowchart.

The first thing to note is that every time the API is queried, we need to store the result in the cache. As we don't need to store anything in the cache *unless* the API is called, we can combine these two actions in the same method. We also often need to check whether there are contents in the cache for a particular path and either load it or retrieve it from the API. We can add this to its own method that returns the data.

Let's map out the methods we need to create:

- `getFolderStructure`: This method will accept a single parameter of the path and return an object of the folder entries. This will be responsible for checking if the data is in the cache and, if not, querying the Dropbox API.
- `displayFolderStructure`: This method will fire the preceding function and use the data to update the `structure` object on the component to display the files and folders in the View.
- `cacheFolderStructure`: This method will include the `getFolderStructure` method to cache each subfolder—we'll explore a couple of ways this can be triggered.

We may need to create more methods than this, but these three will be the backbone of the component. We will keep the path and slug-computed properties, along with the `dropbox()` method. Remove the rest of the objects, methods, and functions so your `dropbox-viewer` is back to basics:

```
Vue.component('dropbox-viewer', {
    template: '#dropbox-viewer-template',
```

```
data() {
  return {
    accessToken: 'XXXX',
    structure: {},
    isLoading: true
  }
},
computed: {
  path() {
    return this.$store.state.path
  },
  slug() {
    return this.path.toLowerCase()
      .replace(/^\/|\/$/g, '')
      .replace(/ /g,'-')
      .replace(/\//g,'-')
      .replace(/[-]+/g, '-')
      .replace(/[^\w-]+/g,'');
  }
},
methods: {
  dropbox() {
    return new Dropbox({
      accessToken: this.accessToken
    });
  },
  }
});
```

Creating the getFolderStructure method

Create a new method on your component called `getFolderStructure`. As mentioned previously, this method needs to accept a single path parameter. This is so we can use with both the current path and children paths:

```
getFolderStructure(path) {
}
```

This method needs to check the cache and return the data. Make a new variable, titled `output`, inside the method and return it:

```
getFolderStructure(path) {
  let output;

  return output;
}
```

When caching the data in Chapter 6, *Caching the Current Folder Structure Using Vuex*, we were using the slug as the key in the store. The slug was generated by using the current path; however, we cannot use this in the new methods as it is fixed to its current location.

Create a new method called generateSlug. This will accept one parameter, the path, and return a converted string using the replacements from the slug-computed function:

```
generateSlug(path) {
    return path.toLowerCase()
        .replace(/^\/|\/$/g, '')
        .replace(/ /g,'-')
        .replace(/\//g,'-')
        .replace(/[-]+/g, '-')
        .replace(/[^\w-]+/g,'');
}
```

We can now delete the computed slug function, so we don't have any repeating code.

Going back to our getFolderStructure method, create a new variable that stores the slug version of the path using the new method. For this, we are going to use const to create a variable that cannot be changed:

```
getFolderStructure(path) {
    let output;

    const slug = this.generateSlug(path);

    return output;
}
```

The last variable we will create is the data path, as we did in Chapter 8, *Introducing Vue-Router and Loading URL-Based Components*. This will use the new slug variable we've just created:

```
getFolderStructure(path) {
    let output;

    const slug = this.generateSlug(path),
        data = this.$store.state.structure[slug];
    return output;
}
```

We can now use the `data` `if` statement from the previous code inside of here, with space for the Dropbox function call. We can assign the `data` to `output` straight away if it exists in the store:

```
getFolderStructure(path) {
    let output;

    const slug = this.generateSlug(path),
        data = this.$store.state.structure[slug];
    if(data) {
      output = data;
    } else {

    }

    return output;
}
```

With the Dropbox API call, however, we can tweak it to suit this new code. Previously, it was retrieving the data from the API and then firing a method that then saved and displayed the structure. As we need to store the data retrieved in the `output` variable, we are going to alter the flow of data. Instead of firing a method, we are going to use this opportunity to first store the response in the cache and then return the data to the `output` variable.

As we only use the entries from the API call, we are also going to update the store to only cache this part of the response. This will reduce the code and complexity of the app:

```
getFolderStructure(path) {
    let output;

    const slug = this.generateSlug(path),
        data = this.$store.state.structure[slug];
    if(data) {
      output = data;
    } else {

      output = this.dropbox().filesListFolder({
        path: path,
        include_media_info: true
      })
      .then(response => {
        let entries = response.entries;
        this.$store.commit('structure', {
          path: slug,
          data: entries
```

```
    });
    return entries;
  })
  .catch(error => {
    this.isLoading = 'error';
    console.log(error);
  });

}


return output;
}
```

The Dropbox `filesListFolder` method uses the passed-in `path` variable, rather than the global one it was previously using. The entries from the response are then stored in a variable before being cached in the Vuex store using the same mutation. The `entries` variable is then returned from the promise, which stores the result in `output`. The `catch()` function is the same as before.

With the data being returned from either the cache or the API, we can trigger and process this data when the component is created and when the path is updated. Before we do that, however, we have a mix of data types to deal with.

When returned from the API, the data is still a promise that needs to be resolved; assigning it to a variable merely passes on the promise to be resolved later. Data from the store, however, is a plain array that is handled very differently. To give us a single data type to deal with, we are going to `resolve` the stored array as a promise, meaning the `getFolderStructure` returns a promise, regardless of where the data is loaded from:

```
getFolderStructure(path) {
  let output;

  const slug = this.generateSlug(path),
      data = this.$store.state.structure[slug];
  if(data) {
    output = Promise.resolve(data);
  } else {

    output = this.dropbox().filesListFolder({
      path: path,
      include_media_info: true
    })
    .then(response => {
      let entries = response.entries;

      this.$store.commit('structure', {
```

```
      path: slug,
      data: entries
    });

    return entries;
  })
  .catch(error => {
    this.isLoading = 'error';
    console.log(error);
  });

  }
  return output;
}
```

With this `getFolderStructure` method, we now have the ability to load some data from the API and store the result in the global cache without updating the view. The function does, however, return the information should we wish to process it further with a JavaScript promise.

We can now proceed with creating our next method, `displayFolderStructure`, which will take the result of the method we have just created and update our View, so the app is navigable once again.

Showing the data with the displayFolderStructure method

With our data now ready to be cached and served up from the store, we can go ahead and actually *display* the data with our new method. Create a new method in your `dropbox-viewer` component labeled `displayFolderStructure`:

```
displayFolderStructure() {
}
```

This method will borrow a lot of code from the previous incarnation of this component. Remember, this method is used purely for displaying the folder and has nothing to do with caching the contents.

The process of the method will be:

1. Set the loading state as active in the app. This lets the user know something is happening.
2. Create an empty structure object.
3. Load the contents of the getFolderStructure method.
4. Loop through the result and add each item to either the folders or files array.
5. Set the global structure object to the new one created.
6. Set the loading state to false so the contents can be displayed.

Set the loading state to true and create an empty structure object

The first step of this method is to hide the structure tree and show the loading message. This can be done as before, by setting the isLoading variable to true. We can also create our empty structure object here, ready to be populated by the data:

```
displayFolderStructure() {
  this.isLoading = true;

  const structure = {
    folders: [],
    files: []
  }
}
```

Load the contents of the getFolderStructure method

As the getFolderStructure method returns a promise, we need to resolve the result before proceeding on to manipulate it. This is done with the .then() function; we have already used this with the Dropbox class. Call the method and then assign the result to a variable:

```
displayFolderStructure() {
  this.isLoading = true;

  const structure = {
    folders: [],
    files: []
  }
  this.getFolderStructure(this.path).then(data => {
```

```
    });
  }
```

This code passes the `path` object of the component into the method. This path is the *current* path that the user is trying to view. Once the data is returned, we can assign it to the `data` variable, which can then be used inside the function.

Loop through the result and add each item to either the folders or files array

We are already familiar with the code that loops through the entries and examines the `.tag` attribute of each one. If this results in a folder, it is added to the `structure.folders` array, otherwise it is appended to `structure.files`.

We are only storing the entries in the cache, so make sure the `for` loop is updated to use the data as is, rather than accessing the property of entries:

```
displayFolderStructure() {
  this.isLoading = true;

  const structure = {
    folders: [],
    files: []
  }
  this.getFolderStructure(this.path).then(data => {
    for (let entry of data) {
      // Check ".tag" prop for type
      if(entry['.tag'] == 'folder') {
        structure.folders.push(entry);
      } else {
        structure.files.push(entry);
      }
    }
  });
}
```

Update the global structure object and remove the loading state

The last task in this method is to update the global structure and remove the loading state. This code is unchanged from before:

```
displayFolderStructure() {
    this.isLoading = true;

    const structure = {
        folders: [],
        files: []
    }
    this.getFolderStructure(this.path).then(data => {
        for (let entry of data) {
            // Check ".tag" prop for type
            if(entry['.tag'] == 'folder') {
                structure.folders.push(entry);
            } else {
                structure.files.push(entry);
            }
        }
        this.structure = structure;
        this.isLoading = false;
    });
}
```

We now have a method that will display the result of our data retrieval.

Instigating the method

This method can now be called when the dropbox-viewer component gets created. The path will already be populated, thanks to the created function on the global Vue instance that commits the URL hash to the store, thus creating the path variable. Because of this, we don't need to pass anything to the function. Add the created function to your component and call the new method inside:

```
Vue.component('dropbox-viewer', {
    template: '#dropbox-viewer-template',
    data() {
        return {
            accessToken: 'XXXX',
            structure: {},
            isLoading: true
        }
```

```
    },
    computed: {
      ...
    },
    methods: {

      ...
    },

    created() {
      this.displayFolderStructure();
    }
});
```

Refreshing the app now will load your folder contents. Updating the URL hash and reloading the page will also show the contents of that folder; however, clicking any folder links will update the breadcrumb, but not the data structure. This can be resolved by watching the computed `path` variable. This will get updated when the hash updates and so can trigger a function in the `watch` object. Add a function that watches for the `path` variable to update and fires the new method when it has:

```
    created() {
      this.displayFolderStructure();
    },

    watch: {
      path() {
        this.displayFolderStructure();
      }
    }
```

With this, we have created an app that, once again, caches any folder you have visited. Clicking through the structure the first time will seem quite slow, but once you navigate back up the tree and re-enter subfolders you will barely see the loading screen.

Despite the app having the same functionality as it did at the beginning of the chapter, we have refactored the code to separate out the retrieval and caching and the displaying of the data. Let's move on to enhancing our app further by pre-caching the subfolders of the selected path.

Caching the subfolders

Now that we have the ability to cache a folder without updating the Vue, we can use our `structure` object to get the contents of the subfolders. Using the `folders` array in the `structure` object, we can loop through this and cache each folder in turn.

We have to make sure we do not hinder the performance of the app; the caching must be done asynchronously, so the user is not aware of this process. We also need to make sure we aren't running the caching unnecessarily.

To achieve this, we can watch the `structure` object. This only gets updated once the data has been loaded from the cache or the API and the Vue has updated. With the user viewing the contents of the folder, we can proceed with looping through the folders to store their contents.

There is a slight issue, however. If we watch the `structure` variable, our code will never run as the direct *contents* of the object does not update, despite the fact we replace the `structure` object with a new one every time. From folder to folder, the structure object always has two keys, of `files` and `folders`, which are both arrays. As far as Vue and JavaScript are concerned, the `structure` object never changes.

Vue can, however, detect nested changes with the `deep` variable. This can be enabled on a per variable basis. Similar to the props on a component, to enable more options on a watch property, you pass it an object instead of a direct function.

Create a new `watch` key for structure, which is an object with two values, `deep` and `handler`. The `deep` key will be set to `true`, while the `handler` will be the function fired when the variable is changed:

```
watch: {
  path() {
    this.displayFolderStructure();
  },

  structure: {
    deep: true,
    handler() {
    }
  }
}
```

Inside this `handler`, we can now loop through each of the folders and run the `getFolderStructure` method for each one, using the `path_lower` property of each one as the function argument:

```
structure: {
  deep: true,
  handler() {
    for (let folder of this.structure.folders) {
      this.getFolderStructure(folder.path_lower);
    }
  }
}
```

With this simple piece of code, our app appears to speed up tenfold. Every subfolder you navigate to loads instantly (unless you have a particularly long folder list and you navigate to the last one very quickly). To give you an idea of the speed and timing of the caching, add a `console.log()` inside your `getFolderStructure` method and open the browser developer tools:

```
if(data) {
  output = Promise.resolve(data);
} else {

  console.log(`API query for ${path}`);
  output = this.dropbox().filesListFolder({
    path: path,
    include_media_info: true
  })
  .then(response => {
    console.log(`Response for ${path}`);

    ...
```

This allows you to see all the API calls are done asynchronously too—the app isn't waiting for the previous folder to be loaded and cached before moving on to the next one. This has the advantage of allowing smaller folders to be cached without waiting for bigger ones to be returned from the API.

Alternative caching method

As with everything, when making an app, there are many approaches to achieving the same result. The downside with this method is that even if your folder contains only files, this function will trigger—albeit with nothing to do.

An alternative approach would be to use our `created` function once again, this time on the `folder` component itself, triggering the parent method with the path as the argument.

One way of doing this is using the `$parent` property. When in the `folder` component, using `this.$parent` will allow access to the variables, methods, and computed values on the `dropbox-viewer` component.

Add a `created` function to the `folder` component and delete the `structure watch` property from the Dropbox component. From there, call the parent `getFolderStructure` method:

```
Vue.component('folder', {
    template: '<li><strong><a :href="\'#\' + f.path_lower">{{ f.name
}}</a></strong></li>',
    props: {
        f: Object
    },
    created() {
        this.$parent.getFolderStructure(this.f.path_lower);
    }
});
```

Previewing the app proves the validity of this method. Only triggering when there are folders in the structure, this cleaner technique ties the folder-caching with the folder itself, rather than getting mixed in with the Dropbox code.

However, `this.$parent` should be avoided unless necessary, and should only be used in edge cases. As we have the opportunity to use props, we should do so. It also gives us the chance to give the function a more meaningful name in the folder context.

Navigate to your HTML view and update the folder component to accept a new prop. We'll call the prop cache and pass the function in as the value. As the property is dynamic, don't forget to add a preceding colon:

```
<folder :f="entry" :cache="getFolderStructure"></folder>
```

Add the `cache` keyword to the props key in the JavaScript `folder` component. Inform Vue that the input will be a function:

```
Vue.component('folder', {
    template: '<li><strong><a :href="\'#\' + f.path_lower">{{ f.name
}}</a></strong></li>',
    props: {
        f: Object,
        cache: Function
```

```
    }
  });
```

Lastly, we can call our new `cache()` method in the `created` function:

```
Vue.component('folder', {
  template: '<li><strong><a :href="\'#\' + f.path_lower">{{ f.name
}}</a></strong></li>',
  props: {
    f: Object,
    cache: Function
  },
  created() {
    this.cache(this.f.path_lower);
  }
});
```

The caching can be verified, once again, by using the console logs as before. This creates cleaner code that is easier for yourself, and any other developers, to read.

With our Dropbox app now progressing, we can move on to caching parent folders, should you enter a subfolder using a hash in the URL.

Caching parent folders

Caching the parent structure is the next preemptive thing we can do to help speed up our app. Say we had navigated to our images directory, /images/holiday/summer, and wished to share this with a friend or colleague. We would send them the URL with this in the URL hash and, on page load, they would see the contents. If they then navigated up the tree using the breadcrumb to /images/holiday, for example, they would need to wait for the app to retrieve the contents.

Using the `breadcrumb` component, we can cache the parent directories and so, on navigating to the `holiday` folder, the user would be presented instantly with its contents. While the user is then browsing this folder, all of its subfolders are being cached with the previous methods.

To cache the parent folders, we already have a component displaying the path with access to the slugs of all the parent folders we can loop through—the breadcrumb.

Before we start the caching process, we need to update the `folders` computed function within the component. This is because currently, we store the path with the hash prepended, which creates an invalid path for the Dropbox API. Remove the hash from the object being pushed to the output array and add it in the template, in a similar fashion to the `folder` component:

```
Vue.component('breadcrumb', {
    template: '<div>' +
      '<span v-for="(f, i) in folders">' +
        '<a :href="\'#\' + f.path">{{ f.name || 'Home' }}</a>' +
        '<i v-if="i !== (folders.length - 1)"> &raquo; </i>' +
      '</span>' +
    '</div>',
    computed: {
      folders() {
        let output = [],
          slug = '',
          parts = this.$store.state.path.split('/');
        for (let item of parts) {
          slug += item;
          output.push({'name': item || 'home', 'path': slug});
          slug += '/';
        }

        return output;
      }
    }
});
```

We can now use the output for both displaying the breadcrumb and caching the parent structure.

The first step is to allow the `breadcrumb` component access to the caching function. In a similar fashion to the `folder` component, add the function as a prop to the `breadcrumb` component in your View:

```
<breadcrumb :cache="getFolderStructure"></breadcrumb>
```

Add the `props` object to the component in the JavaScript code. Declare the `cache` prop as a function so Vue knows what to expect:

```
Vue.component('breadcrumb', {
    template: '...',
    props: {
      cache: Function
    },
```

```
computed: {
  folders() {
    ...
  }
});
```

The parent structure is going to be on the creation of the `breadcrumb` component. However, as we don't want this to hold up the loading process, we are going to trigger it when the component is `mounted`, not `created`.

Add a `mounted` function to your component and assign the folder's computed value to a variable:

```
Vue.component('breadcrumb', {
  template: '...',
  props: {
    cache: Function
  },
  computed: {
    folders() {
      ...
    }
  },
  mounted() {
    let parents = this.folders;
  }
});
```

We now need to start caching the folders; however, we can be smart in the order that we do it. We can assume that the user will generally go back up the folder tree, so we should ideally cache the direct parent before moving onto its parent, and so on and so forth. As our folder's variable goes from the top down, we need to reverse it.

The other thing we can do to improve performance is to remove the current folder; as we are already in it, the app would have cached it already. In your component, reverse the array and remove the first item:

```
mounted() {
  let parents = this.folders;
  parents.reverse().shift();
}
```

If we add a console log to the function of the parent's variable, we can see it contains the folders we now wish to cache. We can now loop through this array, calling the `cache` function for each item in the array:

```
mounted() {
  let parents = this.folders;
  parents.reverse().shift();

  for(let parent of parents) {
    this.cache(parent.path);
  }
}
```

With this, our parent and child folders are being cached by the app, making navigation both up and down the tree lightning fast. However, running a `console.log()` inside the `mounted` function reveals the breadcrumb gets re-mounted every time a folder gets navigated to. This is because of the `v-if` statements in the View, which removes and adds the HTML each time.

As we only need to cache the parent folders once, on initial app load, let's look at changing where it gets triggered. We only need to run this function the first time; once the user has started navigating up and back down the tree, all the folders visited will be cached along the way.

Caching parent folders once

To ensure we are using the least amount of resources, we can keep the array of folders used for the breadcrumb in the store. This means that both the `breadcrumb` component and our parent caching function can access the same array.

Add a `breadcrumb` key to your store state—this is where we will store the array:

```
const store = new Vuex.Store({
  state: {
    path: '',
    structure: {},
    breadcrumb: []
  },
  mutations: {
    updateHash(state) {
      let hash = window.location.hash.substring(1);
      state.path = (hash || '');
    },
    structure(state, payload) {
```

```
        state.structure[payload.path] = payload.data;
      }
    }
  });
```

Next, move the code from the `breadcrumb` component into the `updateHash` mutation so we can update both the `path` and `breadcrumb` variables:

```
updateHash(state) {
  let hash = window.location.hash.substring(1);
  state.path = (hash || '');

  let output = [],
    slug = '',
    parts = state.path.split('/');
  for (let item of parts) {
    slug += item;
    output.push({'name': item || 'home', 'path': slug});
    slug += '/';
  }
  state.breadcrumb = output;
},
```

Note that rather than returning the `output` array, it is getting stored in the `state` object. We can now update the folder's computed function on the `breadcrumb` component to return the store data:

```
computed: {
  folders() {
    return this.$store.state.breadcrumb;
  }
}
```

With the data now available globally, we can create a new method on the `dropbox-viewer` component, `cacheParentFolders`, which triggers the code we wrote for the `breadcrumb` component.

Create a new method on the `Dropbox` component and move your code to it. Update the location of the parents and ensure you are firing the correct path:

```
cacheParentFolders() {
  let parents = this.$store.state.breadcrumb;
  parents.reverse().shift();

  for(let parent of parents) {
    this.getFolderStructure(parent.path);
  }
```

```
}
```

We can now fire this method once when the Dropbox component gets created. Add it after the existing method call in the `created` function:

```
created() {
    this.displayFolderStructure();
    this.cacheParentFolders();
}
```

We can now do some housekeeping and delete the `mounted` method from the `breadcrumb` component, along with the `props` object and the `:cache` prop from the view. This means our `breadcrumb` component is now simpler than it was before:

```
Vue.component('breadcrumb', {
    template: '<div>' +
        '<span v-for="(f, i) in folders">' +
            '<a :href="\'#\' + f.path">{{ f.name || \'Home\' }}</a>' +
            '<i v-if="i !== (folders.length - 1)"> &raquo; </i>' +
        '</span>' +
    '</div>',
    computed: {
        folders() {
            return this.$store.state.breadcrumb;
        }
    }
});
```

The HTML returns to what it was:

```
<breadcrumb></breadcrumb>
```

We can also tidy up the `updateHash` mutation in the store to be a bit neater and more understandable:

```
updateHash(state, val) {
    let path = (window.location.hash.substring(1) || ''),
        breadcrumb = [],
        slug = '',
        parts = path.split('/');

    for (let item of parts) {
        slug += item;
        breadcrumb.push({'name': item || 'home', 'path': slug});
        slug += '/';
    }
```

```
    state.path = path
    state.breadcrumb = breadcrumb;
}
```

All the variables are now being declared at the top, with the `state` being updated at the bottom. The number of variables has also been reduced.

Viewing the app now, it appears to work correctly; however, upon closer inspection, the `breadcrumb` seems to lag a bit with the folder structure on initial page load. Once a folder has been navigated to, it catches up but on the first load it seems to have one fewer item, and when viewing the root of the Dropbox none at all.

This is because the store has not been fully initialized before we are committing the `updateHash` mutation. If we remember back to the Vue instance life cycle, covered in Chapter 4, *Getting a List of Files Using the Dropbox API*, we can see the created function gets fired very early on. Updating the main Vue instance to trigger the mutation on `mounted` instead resolves the issue:

```
const app = new Vue({
  el: '#app',

  store,
  mounted() {
    store.commit('updateHash');
  }
});
```

With all the folders being cached as well as they can be, we can move on to caching more API calls by storing the download link for each file.

We could also look into caching subfolders of subfolders, looping through the contents of each cached folder to eventually cache the whole tree. We won't go into that, but feel free to give it a go yourself.

Caching download links on files

When the user is navigating around the document tree, the Dropbox API is still being queried more than necessary. This is because every time a file is displayed, we query the API to retrieve the download link. Extra API queries can be negated by storing the download link response in the cache and re-displaying the folder it is navigated back into.

Every time a file is displayed, a new component gets initialized using data from the store. We can use this to our advantage as it means we only need to update the component instance and then the result gets cached.

In your file component, update the API response to not only save the result on the `link` property of the data attribute but the on the file instance, `f`, as well. This will be stored as a new key, `download_link`.

When storing the data, rather than having two separate commands, we can combine them into one with two equal signs:

```
Vue.component('file', {
    template: '<li><strong>{{ f.name }}</strong><span v-if="f.size"> - {{
bytesToSize(f.size) }}</span> - <a v-if="link"
:href="link">Download</a></li>',
    props: {
        f: Object,
        d: Object
    },
    data() {
        return {
            byteSizes: ['Bytes', 'KB', 'MB', 'GB', 'TB'],
            link: false
        }
    },
    methods: {
        bytesToSize(bytes) {
            // Set a default
            let output = '0 Byte';
            // If the bytes are bigger than 0
            if (bytes > 0) {
                // Divide by 1024 and make an int
                let i = parseInt(Math.floor(Math.log(bytes) / Math.log(1024)));
                // Round to 2 decimal places and select the appropriate unit from
the array
                output = Math.round(bytes / Math.pow(1024, i), 2) + ' ' +
this.byteSizes[i];
            }
            return output
        }
    },
    created() {
        this.d.filesGetTemporaryLink({path: this.f.path_lower})
            .then(data => {
                this.f.download_link = this.link = data.link;
            });
    }
```

```
});
```

This essentially means `this.f.download_link` is equal to `this.link`, which is also equal to `data.link`, the download link from the API. With this being stored and displayed when the folder is navigated to, we can add an `if` statement to see whether the data exists and, if not, query the API to get it.

```
created() {
  if(this.f.download_link) {
    this.link = this.f.download_link;
  } else {
    this.d.filesGetTemporaryLink({path: this.f.path_lower})
      .then(data => {
        this.f.download_link = this.link = data.link;
      });
  }
}
```

Doing this on file creation saves the API being queried unnecessarily. If we obtained this information when caching the folders, we could slow down the app and be storing non-essential information. Imagine a folder with hundreds of photos in it—we wouldn't want to query the API for every one of these just on the off chance the user might enter that folder.

This means everything in our app only needs to query the API once to get the information. The user can navigate up and down folder structures as many times as they want, with the app only getting faster as they do so.

The complete code—with added documentation

With our app complete, we can now add some much-needed documentation. It's always good to document your code as this gives it reasoning and explanation. Good documentation should not just say what the code does, but why it does it, what is allowed, and what is not allowed.

A popular method for documentation is the JavaScript DocBlock standard. This set of conventions lays out style guide-like rules for you to follow when documenting your code. DocBlock is formatted in a comment block and features keywords starting with an @, such as @author, @example, or listing what parameters a function can accept with the @param keyword. An example would be:

```
/**
 * Displays a folder with a link and cache its contents
 * @example <folder :f="entry" :cache="getFolderStructure"></folder>
 *
 * @param {object} f The folder entry from the tree
 * @param {function} cache The getFolderStructure method from the dropbox-
viewer component
 */
```

Starting off with a description, DocBlock has several keywords to help lay out the documentation. We'll walk through our completed Dropbox app with added documentation.

Let us first take a look at the `breadcrumb` component:

```
/**
 * Displays the folder tree breadcrumb
 * @example <breadcrumb></breadcrumb>
 */
Vue.component('breadcrumb', {
  template: '<div>' +
    '<span v-for="(f, i) in folders">' +
      '<a :href="\'#\' + f.path">{{ f.name || 'Home' }}</a>' +
      '<i v-if="i !== (folders.length - 1)"> &raquo; </i>' +
    '</span>' +
  '</div>',
  computed: {
    folders() {
      return this.$store.state.breadcrumb;
    }
  }
});
```

Moving on to the `folder` component:

```
/**
 * Displays a folder with a link and cache its contents
 * @example <folder :f="entry" :cache="getFolderStructure"></folder>
 *
 * @param {object} f The folder entry from the tree
 * @param {function} cache The getFolderStructure method from the dropbox-
```

```
viewer component
 */
Vue.component('folder', {
  template: '<li><strong><a :href="\'#\' + f.path_lower">{{ f.name
}}</a></strong></li>',
  props: {
    f: Object,
    cache: Function
  },
  created() {
    // Cache the contents of the folder
    this.cache(this.f.path_lower);
  }
});
```

Next, in line, we see the `file` component:

```
/**
 * File component display size of file and download link
 * @example <file :d="dropbox()" :f="entry"></file>
 *
 * @param {object} f The file entry from the tree
 * @param {object} d The dropbox instance from the parent component
 */
Vue.component('file', {
  template: '<li><strong>{{ f.name }}</strong><span v-if="f.size"> - {{
bytesToSize(f.size) }}</span> - <a v-if="link"
:href="link">Download</a></li>',
  props: {
    f: Object,
    d: Object
  },
  data() {
    return {
      // List of file size
      byteSizes: ['Bytes', 'KB', 'MB', 'GB', 'TB'],

      // The download link
      link: false
    }
  },
  methods: {
    /**
     * Convert an integer to a human readable file size
     * @param {integer} bytes
     * @return {string}
     */
    bytesToSize(bytes) {
```

```
    // Set a default
    let output = '0 Byte';
    // If the bytes are bigger than 0
    if (bytes > 0) {
      // Divide by 1024 and make an int
      let i = parseInt(Math.floor(Math.log(bytes) / Math.log(1024)));
      // Round to 2 decimal places and select the appropriate unit from
the array
      output = Math.round(bytes / Math.pow(1024, i), 2) + ' ' +
this.byteSizes[i];
    }
    return output
  }
},
created() {
  // If the download link has be retrieved from the API, use it
  // if not, aquery the API
  if(this.f.download_link) {
    this.link = this.f.download_link;
  } else {
    this.d.filesGetTemporaryLink({path: this.f.path_lower})
      .then(data => {
        this.f.download_link = this.link = data.link;
      });
  }
}
}
});
```

Now we take a look at the dropbox-viewer component:

```
/**
 * The dropbox component
 * @example <dropbox-viewer></dropbox-viewer>
 */
Vue.component('dropbox-viewer', {
  template: '#dropbox-viewer-template',
  data() {
    return {
      // Dropbox API token
      accessToken: 'XXXX',

      // Current folder structure
      structure: {},
      isLoading: true
    }
  },
  computed: {
    // The current folder path
```

```
    path() {
      return this.$store.state.path
    }
  },
  methods: {

    /**
     * Dropbox API instance
     * @return {object}
     */
    dropbox() {
      return new Dropbox({
        accessToken: this.accessToken
      });
    },

    /**
     * @param {string} path The path to a folder
     * @return {string} A cache-friendly URL without punctuation/symbals
     */
    generateSlug(path) {
      return path.toLowerCase()
        .replace(/^\/|\/$/g, '')
        .replace(/ /g,'-')
        .replace(/\//g,'-')
        .replace(/[-]+/g, '-')
        .replace(/[^\w-]+/g,'');
    },

    /**
     * Retrieve the folder structure form the cache or Dropbox API
     * @param {string} path The folder path
     * @return {Promise} A promise containing the folder data
     */
    getFolderStructure(path) {
      let output;

      const slug = this.generateSlug(path),
          data = this.$store.state.structure[slug];
      if(data) {
        output = Promise.resolve(data);
      } else {
        output = this.dropbox().filesListFolder({
          path: path,
          include_media_info: true
        })
        .then(response => {
          let entries = response.entries;
```

```
      this.$store.commit('structure', {
        path: slug,
        data: entries
      });

      return entries;
    })
    .catch(error => {
      this.isLoading = 'error';
      console.log(error);
    });

  }
  return output;
},

/**
 * Display the contents of getFolderStructure
 * Updates the output to display the folders and folders
 */
displayFolderStructure() {
  // Set the app to loading
  this.isLoading = true;

  // Create an empty object
  const structure = {
    folders: [],
    files: []
  }
  // Get the structure
  this.getFolderStructure(this.path).then(data => {

    for (let entry of data) {
      // Check ".tag" prop for type
      if(entry['.tag'] == 'folder') {
        structure.folders.push(entry);
      } else {
        structure.files.push(entry);
      }
    }

    // Update the data object
    this.structure = structure;
    this.isLoading = false;
  });
},

/**
```

```
        * Loop through the breadcrumb and cache parent folders
        */
      cacheParentFolders() {
        let parents = this.$store.state.breadcrumb;
        parents.reverse().shift();

        for(let parent of parents) {
          this.getFolderStructure(parent.path);
        }
      }
    },

    created() {
      // Display the current path & cache parent folders
      this.displayFolderStructure();
      this.cacheParentFolders();
    },

    watch: {
      // Update the view when the path gets updated
      path() {
        this.displayFolderStructure();
      }
    }
});
```

Let us also check the Vuex store:

```
/**
 * The Vuex Store
 */
const store = new Vuex.Store({
  state: {
    // Current folder path
    path: '',

    // The current breadcrumb
    breadcrumb: [],

    // The cached folder contents
    structure: {},
  },
  mutations: {
    /**
     * Update the path & breadcrumb components
     * @param {object} state The state object of the store
     */
    updateHash(state) {
```

```
    let path = (window.location.hash.substring(1) || ''),
        breadcrumb = [],
        slug = '',
        parts = path.split('/');

    for (let item of parts) {
      slug += item;
      breadcrumb.push({'name': item || 'home', 'path': slug});
      slug += '/';
    }

    state.path = path
    state.breadcrumb = breadcrumb;
  },

  /**
   * Cache a folder structure
   * @param {object} state The state objet of the store
   * @param {object} payload An object containing the slug and data to
store
   */
  structure(state, payload) {
    state.structure[payload.path] = payload.data;
  }
  }
});
```

We furthermore move to the Vue app:

```
/**
 * The Vue app
 */
const app = new Vue({
  el: '#app',

  // Initialize the store
  store,

  // Update the current path on page load
  mounted() {
    store.commit('updateHash');
  }
});
```

And in the end, we go through the `window.onhashchange` function:

```
/**
 * Update the path & store when the URL hash changes
 */
window.onhashchange = () => {
  app.$store.commit('updateHash');
}
```

Finally, the HTML from the view looks like this:

```
<div id="app">
  <dropbox-viewer></dropbox-viewer>
</div>
```

And the template for the Dropbox viewer looks like this:

```
<script type="text/x-template" id="dropbox-viewer-template">
  <div>
    <h1>Dropbox</h1>
    <transition name="fade">
      <div v-if="isLoading">
        <div v-if="isLoading == 'error'">
          <p>There seems to be an issue with the URL entered.</p>
          <p><a href="">Go home</a></p>
        </div>
        <div v-else>
          Loading...
        </div>
      </div>
    </transition>

    <transition name="fade">
      <div v-if="!isLoading">
        <breadcrumb></breadcrumb>
        <ul>
          <template v-for="entry in structure.folders">
            <folder :f="entry" :cache="getFolderStructure"></folder>
          </template>
          <template v-for="entry in structure.files">
            <file :d="dropbox()" :f="entry"></file>
          </template>
        </ul>
      </div>
    </transition>

  </div>
</script>
```

You will notice not *everything* has been documented. A simple function or variable assignment doesn't need to re-explain what it does, but a note of the main variables will help anyone looking at it in the future.

Summary

In this section of the book, we've covered quite a lot! We started with querying the Dropbox API to get a list of files and folders. We then moved on to adding navigation, allowing the user to click on folders and download files. We then introduced Vuex and the store into our app, which meant we could centralize the path, breadcrumb, and most importantly, cache the folder contents. Lastly, we looked at caching sub-folders and the file download link.

In the next section of the book, we are going to look at making a shop. This will include browsing products in a category and product pages using a new Vue plugin called Vue router. We will also look at adding products to a basket and storing both the product list and preferences in the Vuex store.

8
Introducing Vue-Router and Loading URL-Based Components

In the next few chapters and the last section of this book, we are going to be creating a shop interface. This shop is going to combine everything we have learned so far while introducing some more techniques, plugins, and functionality. We are going to look at retrieving a list of products from a CSV file, displaying them and their variations, and filtering the products by manufacturer or tags. We will also look at creating a product detail view and allowing the user to add and remove products and product variations, such as size or color, to their online shopping basket.

All of this will be achieved using Vue, Vuex, and a new Vue plugin, Vue-router. Vue-router is used for building **Single Page Applications (SPAs)** and allows you to map components to URLs, or in VueRouter terms, routes, and paths. This is an extremely powerful plugin and handles a lot of the intricate details required for the processing of URLs.

This chapter is going to cover:

- Initializing Vue-router and its options
- Creating links with Vue-router
- Making dynamic routes to update the View based on URL
- Using props with URLs
- Nesting and naming routes
- How to navigate programmatically with Vue-router

Installing and initializing Vue-router

Similar to how we added Vue and Vuex to our applications, you can either directly include the library from unpkg, or head to the following URL and download a local copy for yourself: `https://unpkg.com/Vue-router`. Add the JavaScript to a new HTML document, along with Vue, and your application's JavaScript. Create an application container element, your view, as well. In the following example, I have saved the Vue-router JavaScript file as `router.js`:

```
<!DOCTYPE html>
<html>
<head>
  <title></title>
</head>
<body>
  <div id="app"></div>

  <script type="text/javascript" src="js/vue.js"></script>
  <script type="text/javascript" src="js/router.js"></script>
  <script type="text/javascript" src="js/app.js"></script>
</body>
</html>
```

Initialize a new Vue instance in your application JavaScript:

```
new Vue({
  el: '#app'
});
```

We are now ready to add `VueRouter` and utilize its power. Before we do that, however, we need to create some very simple components which we can load and display based on the URL. As we are going to be loading the components with the router, we don't need to register them with `Vue.component`, but instead create JavaScript objects with the same properties as we would a Vue component.

For this first exercise, we are going to create two pages—Home and About pages. Found on most websites, these should help give you context as to what is loading where and when. Create two templates in your HTML page for us to use:

```
<script type="text/x-template" id="homepage">
  <div>
    <h1>Hello &amp; Welcome</h1>
    <p>Welcome to my website. Feel free to browse around.</p>
  </div>
</script>
```

```html
<script type="text/x-template" id="about">
  <div>
    <h1>About Me</h1>
    <p>Lorem ipsum dolor sit amet, consectetur adipiscing elit. Vivamus sed
metus magna. Vivamus eget est nisi. Phasellus vitae nisi sagittis, ornare
dui quis, pharetra leo. Nullam eget tellus velit. Sed tempor lorem augue,
vitae luctus urna ultricies nec. Curabitur luctus sapien elit, non pretium
ante sagittis blandit. Nulla egestas nunc sit amet tellus rhoncus, a
ultrices nisl varius. Nam scelerisque lacus id justo congue maximus. Etiam
rhoncus, libero at facilisis gravida, nibh nisi venenatis ante, sit amet
viverra justo urna vel neque.</p>
    <p>Curabitur et arcu fermentum, viverra lorem ut, pulvinar arcu. Fusce
ex massa, vehicula id eros vel, feugiat commodo leo. Etiam in sem rutrum,
porttitor velit in, sollicitudin tortor. Interdum et malesuada fames ac
ante ipsum primis in faucibus. Donec ac sapien efficitur, pretium massa at,
vehicula ligula. Vestibulum turpis quam, feugiat sed orci id, eleifend
pretium urna. Nullam faucibus arcu eget odio venenatis ornare.</p>
  </div>
</script>
```

 Don't forget to encapsulate all your content in one "root" element (represented here by the wrapping `<div>` tags). You also need to ensure you declare the templates *before* your application JavaScript is loaded.

We've created a Home page template, with the `id` of `homepage`, and an About page, containing some placeholder text from *lorem ipsum*, with the `id` of `about`. Create two components in your JavaScript which reference these two templates:

```javascript
const Home = {
  template: '#homepage'
};

const About = {
  template: '#about'
};
```

The next step is to give the router a placeholder to render the components in the view. This is done by using a custom `<router-view>` HTML element. Using this element gives you control over where your content will render. It allows us to have a header and footer right in the app view, without needing to deal with messy templates or includes the components themselves.

Add a `header`, `main`, and `footer` element to your app. Give yourself a logo in the header and credits in the footer; in the `main` HTML element, place the `router-view` placeholder:

```
<div id="app">
  <header>
    <div>LOGO</div>
  </header>

  <main>
    <router-view></router-view>
  </main>

  <footer>
    <small>© Myself</small>
  </footer>
</div>
```

Everything in the app view is optional, except the `router-view`, but it gives you an idea of how the router HTML element can be implemented into a site structure.

The next stage is to initialize the Vue-router and instruct Vue to use it. Create a new instance of `VueRouter` and add it to the `Vue` instance—similar to how we added `Vuex` in the previous section:

```
const router = new VueRouter();

new Vue({
  el: '#app',

  router
});
```

We now need to tell the router about our routes (or paths), and what component it should load when it encounters each one. Create an object inside the Vue-router instance with a key of `routes` and an array as the value. This array needs to include an object for each route:

```
const router = new VueRouter({
  routes: [
    {
      path: '/',
      component: Home
    },
    {
      path: '/about',
      component: About
    }
  ]
```

```
});
```

Each route object contains a `path` and `component` key. The `path` is a string of the URL that you want to load the `component` on. Vue-router serves up components based on a first-come-first-served basis. For example, if there are several routes with the same path, the first one encountered is used. Ensure each route has the beginning slash—this tells the router it is a root page and not a sub-page, we will cover sub-pages later on in the chapter.

Press **save** and view your app in the browser. You should be presented with the content of the `Home` template component. If you observe the URL, you will notice that on page load a hash and forward slash (#/) are appended to the path. This is the router creating a method for browsing the components and utilizing the address bar. If you change this to the path of your second route, `#/about`, you will see the contents of the `About` component.

Vue-router is also able to use the JavaScript history API to create prettier URLs. For example, `yourdomain.com/index.html#about` would become `yourdomain.com/about`. This is activated by adding `mode: 'history'` to your `VueRouter` instance:

```
const router = new VueRouter({
  mode: 'history',

  routes: [
    {
      path: '/',
      component: Home
    },
    {
      path: '/about',
      component: About
    }
  ]
});
```

However, it also requires some server configuration to catch all requests and redirect them to your `index.html` page, which is beyond the scope of this book but is fully outlined in the Vue-router documentation.

Changing the folder for Vue-router

There may be scenarios where you want to host your Vue app in a sub-folder of your website. In this instance, you will need to declare the base folder of your project so Vue-router can construct, and listen out for, the correct URLs.

For example, if your app was based on a `/shop/` folder, you would declare it using the `base` parameter on the Vue-router instance:

```
const router = new VueRouter({
  base: '/shop/',

  routes: [
    {
      path: '/',
      component: Home
    },
    {
      path: '/about',
      component: About
    }
  ]
});
```

The value of this needs the slash at both the beginning and end.

Along with `base`, there are several other configuration options available for Vue-router—it is well worth being familiar with them, as they may solve a problem you have later on.

Linking to the different routes

With the router working as expected, we can now proceed with adding links into our application, allowing the user to navigate around the website. Links can be achieved in two ways: we can use a conventional `<a href="#/about">` tag, or alternatively we can utilize a new HTML element provided with the router of `<router-link to="/about">`. When using the router-link element, it works the same as an `<a>` tag, and in fact gets converted to one when running in the browser, but allows a lot more customization and integration with the router.

It is highly advised to use the `router-link` element wherever possible, as it carries several advantages over the standard link:

- **Mode changes**: The first advantage is linked to the `mode` of the router. Using the router link allows you to change the mode of your router, say from hash to history, and not have to change every single link in your app.
- **CSS classes**: Another advantage that comes with using the router link is a CSS class that gets applied to links active in the "tree" and pages which are currently being viewed. Links in the tree are parent pages which also include the root page (for example, any links to "/" will always have the active class). This is one of the big benefits of using the router, as adding and removing these classes manually would require complex coding. These classes can be customized and we will do that later.
- **URL parameters and named routes**: The other advantage to using the router element is the power it gives you over using named routes and passing URL parameters. This further allows you to have one source of truth for the URL of a page and use names and shortcuts to reference a route. More on this will be covered later in the chapter.

Add the links to your pages within your view so you can navigate between pages. Within the `<header>` of your website, create a new `<nav>` element that contains an unordered list. For each page, add a new list item with a `router-link` element inside. Add a `to` attribute to the link path:

```
<nav>
  <ul>
    <li>
      <router-link to="/">Home</router-link>
    </li>
    <li>
      <router-link to="/about">About</router-link>
    </li>
  </ul>
</nav>
```

Viewing the app in the browser should show your two links, allowing you to switch between the two content pages. You will also notice that, by clicking the link, the URL updates too.

If you inspect the links with the browser's HTML inspector, you will notice the change in CSS classes. The **Home** link will always have a class of `router-link-active`—this is because it is either active itself, or it has an active child, such as the About page. There is another CSS class which gets added and removed as you navigate between the two pages—`router-link-exact-active`. This *only* gets applied to the links on the currently active page.

Let's customize the classes that get applied to the view. Head to the initialization of the router in your JavaScript and add two new keys to the object - `linkActiveClass` and `linkExactActiveClass`:

```
const router = new VueRouter({
    routes: [
        {
            path: '/',
            component: Home
        },
        {
            path: '/about',
            component: About
        }
    ],
    linkActiveClass: 'active',
    linkExactActiveClass: 'current'
});
```

The keys should be fairly self-explanatory, but `linkExactActiveClass` gets applied to the current page, the one being viewed, while `linkActiveClass` is the class that gets applied when the page, or one of its children, is active.

Linking to sub-routes

There may be times you want to have links to children pages. For example `/about/meet-the-team`. Fortunately, there is not much work required to get this working. Create a new object in the `routes` array, pointing to a new component with a template:

```
const router = new VueRouter({
    routes: [
        {
            path: '/',
            component: Home
        },
        {
```

```
      path: '/about',
      component: About
   },
   {
      path: '/about/meet-the-team',
      component: MeetTheTeam
   }
 ],

 linkActiveClass: 'active',
 linkExactActiveClass: 'current'
});
```

When navigating to this page, you will notice both the Home and About links have the `active` class and neither have the `current` class we created. If you were to create a link in your navigation to this page, a `current` class would be applied to that.

Dynamic routes with parameters

Vue router easily allows you to have dynamic URLs. A dynamic URL allows you to use the same component to display different data while using the same template. An example of this would be for a shop, where all the category pages look the same but display different data based on the URL. Another example would be a product detail page—you don't want to have to create a component for every product, so instead, you use one component with a URL parameter.

URL parameters can appear anywhere in the path, and there can be one or many. Each parameter gets assigned a key, so it can be created and accessed consistently. We'll go into dynamic routes and parameters in more detail during the Chapter 9, *Using Vue-Router Dynamic Routes to Load Data*. For now, we'll build a basic example.

Before we head into creating the component, let's examine a new variable available to us—`this.$route`. In a similar way to how we accessed the global store with Vuex, this variable allows us to access a lot of information about the routes, URLs, and parameters.

In your Vue instance, as a test, add a `mounted()` function. Inside `console.log`, insert the `this.$route` parameter:

```
new Vue({
   el: '#app',

   router,
   mounted() {
```

```
    console.log(this.$route);
  }
});
```

If you open up your browser and look at the developer tools, you should see an object being output. Viewing this object will reveal several bits of information, such as the path and the components which match the current path. Heading to the /about URL will reveal different information about the object:

```
▼ {name: undefined, meta: {…}, path: "/about", hash: "", query: {…}, …}
    fullPath: "/about"
    hash: ""
  ▼ matched: Array(1)
    ▼ 0:
        beforeEnter: undefined
      ▼ components:
        ▼ default:
          ▶ methods: {someAction: f}
            name: "About"
            template: "#about"
          ▶ _Ctor: {0: f}
          ▶ __proto__: Object
        ▶ __proto__: Object
      ▶ instances: {default: VueComponent}
        matchAs: undefined
      ▶ meta: {}
        name: undefined
        parent: undefined
        path: "/about"
      ▶ props: {}
        redirect: undefined
      ▶ regex: /^\/about(?:\/(?=$))?$/i
      ▶ __proto__: Object
        length: 1
      ▶ __proto__: Array(0)
    ▶ meta: {}
      name: undefined
    ▶ params: {}
      path: "/about"
    ▶ query: {}
```

Let's create a component that uses the parameters from this object. Create a new object in your routes array:

```
const router = new VueRouter({
  routes: [
    {
      path: '/',
      component: Home
    },
    {
      path: '/about',
      component: About
    },
    {
      path: '/user/:name',
      component: User
    }
  ],

  linkActiveClass: 'active',
  linkExactActiveClass: 'current'
});
```

The thing you'll notice that is different with this path is the colon preceding the name in the path. This tells Vue-router that this part of the URL is dynamic, but the variable name for that section is name.

Now create a new component called User, and create a template for it. For this example, our template will be inline and we will be using the ES2015 template syntax. This uses backticks and allows the passing of variables and new lines directly into the template without the need to escape them:

```
const User = {
  template: `<h1>Hello {{ $route.params.name }}</h1>`
};
```

The variable being output within the template is from the global router instance and is the name variable within the parameters object. The variable name references the variable preceded by the colon in the route path, within the routes array. Within the component template, we can also omit the this variable from the $route.

Head back to your browser and enter `#/user/sarah` at the end of your URL. You should see **Hello sarah** in the main body of your web page. Viewing the JavaScript browser console, you should see the `params` object has a key/value pair of `name: sarah` within it:

```
▼ {name: undefined, meta: {…}, path: "/user/sarah", hash: "", query: {…}, …} ⓘ
    fullPath: "/user/sarah"
    hash: ""
  ▶ matched: [{…}]
  ▶ meta: {}
    name: undefined
  ▼ params:
       name: "sarah"
     ▶ __proto__: Object
    path: "/user/sarah"
  ▶ query: {}
```

This variable is also available to us within the component itself. For example, if we wanted to capitalize the first letter of our user's name, we could make a computed variable which takes the route parameter and transforms it:

```
const User = {
  template: `<h1>Hello {{ name }}</h1>`,
  computed: {
    name() {
      let name = this.$route.params.name;
      return name.charAt(0).toUpperCase() + name.slice(1);
    }
  }
};
```

If you're not familiar with what the preceding code is doing, it takes the first character of the string and makes it uppercase. It then splits the string after the first character (that is, the rest of the word) and appends it on the uppercase letter.

Adding this `computed` function and refreshing the app will yield **Hello sarah**.

As mentioned, the route can accept as many parameters as you want and can be separated by static or dynamic variables.

Changing the path to the following (while keeping the component name the same):

```
/:name/user/:emotion
```

Would mean you would need to go to /sarah/user/happy to see the user component. You would, however, have access to a new parameter titled emotion, which means you could use the following template to render **sarah is happy!**:

```
const User = {
  template: `<h1>{{ name }} is {{ $route.params.emotion }}</h1>`,

  computed: {
    name() {
      let name = this.$route.params.name;
      return name.charAt(0).toUpperCase() + name.slice(1);
    }
  }
};

const router = new VueRouter({
  routes: [
    {
      path: '/',
      component: Home
    },
    {
      path: '/about',
      component: About
    },
    {
      path: '/:name/user/:emotion',
      component: User
    }
  ],

  linkActiveClass: 'active',
  linkExactActiveClass: 'current'
});
```

Dynamic routes will come in handy when we come to build our shop over the next few chapters, as we'll be using it for both products and categories.

GET parameters

Along with the dynamic routes, Vue-router handles GET parameters in a really simple way. GET parameters are extra URL parameters you can pass to a web page that appear as key/value pairs. With GET parameters, the first one is preceded by a ?—this tells the browser to expect parameters. Any further parameters are separated by an ampersand. An example would be:

```
example.com/?name=sarah&amp;emotion=happy
```

This URL would yield `sarah` as the value of `name` and `happy` as the value for `emotion`. They are normally used for filtering or search—next time you search for something on Google, take a look at the URL and you will notice `?q=Your+search+query` in the address bar.

Vue router makes these parameters available to the developer within the `query` object in the `this.$route` variable. Try adding `?name=sarah` to the end of your URL and opening the JavaScript developer tool. Inspecting the query object will reveal an object with `name` as the key and `sarah` as the value:

```
▼ {name: undefined, meta: {…}, path: "/user/sarah", hash: "", query: {…}, …} ⊡
    fullPath: "/user/sarah?name=sarah&emotion=happy"
    hash: ""
  ▶ matched: [{…}]
  ▶ meta: {}
    name: undefined
  ▶ params: {name: "sarah"}
    path: "/user/sarah"
  ▼ query:
      emotion: "happy"
      name: "sarah"
```

We'll be using the query object when we build the filtering in our shop categories.

Using props

Although using router parameters directly within the component works perfectly fine, it is not good practice as it ties the component directly to the route. Instead, `props` should be used—in the same way, we used them earlier in the book for HTML components. When enabled and declared, the parameter passed in via the URL becomes available to use as though it had been passed in via an HTML attribute.

Using props for your route component is a better way to pass options and parameters into your route, as it has many benefits. Firstly, it decouples the component from a specific URL structure—as you'll see, we can pass props straight to the component itself. It also helps make your route component clearer; the incoming parameters are clearly laid out within the component itself, and the code is cleaner throughout the component.

Props only work with the dynamic routes—GET parameters would still be accessed with the preceding technique.

Using the preceding example, declare the `props` for both the `name` and `emotion` parameters. When using props with a URL-based variable, you will want to use the `String` data type:

```
const User = {
    template: `<h1>{{ name }} is {{ $route.params.emotion }}</h1>`,
    props: {
        name: String,
        emotion: String
    },
    computed: {
        name() {
            let name = this.$route.params.name;
            return name.charAt(0).toUpperCase() + name.slice(1);
        }
    }
};
```

We now have `this.name` available to us twice—through the `props` and through the computed value. However, as we have `this.name` and `this.emotion` via the `props`, we can update our component to use these variables, rather than the `$route` parameters.

To avoid conflicts with the prop, update the computed function to be called `formattedName()`. We can also remove the variable declaration from the function, as the new variable is a lot more readable:

```
const User = {
    template: `<h1>{{ formattedName }} is {{ this.emotion }}</h1>`,
    props: {
        name: String,
        emotion: String
    },
    computed: {
        formattedName() {
            return this.name.charAt(0).toUpperCase() + this.name.slice(1);
        }
```

```
      }
   };
```

Before the `props` work, Vue-router needs to be told to use them with a particular route. This is enabled within the `routes` array, on a route-by-route basis and, initially, is set with a `props: true` value:

```
const router = new VueRouter({
  routes: [
    {
      path: '/',
      component: Home
    },
    {
      path: '/about',
      component: About
    },
    {
      path: '/:name/user/:emotion',
      component: User,
      props: true
    }
  ],

  linkActiveClass: 'active',
  linkExactActiveClass: 'current'
});
```

Setting prop defaults

With the route parameters now available as `props`, this gives us the flexibility of easily creating a default. If we had wanted to make a parameter optional, we would have needed to add several `if()` statements to check the existence of the variables.

With props, however, we can declare defaults as we did earlier. Add a default for the emotion variable:

```
const User = {
  template: `<h1>{{ formattedName }} is {{ this.emotion }}</h1>`,
  props: {
    name: String,
    emotion: {
      type: String,
      default: 'happy'
    }
```

```
    },
    computed: {
      formattedName() {
        return this.name.charAt(0).toUpperCase() + this.name.slice(1);
      }
    }
};
```

We can now create a new route within our router, which uses the same component without the final variable. Don't forget to enable `props` for the new route too:

```
const router = new VueRouter({
  routes: [
    {
      path: '/',
      component: Home
    },
    {
      path: '/about',
      component: About
    },
    {
      path: '/:name/user',
      component: User,
      props: true
    },
    {
      path: '/:name/user/:emotion',
      component: User,
      props: true
    }
  ],

  linkActiveClass: 'active',
  linkExactActiveClass: 'current'
});
```

Now, by visiting `/sarah/user`, we should be presented with text that declares **sarah is happy**.

Using static props

Along with a Boolean value, the props parameter in the route can also accept an object with a list of the props to pass. This allows you to utilize the same component and alter its state based on the URL, without requiring the variables to be passed via the path for example, if you want to activate or deactivate part of the template.

 When passing the props object in via the URL, it overwrites the whole props object, meaning you either have to declare none or all of them. The props variables will also take priority over the dynamic, URL-based variables.

Update your new /:name/user path to include the props in the route - remove the :name variable from the path so it becomes just /user:

```
const router = new VueRouter({
  routes: [
    {
      path: '/',
      component: Home
    },
    {
      path: '/about',
      component: About
    },
    {
      path: '/user',
      component: User,
      props: {
        name: 'Sarah',
        emotion: 'happy'
      }
    },
    {
      path: '/:name/user/:emotion',
      component: User,
      props: true
    }
  ],

  linkActiveClass: 'active',
  linkExactActiveClass: 'current'
});
```

Navigating to `/user` should reveal the same sentence as we had before. Passing `props` "behind the scenes" (not using the URL) is ideal in some scenarios where you may not want the user to share the specific URL or alter the app's state based on easily altered parameters.

Nested routes

Nested routes differ from sub-routes as they exist *within* a component already matching the beginning part of a route. This allows you to show different content within an existing view.

A good example of this would be Twitter. If you visit a Twitter user's profile page, you are able to view who they are following, who follows them, and what lists they've created. If you observe the URL while you navigate through the pages, you will notice a recurring pattern: the username followed by the different page. The difference between nested routes and sub-routes is that nested routes allow you to keep components the same throughout the different sub-pages (for example, the header and sidebar).

The advantages of this are that the user can bookmark and share the link, it makes the page more accessible, and is good for SEO reasons. None of these advantages could be easily achieved using simple toggle or tab boxes to show different content in the view.

To reproduce the Twitter pattern into a Vue route, it would look like the following:

```
https://twitter.com/:user/:page
```

If we were to create this with the previous route method, we would have to build components for each page which contain the header and user information in the sidebar in their templates—that would be a pain if you needed to update the code!

Let's make some nested routes for our About page. We won't be using nested routes in our shop app, but it's important to understand the capabilities of Vue router.

Create two new components—`AboutContact`, which will display contact information, and `AboutFood`, a component that will detail the food you like to eat! Although not required, it's a good idea to keep a reference to the parent component (in this case, About) in the component name—this ties together the components when you come to look at them later on! Give each component a template with some fixed content:

```
const AboutContact = {
  template: `<div>
    <h2>This is some contact information about me</h2>
    <p>Find me online, in person or on the phone</p>
```

```
    </div>`
};

const AboutFood = {
  template: `<div>
    <h2>Food</h2>
    <p>I really like chocolate, sweets and apples.</p>
  </div>`
};
```

The next step is to create the placeholder in your `#about` template for the nested routes to render in. The element is exactly the same as one we've seen before—the `<router-view>` element. To demonstrate that this can be placed anywhere, add it between two paragraphs in your template:

```
<script type="text/x-template" id="about">
  <div>
    <h1>About Me</h1>
    <p>Lorem ipsum dolor sit amet, consectetur adipiscing elit. Vivamus sed
metus magna. Vivamus eget est nisi. Phasellus vitae nisi sagittis, ornare
dui quis, pharetra leo. Nullam eget tellus velit. Sed tempor lorem augue,
vitae luctus urna ultricies nec. Curabitur luctus sapien elit, non pretium
ante sagittis blandit. Nulla egestas nunc sit amet tellus rhoncus, a
ultrices nisl varius. Nam scelerisque lacus id justo congue maximus. Etiam
rhoncus, libero at facilisis gravida, nibh nisi venenatis ante, sit amet
viverra justo urna vel neque.</p>

    <router-view></router-view>

    <p>Curabitur et arcu fermentum, viverra lorem ut, pulvinar arcu. Fusce
ex massa, vehicula id eros vel, feugiat commodo leo. Etiam in sem rutrum,
porttitor velit in, sollicitudin tortor. Interdum et malesuada fames ac
ante ipsum primis in faucibus. Donec ac sapien efficitur, pretium massa at,
vehicula ligula. Vestibulum turpis quam, feugiat sed orci id, eleifend
pretium urna. Nullam faucibus arcu eget odio venenatis ornare.</p>
  </div>
</script>
```

Viewing the About page in the browser won't render anything, nor will it break the app. The next step is to add the nested routes for these components to the router. Rather than adding them to the top level `routes` array, we create an array inside the `/about` route—with the key of `children`. The syntax of this array is an exact replica of the main array—that is, an array of route objects.

Add an object for each of the routes containing the path and component keys. The thing to note about the path is that it shouldn't start with a / if you want the path to be added to the end of the parent.

For example, if you wanted the URL to be /about/contact to render the AboutContact component, you would make the route component like the following:

```
const router = new VueRouter({
  routes: [
    {
      path: '/',
      component: Home
    },
    {
      path: '/about',
      component: About,
      children: [
        {
          path: 'contact',
          component: AboutContact
        },
        {
          path: 'food',
          component: AboutFood
        }
      ]
    }
  ],

  linkActiveClass: 'active',
  linkExactActiveClass: 'current'
});
```

However, if you wanted the URL to be simply /contact, but still render the AboutContact component inside the About component, you could add the preceding slash. Try viewing the app without the slash, and then with it added, to see the difference it makes. If you wanted a sub-route to show when the parent is loaded without a second part of the URL, you would use an empty path—path: ''.

For now, leave it without the slash and add the preceding children array. Head to your browser and navigate to the About page. Add /contact or /food to the end of the URL, and notice the new content appear in place of the <router-link> element you added to the template earlier.

Links can be created to these components from anywhere, in the same fashion that you linked the Home and About pages. You can either add them to the about template, so they only appear when that page has been navigated to, or add them to the main navigation in your app view.

Creating a 404 page

When building an app or website, despite all good intentions, problems, issues, and mistakes do happen. For this reason, it's a good idea to have error pages in place. The most common page would be a 404 page—a message displayed when a link is incorrect or a page has moved. 404 is the official HTTP code for page not found.

As mentioned earlier, Vue-router will match the routes based on a first-come-first-served principle. We can use this to our advantage by using a wildcard (*) character as the last route. As the wildcard matches *every* route, only URLs which have not matched a previous route will be caught by this one.

Create a new component titled PageNotFound with a simple template, and add a new route which uses the wildcard character as the path:

```
const PageNotFound = {
  template: `<h1>404: Page Not Found</h1>`
};

const router = new VueRouter({
  routes: [
    {
      path: '/',
      component: Home
    },
    {
      path: '/about',
      component: About,
      children: [
        {
          path: 'contact',
          component: AboutContact
        },
        {
          path: 'food',
          component: AboutFood
        }
      ]
```

```
      },
      {
        path: '*',
        component: PageNotFound
      }
    ],

    linkActiveClass: 'active',
    linkExactActiveClass: 'current'
});
```

Open the app up in the browser and type anything at the end of the URL (except about) and press *Enter*—you should be presented with the 404 heading.

 Although this is simulating a page not found request, it is not actually sending the correct HTTP code to the browser. If you are using a Vue web app in production it is a good idea to set up server-side error checking, so in the instance of an incorrect URL the browser can be correctly notified.

Naming components, routes, and views

Adding names to your routes and components is not required when using Vue-router, but is good practice to do so and a good habit to get into.

Naming components

Components with names allow you to debug your errors more easily. In Vue, when a JavaScript error is thrown from a component, it will give you the name of that component, rather than listing Anonymous as the component.

An example of this would be if you tried to output a variable of {{ test }} in the food component—one that isn't available. By default, a JavaScript console error would look like the following:

```
❌ ▶ [Vue warn]: Property or method "test" is not defined on the instance but      vue.js:440
   referenced during render. Make sure to declare reactive data properties in the data option.

   found in

   ---> <Anonymous>
          <Anonymous>
            <Root>
```

Note the two <Anonymous> components in the stack.

By adding names to our components, we can easily identify where the problem lies. Names have been added to both the About and AboutFood components in the following example:

```
⊗ ▶ [Vue warn]: Property or method "test" is not defined on the instance but        vue.js:440
    referenced during render. Make sure to declare reactive data properties in the data option.

    found in

    ---> <AboutFood>
           <About>
             <Root>
```

You can easily see the error is in the <AboutFood> component.

Adding a name to a component is as simple as adding a key of name to your object, with the name as the value. These names adhere to the same rules as to when we were creating our HTML element components: no spaces, but hyphens and letters are allowed. To allow me to quickly identify the code, I chose to name my component the same as the variable defining it:

```
const About = {
  name: 'About',
  template: '#about'
};

const AboutFood = {
  name: 'AboutFood',
  template: `<div>
    <h2>Food</h2>
    <p>I really like chocolate, sweets and apples.</p>
  </div>`
}
```

Naming routes

Another object you are able to name when using VueRouter is the route itself. This gives you the ability to simplify a route's location and update the path, without needing to find and replace all the instances in the app.

Add the name key to your routes, as shown in the following example:

```
const router = new VueRouter({
  routes: [
    {
      path: '/',
      component: Home
    },
    {
      path: '/about',
      component: About,
      children: [
        {
          name: 'contact',
          path: 'contact',
          component: AboutContact
        },
        {
          name: 'food',
          path: 'food',
          component: AboutFood
        }
      ]
    },
    {
      path: '*',
      component: PageNotFound
    }
  ],

  linkActiveClass: 'active',
  linkExactActiveClass: 'current'
});
```

You can now use that name when creating your router-link component, like so:

```
<router-link :to="{name: 'food'}">Food</router-link>
```

Note the colon before the to attribute. This ensures the contents are parsed as an object, not a literal string. Another advantage of using named routes is being able to pass specific attributes to our dynamic paths. Using the example from earlier in this chapter, we can build the URL in a programmatic way, abstracting the data away from the path construction. This is where named routes really come into their own. Say we had the following path:

```
{ name: 'user', path: '/:name/user/:emotion', component: User }
```

We need to pass in a name and emotion variable to the URL for the component to render. We can pass in as we did before, directly to the URL or, alternatively, use the `to` object notation with a named route:

```
<router-link :to="{name: 'user', params: { name: 'sarah', emotion: 'happy'
}}">
   Sarah is Happy
</router-link>
```

Viewing this in the browser will show the anchor link has been generated correctly:

```
/sarah/user/happy
```

This gives us the flexibility to rearrange the URL, using the variables, without needing to update the rest of the app. If you wanted to pass parameters at the end of the URL (for example, `?name=sarah`), the `params` key can be changed to `query`, as it follows the same format:

```
<router-link :to="{name: 'user', query: { name: 'sarah', emotion: 'happy'
}}">
   Sarah is Happy
</router-link>
```

With the path reconfigured not to accept parameters, it will generate the following link:

```
/user?name=sarah&amp;emotion=happy
```

> Be careful when interchanging `params` and `query` - as they can affect whether you use `path` or `name`. When using `path`, the `params` object will be ignored, whereas the `query` one will not. To use the `params` object, you need to use a named route. Alternatively, pass the parameters into the `path` with the `$` variable.

Named views

Vue router also allows you to name the views, letting you pass in different components to different sections of the app. An example of this might be a shop, where you have a sidebar and main content area. Different pages may utilize these areas in different ways.

The About page may use the main content to show the About content while using the sidebar to show contact details. The shop page, however, will use the main content to list the products and the sidebar for displaying the filters.

To do this, create a second `router-view` element as a sibling to your original one. Leave the original one in place, but add a `name` attribute to the second, with an appropriate title:

```
<main>
  <router-view></router-view>
</main>

<aside>
    <router-view name="sidebar"></router-view>
</aside>
```

When declaring your routes in the router instance, we are now going to use a new key, `components`, and remove the previous singular `component` key. This accepts an object with key-value pairs of the name of the view and the name of the component.

> It's advisable to leave your main route unnamed, so you don't need to update every route. If you decide to name your main route, you would be required to do this next step for every route in your app.

Update the `About` route to use this new key and make it into an object. The next step is to tell the code where each component will go.

Using default as the key, set the `About` component as the value. This puts the content from the About component in your unnamed `router-view`, the main one. This is also what using the singular `component` key is shorthand for:

```
const router = new VueRouter({
  routes: [
    {
      path: '/',
      component: Home
    },
    {
      path: '/about',
      components: {
        default: About
      }
    },
    {
      path: '*',
      component: PageNotFound
    }
  ],

  linkActiveClass: 'active',
```

```
    linkExactActiveClass: 'current'
});
```

Next, add a second key-value, specifying the name of the second router-view, `sidebar`.
Name the component you want to populate this area when the `/about` URL is navigated to.
For this, we will use the `AboutContact` component:

```
const router = new VueRouter({
  routes: [
    {
      path: '/',
      component: Home
    },
    {
      path: '/about',
      components: {
        default: About,
        sidebar: AboutContact
      }
    },
    {
      path: '*',
      component: PageNotFound
    }
  ],

  linkActiveClass: 'active',
  linkExactActiveClass: 'current'
});
```

Running the app in your browser will render both components, with the contents of the
contact component appearing in the sidebar.

Programmatically navigating with, redirecting, and adding an alias

While building your app, there may be situations that require some different navigation
techniques. These may be navigating programmatically, for example in a component or the
main Vue instance, redirecting users when they hit a specific URL, or loading the same
component with various URLs.

Navigating programmatically

You may want to alter the path, URL, or user flow from the code, a component, or action. An example of this might be sending the user to the basket after they've added an item.

To do this, you use a push() function on the router instance. The value of push can either be a string for a direct URL or it can accept an object to pass named routes or route parameters. The allowed contents of the push function are exactly the same as the to="" attribute on the router-link element. For example:

```
const About = {
  name: 'About',
  template: '#about',
  methods: {
    someAction() {
      /* Some code here */
      // direct user to contact page
      this.$router.push('/contact');
    }
  }
};
```

Alternatively, you could direct to a named route with parameters:

```
this.$router.push({name: 'user', params: { name: 'sarah', emotion: 'happy' }});
```

Redirecting

Redirecting using VueRouter is fairly straightforward. An example of a redirect might be if you move your /about page to the /about-us URL. You will want to redirect the first URL to the second, in case anyone has shared or bookmarked your link, or in case a search engine has cached the URL.

You may be tempted to create a basic component which, when created, uses the router.push() function to send the user to the new URL.

Instead, you can add a route and specify the redirect within that:

```
const router = new VueRouter({
  routes: [
    {
      path: '/',
      component: Home
    },
    {
      path: '/about',
      redirect: '/about-us'
    },
    {
      path: '/about-us',
      component: About
    },
    {
      path: '*',
      component: PageNotFound
    }
  ],

  linkActiveClass: 'active',
  linkExactActiveClass: 'current'
});
```

Once again, the contents of the redirect key can be a literal string or an object—much like the push() function. With the preceding, if the user visits /about, they will instantly be redirected to /about-us and the About component shown.

Alias routes

There may be circumstances where you want to show the same component under two URLs. Although not recommended as standard practice, there are some edge cases where this is required.

The alias key gets added to an existing route and accepts just a string of the path. Using the preceding example, the following will show the About component, whether the user visits /about or /about-us:

```
const router = new VueRouter({
  routes: [
    {
      path: '/',
      component: Home
    },
    {
      path: '/about',
      alias: '/about-us',
      component: About,
    },
    {
      path: '*',
      component: PageNotFound
    }
  ],

  linkActiveClass: 'active',
  linkExactActiveClass: 'current'
});
```

Summary

You should now be familiar with Vue-router, how to initialize it, what options are available, and how to create new routes—both static and dynamic. In the next few chapters, we'll begin creating our shop, starting with loading some shop data and creating a product page.

9

Using Vue-Router Dynamic Routes to Load Data

In `Chapter 8`, *Introducing Vue-Router and Loading URL-Based Components*, we explored Vue-router and its capabilities and functionality. With that knowledge, we can now progress on to making our shop with Vue. Before we jump into the code and start creating, we should first plan how our shop is going to work, what URLs we need, and what components we need to make. Once we've planned our app we can move on to creating a product page.

In this chapter, we are going to:

- Outline our components and routes, and create placeholder files
- Load a product CSV file, process it, and cache in Vuex
- Create an individual product page with images and product variations

Outline and plan your app

First, let's think about the overall app and the user flow.

We are going to be creating a shop without a payment processing gateway. The shop homepage will display a hand-picked list of products. The user will be able to browse the products using categories and narrow down the selection using filters we've made. They will be able to select a product and view more details about it. The product will have variations (size, color, and such) and may have several product images. The user will be able to add a variation to their basket. From there, they can either continue browsing the products and add more to their basket, or proceed to checkout, where they will be asked for their name and address, and to pay. An order confirmation screen will be shown.

The whole shop app will be created in Vue and will run client-side. This will not cover any server-side code needed for payment, user accounts, stock management, or validation.

The app will use Vue-router for handling URLs and Vuex for storing products, basket contents, and user details.

Components

With a user flow outlined, we need to plan which components we need to make for our shop and what they will be called. This helps with developing the app, as we have a clear idea of what components we need to create. We will also decide on the component names. Following the Vue style guide (`https://vuejs.org/v2/style-guide/index.html`), all our components will consist of two names.

Route components

The following components will be used in conjunction with Vue-router to form the pages for our app:

- **Shop homepage**—`HomePage`: The shop homepage will display a list of products that are curated by the shop owner. This will use a pre-selected list of product handles to display.
- **Category page**—`CategoryPage`: This will list the products from a specific category. The category listing page will also have filters.
- **Product page**—`ProductPage`: The product page will display product details, images, and variations of the product.
- **Basket**—`OrderBasket`: In the basket, the user will be able to review the products they've added, remove unwanted items, and alter the quantity of each item. It will also show the overall cost of the order.
- **Checkout**—`OrderCheckout`: The checkout will lock down the basket – taking away the ability to remove and update products, and will have a form for the user to enter their address.
- **Order confirmation**—`OrderConfirmation`: This component will be displayed after the order has been placed, confirming the products purchased, the delivery address, and the total price.
- `404` **page**—`PageNotFound`: An error page when an incorrect URL is entered.

HTML components

The HTML components will be used within the page components to help reduce repetition in our code for recurring layouts:

- **Product in a list**—`ListProducts`: This will display a paginated list of products when viewing in a list view – such as in the `HomePage` or `CategoryPage` components.
- **Category listing**—`ListCategories`: This will create a list of categories for navigation.
- **List of Purchases**—`ListPurchases`: This component will appear in the basket, checkout, and order confirmation page; it will list the products in a table form – detailing the variation, price, and quantity. It will also feature the total price of all the products in the basket.
- **Filtering**—`ProductFiltering`: A component used on the side of a category page will offer the user the ability to filter and will update the URL, using the GET parameters we covered in `Chapter 8`, *Introducing Vue-Router and Loading URL-Based Components*.

Paths

With our components outlined, we can plan the paths and URLs to our shop, and which components or actions they are going to take. We also need to consider erroneous URLs and whether we should redirect the user to a suitable place or display an error message:

- `/`: Home
- `/category/:slug`: CategoryPage, using the `:slug` unique identifier to identify which products to show
- `/category`: This will redirect to `/`
- `/product/:slug`: ProductPage – once again, using the `:slug` to identify the product
- `/product`: This will redirect to `/`
- `/basket`: OrderBasket
- `/checkout`: OrderCheckout – if there are no products, however, it will redirect the user to `/basket`
- `/complete`: OrderConfirmation – if the user did not come from the OrderCheckout component, then they will be redirected to `/basket`

- `*: PageNotFound` – this will catch any unspecified routes

With our routes and components decided upon, we can begin to create our app.

Create initial files

With the app outlined in the preceding section, we can create the skeletons for our file structure and components. With this app being a large-scale app, we are going to split our files into individual files for each component. This means our files are much more manageable and our main app JavaScript file does not grow out of control.

Although acceptable for development, deploying an app with this number of files could potentially increase your load times depending on how your server is set up. With the traditional HTTP/1.1, browsers have to request and load each file – which is a hindrance if there are multiple files. However, with HTTP/2, you are able to push several files to the user at the same time – in which case, multiple files can somewhat improve the performance of your app.

Whichever method you choose to use with your deployment, it is highly advised you minify your JavaScript when deploying the code to a production environment. This ensures your code is as small as possible when being served up to your user:

Create a file for each component, view, and library, such as Vue, Vuex, and Vue-router. Then, create a folder for each type of file. Finally, add an app.js—which is where the libraries will be initialized.

You may also consider using the
vue-cli (https://github.com/vuejs/vue-cli) for building your app.
Beyond the scope of this book, as we only cover building a Vue app using
the included JavaScript files, the vue-cli application allows you to develop
your app in a more modular way and, once developed, deploy it in a
similar fashion to how we have been developing the app.

Create an index.html and include your JavaScript files, ensuring Vue is loaded first and your app's JavaScript last. Add a container for your app to form the view of our shop:

```
<!DOCTYPE html>
<html>
<head>
  <title>Vue Shop</title>
</head>
<body>
  <div id="app"></div>

  <!-- Libraries -->
  <script type="text/javascript" src="js/libs/vue.js"></script>
  <script type="text/javascript" src="js/libs/vuex.js"></script>
  <script type="text/javascript" src="js/libs/router.js"></script>

  <!-- Components -->
  <script src="js/components/ListCategories.js"></script>
  <script src="js/components/ListProducts.js"></script>
  <script src="js/components/ListPurchases.js"></script>
  <script src="js/components/ProductFiltering.js"></script>

  <!-- Views -->
  <script src="js/views/PageNotFound.js"></script>
  <script src="js/views/CategoryPage.js"></script>
  <script src="js/views/HomePage.js"></script>
  <script src="js/views/OrderBasket.js"></script>
  <script src="js/views/OrderCheckout.js"></script>
  <script src="js/views/OrderConfirmation.js"></script>
  <script src="js/views/ProductPage.js"></script>

  <!-- App -->
  <script type="text/javascript" src="js/app.js"></script>
</body>
</html>
```

Ensure the PageNotFound component is loaded first, as we are going to be utilizing it within other components, as well as specifying it as the 404 page in our routes.

Within each file, initialize the type of component it's going to be by either declaring a variable or using Vue.component. For the views, add a name attribute too – to help with debugging later on.

For example, all of the files located in the js/components/ folder should be initialized like the following. Make sure these components are lowercase and are hyphenated:

```
Vue.component('list-products', {
});
```

Whereas the components for the routes and views, located in js/views, should look like the following:

```
const OrderConfirmation = {
name: 'OrderConfirmation'
};
```

The last step is to initialize our Vuex store, Vue-router, and Vue application. Open app.js and initialize the libraries:

```
const store = new Vuex.Store({});

const router = new VueRouter({});

new Vue({
  el: '#app',

  store,
  router
});
```

With the Vue components and routes ready to go, our store, route, and app initialized, let's look at setting up a server (if required) and loading in data.

Server setup

With our shop, we are going to be loading in a CSV of products on page load. This will simulate gathering stock and product data from a database or API from a point-of-sale system, something online shops with a physical shop might have to deal with.

In a similar way to our Dropbox app earlier in the book, we will be loading external data and saving it into the Vuex store. The issue we will face, however, is when loading a resource via JavaScript; the browsers demand the protocol for the file being requested is via HTTP, HTTPS, or is a CORS request.

This means that we are unable to load a *local* file using the `fetch()` technique we used with the Dropbox API as, when viewing our app in the browser, we are loading local assets over the `file://` protocol.

We can resolve this issue in a few different ways – which one you choose depends on your circumstance. We are going to be loading a CSV file and, using two plugins, converting it into a useable JSON object. The three options you have are:

1. Storing the file locally
2. Using a remote server or
3. Using a local server

Let's run through each option, with the advantages and disadvantages for each.

Storing the file locally

The first option is to convert the CSV to JSON appropriately once, and then save the output in a file. You'll need to assign it to a variable in the file and load the JSON before your libraries. An example might be creating a `data.json` and updating it to be assigned to a variable:

```
const products = {...}
```

You can then load the JSON file in your HTML:

```
<script type="text/javascript" src="data.json"></script>
```

You then have the `products` variable available to you in your `app.js`.

Advantages:

- Less load in your code
- No need to load the extra files required for processing the CSV
- No extra steps required

Disadvantages:

- Does not simulate the real world
- If you want to update the CSV data, you need to convert, save, and assign to a variable

Using a remote server

Another option is to upload the files to a remote, existing server and develop your app there.

Advantages:

- Simulates real-world development of loading CSV
- Can be developed anywhere, with any machine

Disadvantages:

- Can be slow
- Needs to be connected to the internet
- Needs to either set up a deployment process or edit files on a live server

Setting up local server

The last option is to set up a local server on your machine. There are several small, lightweight, zero configuration modules, and applications, or there are bigger, beefier applications too. If you have npm installed on your machine, the node HTTP server is recommended. If not, there are other options available.

The other option would be to use a more heavyweight application, which can provide you with an SQL database and the ability to run PHP applications. An example of this would be MAMP or XAMPP.

Advantages:

- Simulates real-world development of loading CSV
- Quick, instant updates
- Can be developed offline

Disadvantages:

- Requires installing software
- May require some configuration and/or command-line knowledge

The option we are going to choose is the last one, using an HTTP server. Let's load and process the CSV so we can start creating our shop.

Loading CSV

To simulate gathering data from a shop database or point-of-sale, our app is going to load product data from a CSV. CSV, or Comma Separated Values, is a file format often used for sharing data in a database-style way. Think of how you would lay out a list of products in excel or numbers: that is how a CSV file is formatted.

This next step is going to require downloading and including a couple more JavaScript files. If you chose option 1 in the *Server setup* section – to have your files stored in a JSON file locally – you can skip this step.

The data we're going to be using is example shop data from Shopify. These CSVs have a wide selection of product types and different data, which will test our Vue skills. Shopify has made their example data available for download from a GitHub repository (`https://github.com/shopifypartners/shopify-product-csvs-and-images`). Download any CSV file that takes your interest and save it in a `data/` folder in your file system. For this app, I will be using the `bicycles.csv` file.

JavaScript cannot natively load and process CSV files without a significant amount of coding and processing of comma-separated and quote-encapsulated values. To save this book digressing into how to load, parse, and process CSV files, we are going to use a library to do the heavy lifting for us. There are two noteworthy libraries, CSV Parser (`https://github.com/okfn/csv.js`) and d3 (`https://d3js.org/`). CSV Parser simply does CSV parsing and nothing else, while d3 has the ability to generate charts and data visualizations.

It is worth considering which one suits you best; CSV Parser only adds just over 3 KB of weight to your app, whereas d3 is around 60 KB. Unless you anticipate adding visualizations later, it is recommended you go to the smaller library – especially as they execute the same function. However, we'll run through examples for both libraries.

We want to load our product data when the app loads, so our CSV will be loaded and parsed by the time our components require the data. Because of this, we will be loading our data in the created() method of Vue.

Loading a CSV with d3

Both plugins load the data in a very similar way, but the data returned varies somewhat – however, we'll deal with that once we have loaded our data.

Load the d3 library – if you want to try it out, you can use the hosted version:

```
<script src="https://d3js.org/d3.v4.min.js"></script>
```

Using d3, we use a function on the d3 object of csv(), which accepts one parameter – the path to the CSV file. Add the created() function to your Vue instance and initialize the CSV loader:

```
new Vue({
  el: '#app',

  store,
  router,
  created() {
    d3.csv('./data/csv-files/bicycles.csv', (error, data) => {
      console.log(data);
    });
  }
});
```

 Remember the path to your file is relative to the HTML file which is including your JavaScript file – in this case, index.html.

Opening the file in your browser will not render any output. However, if you open the Javascript console and expand the object being output, you will see something similar to this:

```
▼ (1399)
▼ [{…}, {…}, {…}, {…}, {…}, {…}, {…}, {…}, {…}, {…}, {…}, {…}, {…}, {…}, {…}, {…},
  ▼ [0 … 99]
    ▼ 0:
        Body (HTML): "<p><em>This is a demonstration store. You can purchase products li
        Gift Card: "false"
        Google Shopping / AdWords Grouping: ""
        Google Shopping / AdWords Labels: ""
        Google Shopping / Age Group: ""
        Google Shopping / Condition: ""
        Google Shopping / Custom Label 0: ""
        Google Shopping / Custom Label 1: ""
        Google Shopping / Custom Label 2: ""
        Google Shopping / Custom Label 3: ""
        Google Shopping / Custom Label 4: ""
        Google Shopping / Custom Product: ""
        Google Shopping / Gender: ""
        Google Shopping / Google Product Category: ""
        Google Shopping / MPN: ""
        Handle: "15mm-combo-wrench"
        Image Alt Text: ""
        Image Src: "https://cdn.shopify.com/s/files/1/0923/8062/products/15mm-icetoolz-c
        Option1 Name: "Title"
        Option1 Value: "15mm Combo Wrench"
        Option2 Name: ""
        Option2 Value: ""
        Option3 Name: ""
        Option3 Value: ""
        Published: "true"
        SEO Description: ""
        SEO Title: ""
        Tags: "15mm, Accessories, Essential, Essentials, Safety Gear, Tool, Tools, Tools
        Title: "15mm Combo Wrench"
        Type: "Tools"
        Variant Barcode: ""
        Variant Compare At Price: ""
        Variant Fulfillment Service: "manual"
        Variant Grams: "272"
        Variant Image: "https://cdn.shopify.com/s/files/1/0923/8062/products/15mm-icetoo
        Variant Inventory Policy: "deny"
        Variant Inventory Qty: "1"
        Variant Inventory Tracker: "shopify"
        Variant Price: "10.99"
        Variant Requires Shipping: "true"
        Variant SKU: "Tool - Ice 15mm Wrench"
        Variant Taxable: "true"
        Variant Weight Unit: "lb"
        Vendor: "IceToolz"
```

This gives you a breakdown of all of the properties available on each product in a `key: value` format. This allows us to access each `value` in red, using a consistent `key` found on each product. For example, if we wanted `15mm-combo-wrench` from the product above, we could use the `Handle` key. More on this will be covered later

Loading a CSV with CSV Parser

CSV Parser works in a slightly different way, in that it can accept many different parameters and the library contains several different methods and functions. The data output is also in a different format, providing a table/CSV style structure in return, with a `headers` and `fields` object:

```
new Vue({
  el: '#app',

  store,
  router,
  created() {
    CSV.fetch({url: './data/csv-files/bicycles.csv'}).then(data => {
      console.log(data);
    });
  }
});
```

Viewing the output this time will reveal a much different structure and will require matching up the `key` of the fields, with the index of the `headers` object.

Unifying Shopify CSV data

Before we can save and utilize the Shopify data, we need to unify the data and manipulate it into a more manageable state. If you inspect the data being output by either library, you will notice there is an entry for each variation or additional image of a product, with the handle being the linking factor between each entry. For example, there are around 12 entries with the handle of `pure-fix-bar-tape`, each one a different color. Ideally, we would like each variation grouped under the same item, also showing the images as a list of one product.

The other issue with the Shopify CSV data is that the punctuation and grammar of the field headings do not make great object keys. Ideally object keys would be like URL slugs, lowercase and contain no spaces. For example, `Variant Inventory Qty` should ideally be `variant-inventory-qty`.

To save manually processing the data ourselves and updating the keys, we can use a Vue plugin to process the output from either loading library and return an object of products formatted exactly how we want. The plugin is `vue-shopify-products` and is available from unpkg:

```
https://unpkg.com/vue-shopify-products
```

Download and include the library into your `index.html` file. The next step is to tell Vue to use this plugin – at the top of your `app.js` file, include the following line:

```
Vue.use(ShopifyProducts);
```

This now exposes a new method on the Vue instance of `$formatProducts()`, which allows us to pass in the output of our CSV loading library and get a more useful collection of objects:

```
Vue.use(ShopifyProducts);

const store = new Vuex.Store({});

const router = new VueRouter({});

new Vue({
  el: '#app',

  store,
  router,

  created() {
    CSV.fetch({url: './data/csv-files/bicycles.csv'}).then(data => {
      let products = this.$formatProducts(data);
      console.log(products);
    });
  }
});
```

Inspecting the output now reveals a collection grouped by `handle`, with variations and images as objects:

```
▼ {15mm-combo-wrench: {…}, 4mm-5mm-6mm-y-wrench: {…}, adjustable-stem: {…}, ass-savers: {…}
  ▶ 4mm-5mm-6mm-balldriver-y-wrench: {title: "4mm 5mm 6mm Balldriver Y-Wrench", body: "<p><e
  ▶ 4mm-5mm-6mm-y-wrench: {title: "4mm 5mm 6mm Y-Wrench", body: "<p><em>This is a demonstrat
  ▶ 15mm-combo-wrench: {title: "15mm Combo Wrench", body: "<p><em>This is a demonstration st
  ▼ 650c-micro-wheelset:
      body: "<p><em>This is a demonstration store. You can purchase products like this from
      handle: "650c-micro-wheelset"
    ▶ images: (4) [{…}, {…}, {…}, {…}]
      tags: "650C, 650C Wheelsets, Black, Blue, Micro, Orange, Wheels, Wheelset, Wheelsets a
      title: "650C 45mm Micro Wheelset"
      type: "Wheelsets"
    ▼ variations:
      ▼ items: Array(4)
        ▶ 0: {title: "Orange", barcode: "'741360638785", comaprePrice: null, grams: 13608, q
        ▶ 1: {title: "Black", barcode: "'741360638761", comaprePrice: null, grams: 13608, qu
        ▶ 2: {title: "Blue", barcode: "'741360638792", comaprePrice: null, grams: 13608, qua
        ▶ 3: {title: "White", barcode: "'741360638778", comaprePrice: null, grams: 13608, qu
          length: 4
        ▶ __proto__: Array(0)
          title: "Color"
      ▶ __proto__: Object
        vendor: "Pure Fix Cycles"
    ▶ __proto__: Object
  ▶ 700c-aerospoke: {title: "700C Aerospoke - Lime Green Front", body: "<p><em>This is a dem
  ▶ acs-crossfire-chain: {title: "ACS Crossfire Chain", body: "<p><em>This is a demonstratio
  ▶ acs-crossfire-freewheel: {title: "ACS Crossfire Freewheel", body: "<p><em>This is a demo
  ▶ acs-crossfire-headset: {title: "ACS Crossfire Headset", body: "<p><em>This is a demonst
  ▶ acs-crossfire-pro-freewheel: {title: "ACS Crossfire Pro Freewheel", body: "<p><em>This i
  ▶ acs-crossfire-spanner: {title: "ACS Crossfire Spanner", body: "<p><em>This is a demonst
  ▶ acs-maindrive-freewheel: {title: "ACS MainDrive Freewheel", body: "<p><em>This is a demo
  ▶ acs-maindrive-headset: {title: "ACS MainDrive Headset", body: "<p><em>This is a demonst
  ▶ adjustable-stem: {title: "Adjustable Stem", body: "<p><em>This is a demonstration store.
  ▶ airboy-mini-pump: {title: "Airboy Mini Pump", body: "<p><em>This is a demonstration stor
```

With our products grouped more effectively, we can proceed with storing and recalling as desired.

Storing the products

Once we have retrieved and formatted the CSV data, we can cache the contents in the Vuex store. This will be done via a simple mutation that takes a payload and stores it without any modifications.

Create a `state` and `mutations` object in your store. Add a key of `products` as an object in the `state`, and create a function in the `mutations` object, also titled `products`. The mutation should accept two parameters – the state and a payload:

```
const store = new Vuex.Store({
  state: {
    products: {}
  },

  mutations: {
    products(state, payload) {

    }
  }
});
```

Update the `state.products` object to the contents of the `payload`:

```
const store = new Vuex.Store({
  state: {
    products: {}
  },

  mutations: {
    products(state, payload) {
      state.products = payload;
    }
  }
});
```

Replace the `console.log` in the main Vue instance with a commit function, calling the new mutation and passing in the formatted product data:

```
new Vue({
  el: '#app',

  store,
  router,

  created() {
    CSV.fetch({url: './data/csv-files/bicycles.csv'}).then(data => {
      let products = this.$formatProducts(data);
      this.store.commit('products', products);
    });
  }
});
```

This can be reduced somewhat, by passing the `$formatProducts` function directly into the store `commit()` function, rather than storing it as a variable:

```
new Vue({
  el: '#app',

  store,
  router,

  created() {
    CSV.fetch({url: './data/csv-files/bicycles.csv'}).then(data => {
      this.$store.commit('products', this.$formatProducts(data));
    });
  }
});
```

Displaying a single product

With our data stored, we can now begin making our components and displaying content on the frontend. We're going to start by making a product view – displaying product details, variations, and images. We'll move on to creating the category listing page in Chapter 10, *Building an E-Commerce Store – Browsing Products*.

The first step in making our product view is to create the route, to allow the component to be displayed via a URL. Referring back to our notes at the beginning of the chapter, the product component is to be loaded on the `/product/:slug` path.

Create a `routes` array in your Vue-router, with the path and component specified:

```
const router = new VueRouter({
  routes: [
    {
      path: '/product/:slug',
      component: ProductPage
    }
  ]
});
```

With the layout of the `products` object explained, we can start to understand how the route and products link. We will pass the handle of the product into the URL. This will select the product with that handle and display the data. This means we do not need to explicitly link `slug` with `products`.

Page Not Found

With our first route created, we should also create our PageNotFound route, to catch any URLs that are non-existent. We can also redirect to this page when there is no product that matches.

We're going to create the PageNotFound component in a slightly different way than we did before. Rather than having the component on *, we're going to create a /404 path as a named route. This allows us to alias and redirect several different routes as required.

Add a new object to the routes array, with /404 as the path, the PageNotFound component as the specified component. Add a name to your route, so we can utilize if required, and lastly, add an alias attribute, which contains our global, catchall route.

Don't forget to put this *at the end* of the routes array – to catch any previously unspecified route. When adding new routes, always remember to put them before the PageNotFound route:

```
const router = new VueRouter({
  routes: [
    {
      path: '/product/:slug',
      component: ProductPage
    },

    {
      path: '/404',
      alias: '*',
      component: PageNotFound
    }
  ]
});
```

Add a template to your PageNotFound component. For now, give it some basic content – we can improve it later, once we have the rest of our app set out:

```
const PageNotFound = {
  name: 'PageNotFound',
  template: `<div>
    <h1>404 Page Not Found</h1>
    <p>Head back to the <router-link to="/">home page</router-link> and
start again.</p>
  </div>`
};
```

Note the use of the router link in the content. The last thing we need to do to get our app started is to add the `<router-view>` element inside our app. Head to the view, and include it in the app space:

```
<div id="app">
  <router-view></router-view>
</div>
```

Load up the app in your browser, not forgetting to start the HTTP server if required. You should be, at first, presented with your `PageNotFound` component contents. Navigating to the following product URL should result in a JavaScript error instead of the `404` page. This shows the route is correctly picking up the URL but the error is because our `ProductPage` component does not contain a template:

```
#/product/15mm-combo-wrench
```

If you are presented with the `PageNotFound` component, check your route's code, as it means the `ProductPage` route is not being picked up.

Selecting the right product

With our initial routes set up, we can now proceed with loading the desired product and displaying the information from the store. Open `views/Product.js` and create a template key. To begin with, create a simple `<div>` container that displays the title of the product:

```
const ProductPage = {
  name: 'ProductPage',
  template: `<div>{{ product.title }}</div>`
};
```

Viewing this in the browser will instantly throw a JavaScript error as Vue is expecting the `product` variable to be an object – but it is currently undefined as we have yet to declare it. Although the fix for this seems fairly simple at the moment, we need to consider the case where the product is not yet defined.

Our shop app loads the data CSV asynchronously. This means that the execution of the rest of the app does not stop while the products are being loaded. Overall, this increases the speed of our app at the moment we have the products, we can start manipulating and displaying the list, without waiting for the rest of the app to start.

Because of this, there is a distinct possibility that the user could visit the product details page, be it from a link that was shared or a search result, without the product list being loaded. To prevent the app trying to display the product data without being fully initialized, add a conditional attribute to the template to check if the product variable exists before trying to display any of its attributes.

When loading our product data, we can then ensure the product variable is set to `false`, until everything is fully loaded. Add the `v-if` attribute to the containing element in your template:

```
const ProductPage = {
  name: 'ProductPage',
  template: `<div v-if="product">{{ product.title }}</div>`
};
```

We can now start loading the correct product from the store and assign it to a variable.

Create a `computed` object with a `product()` function inside. Within that, create a blank variable of the product, and return it afterward. This now defaults to returning `false`, which means our template will not generate the `<div>`:

```
const ProductPage = {
  name: 'ProductPage',
  template: `<div v-if="product">{{ product.title }}</div>`,

  computed: {
    product() {
      let product;

      return product;
    }
  }
};
```

Selecting the product is now a fairly simple procedure, thanks to our helpfully-formatted product store and the `slug` variable, available to us within the `Product` component. The `products` object in the store is formatted with the handle as the key and the `product details` object as the value. With this in mind, we can select the desired product using the square bracket format. For example:

```
products[handle]
```

Using the router `params` object, load the desired product from the store and assign it to the `product` variable to be returned:

```
const ProductPage = {
  name: 'ProductPage',
  template: `<div v-if="product">{{ product.title }}</div>`,

  computed: {
    product() {
      let product;

      product = this.$store.state.products[this.$route.params.slug];

      return product;
    }
  }
};
```

The reason we don't assign the value of `product` straightaway is so we can add some conditional statements. To ensure we are only loading the product if the store has the data available, we can add an `if()` statement to make sure the product's object has keys available; in other words, has the data loaded?

Add an `if` statement checking the length of the store product keys. If they exist, assign the data from the store to the `product` variable to be returned:

```
const ProductPage = {
  name: 'ProductPage',
  template: `<div v-if="product">{{ product.title }}</div>`,

  computed: {
    product() {
      let product;

      if(Object.keys(this.$store.state.products).length) {
        product = this.$store.state.products[this.$route.params.slug];
      }

      return product;
    }
  }
};
```

Viewing the app in the browser now, you will be presented with the title of the product – once the data has loaded. This should only take a split second to load and should be gracefully handled by our `if` statement.

Before proceeding with displaying all our product data, we need to handle the situation where a product does not exist with the handle in the URL. Because our `ProductPage` route is picking up anything after `/product` in the URL, the `PageNotFound` wildcard path will not be able to be used – as it is our `ProductPage` component that is loading the data and determining whether the product exists.

Catching products not found

In order to show the `PageNotFound` page when a product is not available, we are going to load the component with our `ProductPage` component and display it conditionally.

To do this, we need to register the component so we can use it in our template. We need to register it since our `PageNotFound` component currently lives as an object and not a Vue component (for example, when we use `Vue.component`).

Add a `components` object to your `ProductPage` component and include `PageNotFound`:

```
const ProductPage = {
  name: 'ProductPage',

  template: `<div v-if="product"><h1>{{ product.title }}</h1></div>`,

  components: {
    PageNotFound
  },

  computed: {
    product() {
      let product;

      if(Object.keys(this.$store.state.products).length) {
        product = this.$store.state.products[this.$route.params.slug];
      }

      return product;
    }
  }
};
```

This now gives us a new HTML element to use in the form of `<page-not-found>`. Add this element to your template after the existing `<div>`. As our templates need a single root element, wrap both of them in an extra container:

```
const ProductPage = {
  name: 'ProductPage',

  template: `<div>
    <div v-if="product"><h1>{{ product.title }}</h1></div>
    <page-not-found></page-not-found>
  </div>`,

  components: {
    PageNotFound
  },
  computed: {
    product() {
      let product;

      if(Object.keys(this.$store.state.products).length) {
        product = this.$store.state.products[this.$route.params.slug];
      }

      return product;
    }
  }
};
```

Viewing this in the browser will render the 404 page template and, once the data has loaded, the product title above that. We now need to update the component to only show the `PageNotFound` component when there is no data to show. We could use the existing product variable with a `v-if` attribute and, if false, show the error message like so:

```
<page-not-found v-if="!product"></page-not-found>
```

However, this would mean that if the user visited the product page without the product data loading yet, they would see a flash of the 404 information before being replaced with the product information. This isn't a very good user experience, so we should only show the error if we are sure the product data has loaded and that there isn't a matching item.

To combat this, we will create a new variable which will determine if the component displays. Create a data function in the `ProductPage` component that returns an object with a key of `productNotFound`, set to false. Add a `v-if` condition to the `<page-not-found>` element, checking against the new `productNotFound` variable:

```
const ProductPage = {
  name: 'ProductPage',

  template: `<div>
    <div v-if="product"><h1>{{ product.title }}</h1></div>
    <page-not-found v-if="productNotFound"></page-not-found>
  </div>`,

  components: {
    PageNotFound
  },
  data() {
    return {
      productNotFound: false
    }
  },

  computed: {
    product() {
      let product;

      if(Object.keys(this.$store.state.products).length) {
        product = this.$store.state.products[this.$route.params.slug];
      }

      return product;
    }
  }
};
```

The last step is to set the variable to `true` if a product doesn't exist. As we only want to do this once the data has loaded, add the code to the `$store.state.products` check. We are already assigning the data to the `product` variable, so we can add a check to see if this variable exists – if not, change the polarity of our `productNotFound` variable:

```
const ProductPage = {
  name: 'ProductPage',

  template: `<div>
    <div v-if="product"><h1>{{ product.title }}</h1></div>
    <page-not-found v-if="productNotFound"></page-not-found>
```

```
  </div>`,

  components: {
    PageNotFound
  },
  data() {
    return {
      productNotFound: false
    }
  },

  computed: {
    product() {
      let product;

      if(Object.keys(this.$store.state.products).length) {
        product = this.$store.state.products[this.$route.params.slug];

        if(!product) {
          this.productNotFound = true;
        }
      }

      return product;
    }
  }
};
```

Try entering an erroneous string at the end of the URL – you should be faced with our, now familiar, 404 error page.

Displaying product information

With our product loading, filtering, and error-catching in place, we can proceed with displaying the information we need for our product. Each product could contain one or many images, and one or many variations and any combination in-between – so we need to make sure we cater for each of these scenarios.

To see the data available to us, add a console.log(product) just before the return:

```
product() {
  let product;

  if(Object.keys(this.$store.state.products).length) {
    product = this.$store.state.products[this.$route.params.slug];
```

```
        if(!product) {
            this.productNotFound = true;
        }
    }

    console.log(product);
    return product;
}
```

Open up the JavaScript console and inspect the object that should now be there. Familiarize yourself with the keys and values available to you. Take note that the images key is an array and the variations an object, containing a string and a further array.

Before we tackle the variations and images – let's output the simple stuff. What we need to remember is that every field we output might not exist on every product – so it's best to wrap it in conditional tags where necessary.

Output the body, type, and vendor.title from the product details. Prepend both the vendor.title and type with a description of what they are, but make sure you only render that text if it exists in the product details:

```
template: `<div>
  <div v-if="product">
    <h1>{{ product.title }}</h1>
    <div class="meta">
      <span>
        Manufacturer: <strong>{{ product.vendor.title }}</strong>
      </span>
      <span v-if="product.type">
        Category: <strong>{{ product.type }}</strong>
      </span>
    </div>
    {{ product.body }}
  </div>
  <page-not-found v-if="productNotFound"></page-not-found>
</div>`,
```

Notice we've got the flexibility to prepend the type and vendor with more user-friendly names. Once we have our categories and filtering set up, we can link both the vendor and type to appropriate product listing.

Viewing this in the browser will reveal the body outputting all HTML tags as text – meaning we can see them on the page. If you cast your mind back to the beginning of the book where we were discussing output types, we need to use `v-html` to tell Vue to render the block as raw HTML:

```
template: `<div>
  <div v-if="product">
    <h1>{{ product.title }}</h1>
    <div class="meta">
      <span>
        Manufacturer: <strong>{{ product.vendor.title }}</strong>
      </span>
      <span v-if="product.type">
        Category: <strong>{{ product.type }}</strong>
      </span>
    </div>
    <div v-html="product.body"></div>
  </div>
  <page-not-found v-if="productNotFound"></page-not-found>
</div>`,
```

Product images

The next step is to output the images for our product. If you are using the bicycles CSV file, a good product to test with is `650c-micro-wheelset` – navigate to this product as it has four images. Don't forget to go back to your original product to check that it works with one image.

The images value will always be an array, whether there is one image or 100, so to display them, we will always need to do a `v-for`. Add a new container and loop through the images. Add a width to each image so it doesn't take over your page.

The images array contains an object for each image. This has an `alt` and `source` key that can be input directly into your HTML. There are some instances, however, where the `alt` value is missing – if it is, insert the product title instead:

```
template: `<div>
  <div v-if="product">

    <div class="images" v-if="product.images.length">
      <template v-for="img in product.images">
        <img
          :src="img.source"
          :alt="img.alt || product.title"
```

```
      width="100">
    </template>
  </div>

  <h1>{{ product.title }}</h1>

  <div class="meta">
    <span>
      Manufacturer: <strong>{{ product.vendor.title }}</strong>
    </span>
    <span v-if="product.type">
      Category: <strong>{{ product.type }}</strong>
    </span>
  </div>

  <div v-html="product.body"></div>

</div>
<page-not-found v-if="productNotFound"></page-not-found>
</div>`,
```

With our images displaying, it would be a nice addition to create a gallery. Shops often show one big image, with a set of thumbnails underneath. Clicking each thumbnail then replaces the main image so the user can get a better look at the bigger image. Let's recreate that functionality. We also need to ensure we don't show the thumbnails if there is only one image.

We do this, by setting an image variable to the first image in the images array, this is the one that will form the big image. If there is more than one image in the array, we will show the thumbnails. We will then create a click method that updates the image variable with the selected image.

Create a new variable in your data object and update it with the first item from the images array when the product has loaded. It's good practice to ensure the images key is, in fact, an array of items before trying to assign a value:

```
const ProductPage = {
  name: 'ProductPage',

  template: `<div>
    <div v-if="product">
      <div class="images" v-if="product.images.length">
        <template v-for="img in product.images">
          <img
            :src="img.source"
            :alt="img.alt || product.title"
```

```
              width="100">
          </template>
        </div>
        <h1>{{ product.title }}</h1>
        <div class="meta">
          <span>
            Manufacturer: <strong>{{ product.vendor.title }}</strong>
          </span>
          <span v-if="product.type">
            Category: <strong>{{ product.type }}</strong>
          </span>
        </div>
        <div v-html="product.body"></div>
      </div>
      <page-not-found v-if="productNotFound"></page-not-found>
    </div>`,

  components: {
    PageNotFound
  },
  data() {
    return {
      productNotFound: false,
      image: false
    }
  },

  computed: {
    product() {
      let product;

      if(Object.keys(this.$store.state.products).length) {

        product = this.$store.state.products[this.$route.params.slug];
        this.image = (product.images.length) ? product.images[0] : false;

        if(!product) {
          this.productNotFound = true;
        }
      }

      console.log(product);
      return product;
    }
  }
};
```

Next, update your existing images loop in your template to only display when there is more than one image in the array. Also, add the first image as the main image in your template – not forgetting to check whether it exists first:

```
template: `<div>
  <div v-if="product">

    <div class="images" v-if="image">
      <div class="main">
        <img
          :src="image.source"
          :alt="image.alt || product.title">
      </div>

      <div class="thumbnails" v-if="product.images.length > 1">
        <template v-for="img in product.images">
          <img
            :src="img.source"
            :alt="img.alt || product.title"
            width="100">
        </template>
      </div>
    </div>

    <h1>{{ product.title }}</h1>

    <div class="meta">
      <span>
        Manufacturer: <strong>{{ product.vendor.title }}</strong>
      </span>
      <span v-if="product.type">
        Category: <strong>{{ product.type }}</strong>
      </span>
    </div>

    <div v-html="product.body"></div>

  </div>
  <page-not-found v-if="productNotFound"></page-not-found>
</div>`,
```

The last step is to add a click handler to each of the thumbnail images, to update the image variable when interacted with. As the images will not natively have the `cursor: pointer` CSS attribute, it might be worth considering adding this.

The click handler will be a method that accepts each image in the thumbnail loop as a parameter. On click, it will simply update the image variable with the object passed through:

```
const ProductPage = {
  name: 'ProductPage',

  template: `<div>
    <div v-if="product">
      <div class="images" v-if="image">
        <div class="main">
          <img
            :src="image.source"
            :alt="image.alt || product.title">
        </div>

        <div class="thumbnails" v-if="product.images.length > 1">
          <template v-for="img in product.images">
            <img
              :src="img.source"
              :alt="img.alt || product.title"
              width="100"
              @click="updateImage(img)">
          </template>
        </div>
      </div>

      <h1>{{ product.title }}</h1>

      <div class="meta">
        <span>
          Manufacturer: <strong>{{ product.vendor.title }}</strong>
        </span>
        <span v-if="product.type">
          Category: <strong>{{ product.type }}</strong>
        </span>
      </div>

      <div v-html="product.body"></div>
    </div>
    <page-not-found v-if="productNotFound"></page-not-found>
  </div>`,

  components: {
    PageNotFound
  },
  data() {
```

```
      return {
        productNotFound: false,
        image: false
      }
    },

  computed: {
    product() {
      let product;

      if(Object.keys(this.$store.state.products).length) {

        product = this.$store.state.products[this.$route.params.slug];
        this.image = (product.images.length) ? product.images[0] : false;

        if(!product) {
          this.productNotFound = true;
        }
      }

      console.log(product);
      return product;
    }
  },

  methods: {
    updateImage(img) {
      this.image = img;
    }
  }
};
```

Load the product up in your browser and try clicking on any of the thumbnails - you should be able to update the main image. Don't forget to validate your code on a product with one image or even zero images, to make sure the user isn't going to encounter any errors.

Don't be afraid of whitespace and adding new lines for readability. Being able to easily understand your code is better than the few bytes you would have saved on file load. When deploying to production, files should be minified, but during development white space takes precedence.

Product variations

With this particular dataset, each of our products contains at least one variation but can contain several. This normally goes hand-in-hand with the number of images but does not always correlate. Variations can be things such as color or size.

On our `Product` object, we have two keys which are going to help us display the variations. These are `variationTypes`, which list the names of the variations such as size and color, and `variationProducts`,which contains all of the variations. Each product within the `variationProducts` object has a further object of `variant`, which lists all of the changeable properties. For example, if a jacket came in two colors and each color had three sizes, there would be six `variationProducts`, each with two `variant` properties.

Every product will contain at least one variation, although if there is only one variation, we may need to consider the UX of the product page. We are going to display our product variations in both a table and drop-down, so you can experience creating both elements.

Variations display table

Create a new container in your product template that will display the variations. Within this container, we can create a table to display the different variations of the product. This will be achieved with a `v-for` declaration. However, now that you are more familiar with the functionality, we can introduce a new attribute.

Using a key with loops

When using loops in Vue, it is advised you use an extra attribute to identify each item, `:key`. This helps Vue identify the elements of the array when re-ordering, sorting, or filtering. An example of `:key` use would be:

```
<div v-for="item in items" :key="item.id">
  {{ item.title }}
</div>
```

The key attribute should be a unique attribute of the item itself and not the index of the item in the array, to help Vue identify the specific object. More information about using a key with a loop is available in the `official Vue documentation`.

We'll be utilizing the `key` attribute when displaying our variations, but using the `barcode` attribute.

Displaying the variations in a table

Add a table element to your variations container and loop through the `items` array. For now, display the `title`, `quantity` and `price`. Add an additional cell that contains a button with the value of **Add to basket**. We'll configure that in `Chapter 11`, *Building an E-commerce Store – Adding a Checkout*. Don't forget to add a $ currency symbol in front of your price, as it's currently just a "raw" number.

Watch out – when using the $ sign within the template literals, JavaScript will try and interpret it, along with the curly brackets, as a JavaScript variable. To counteract this, prepend the currency with a backslash – this tells JavaScript that the next character is literal, and should not be interpreted in any other way:

```
template: `<div>
  <div v-if="product">
    <div class="images" v-if="image">
      <div class="main">
        <img
          :src="image.source"
          :alt="image.alt || product.title">
      </div>

      <div class="thumbnails" v-if="product.images.length > 1">
        <template v-for="img in product.images">
          <img
            :src="img.source"
            :alt="img.alt || product.title"
            width="100"
            @click="updateImage(img)">
        </template>
      </div>
    </div>

    <h1>{{ product.title }}</h1>

    <div class="meta">
      <span>
        Manufacturer: <strong>{{ product.vendor.title }}</strong>
      </span>
      <span v-if="product.type">
        Category: <strong>{{ product.type }}</strong>
      </span>
    </div>

    <div class="variations">
      <table>
```

```
            <tr v-for="variation in product.variationProducts"
   :key="variation.barcode">
                <td>{{ variation.quantity }}</td>
                <td>\${{ variation.price }}</td>
                <td><button>Add to basket</button></td>
            </tr>
        </table>
    </div>

    <div v-html="product.body"></div>

  </div>
  <page-not-found v-if="productNotFound"></page-not-found>
</div>`,
```

Although we're displaying the price and quantity, we aren't outputting the actual variant properties of the variation (such as color). To do this, we are going to need to do some processing on our variation with a method.

The variant object contains a child object for each variation type, with a name and a value for each type. They are also stored with a slug-converted key within the object. See the following screenshot for more details:

```
▼ product: Object
    body: "<p><em>This is a demonstration store. You can purchase products like this from
    handle: "keirin-pro-track-frame"
  ▶ images: Array[9]
    tags: "Alloy, Black, Chrome, Framesets, Keirin, Parts, Pro, Racing, Track, Track Fram
    title: "Keirin Pro Track Frameset"
    type: "Framesets"
  ▼ variationProducts: Array[20]
    ▼ 0: Object
        barcode: "'712392689311"
        grams: 9072
        price: 325
        quantity: 0
        shipping: "true"
        sku: "Keirin Pro - Polished Raw - 49c"
        taxable: "true"
      ▼ variant: Object
        ▼ color: Object
            name: "Color"
            value: "Alloy"
        ▼ size: Object
            name: "Size"
            value: "49 cm"
```

Add a new cell at the beginning of the table that passes the variation to a method titled
`variantTitle()`:

```
<div class="variations">
  <table>
    <tr v-for="variation in product.variationProducts"
:key="variation.barcode">
      <td>{{ variantTitle(variation) }}</td>
      <td>{{ variation.quantity }}</td>
      <td>\${{ variation.price }}</td>
      <td><button>Add to basket</button></td>
    </tr>
  </table>
</div>
```

Create the new method within your `methods` object:

```
methods: {
  updateImage(img) {
    this.image = img;
  },

  variantTitle(variation) {
  }
}
```

We now need to construct a string with the title of the variant, displaying all available
options. To do this, we are going to construct an array of each of the types and then join
them into a string.

Store the `variants` as a variable and create an empty array. We can now loop through the
keys available within the `variants` object and create a string to output. If you decide to
add HTML into the string, as shown in the following example, we will need to update our
template to output HTML instead of a raw string:

```
variantTitle(variation) {
  let variants = variation.variant,
    output = [];

  for(let a in variants) {
    output.push(`<b>${variants[a].name}:</b> ${variants[a].value}`);
  }
}
```

Our output array will have an item for each variant, formatted like the following:

```
["<b>Color:</b> Alloy", "<b>Size:</b> 49 cm"]
```

We can now join each one together, which transforms the output from an array to a string. The character, string, or HTML you choose to join it with is up to you. For now, use a / with spaces on either side. Alternatively, you could use </td><td> tags to create a new table cell. Add the join() function and update the template to use v-html:

```
const ProductPage = {
  name: 'ProductPage',

  template: `<div>
    <div v-if="product">
      <div class="images" v-if="image">
        <div class="main">
          <img
            :src="image.source"
            :alt="image.alt || product.title">
        </div>

        <div class="thumbnails" v-if="product.images.length > 1">
          <template v-for="img in product.images">
            <img
              :src="img.source"
              :alt="img.alt || product.title"
              width="100"
              @click="updateImage(img)">
          </template>
        </div>
      </div>

      <h1>{{ product.title }}</h1>

      <div class="meta">
        <span>
          Manufacturer: <strong>{{ product.vendor.title }}</strong>
        </span>
        <span v-if="product.type">
          Category: <strong>{{ product.type }}</strong>
        </span>
      </div>

      <div class="variations">
        <table>
          <tr v-for="variation in product.variationProducts"
:key="variation.barcode">
```

```
      <td v-html="variantTitle(variation)"></td>
      <td>{{ variation.quantity }}</td>
      <td>\${{ variation.price }}</td>
      <td><button>Add to basket</button></td>
    </tr>
  </table>
</div>

<div v-html="product.body"></div>

</div>
<page-not-found v-if="productNotFound"></page-not-found>
</div>`,

components: {
  PageNotFound
},
data() {
  return {
    productNotFound: false,
    image: false
  }
},

computed: {
  ...
},

methods: {
  updateImage(img) {
    this.image = img;
  },

  variantTitle(variation) {
    let variants = variation.variant,
      output = [];

    for(let a in variants) {
      output.push(`<b>${variants[a].name}:</b> ${variants[a].value}`);
    }

    return output.join(' / ');
  }

}
};
```

Attach a click event to the **Add to basket** button and create a new method on the component. This method will require the `variation` object to be passed in, so the correct one could be added to the basket. For now, add a JavaScript `alert()` to confirm you have the right one:

```
const ProductPage = {
  name: 'ProductPage',

  template: `<div>
    <div v-if="product">
      <div class="images" v-if="image">
        <div class="main">
          <img
            :src="image.source"
            :alt="image.alt || product.title">
        </div>

        <div class="thumbnails" v-if="product.images.length > 1">
          <template v-for="img in product.images">
            <img
              :src="img.source"
              :alt="img.alt || product.title"
              width="100"
              @click="updateImage(img)">
          </template>
        </div>
      </div>

      <h1>{{ product.title }}</h1>

      <div class="meta">
        <span>
          Manufacturer: <strong>{{ product.vendor.title }}</strong>
        </span>
        <span v-if="product.type">
          Category: <strong>{{ product.type }}</strong>
        </span>
      </div>

      <div class="variations">
        <table>
          <tr v-for="variation in product.variationProducts"
 :key="variation.barcode">
            <td v-html="variantTitle(variation)"></td>
            <td>{{ variation.quantity }}</td>
            <td>\${{ variation.price }}</td>
            <td><button @click="addToBasket(variation)">Add to
```

```
basket</button></td>
        </tr>
      </table>
    </div>

    <div v-html="product.body"></div>

  </div>
  <page-not-found v-if="productNotFound"></page-not-found>
</div>`,

components: {
  PageNotFound
},
data() {
  return {
    productNotFound: false,
    image: false
  }
},

computed: {
  product() {
    let product;

    if(Object.keys(this.$store.state.products).length) {

      product = this.$store.state.products[this.$route.params.slug];
      this.image = (product.images.length) ? product.images[0] : false;

      if(!product) {
        this.productNotFound = true;
      }
    }

    console.log(product);
    return product;
  }
},

methods: {
  updateImage(img) {
    this.image = img;
  },

  variantTitle(variation) {
    let variants = variation.variant,
      output = [];
```

```
        for(let a in variants) {
          output.push(`<b>${variants[a].name}:</b> ${variants[a].value}`);
        }

        return output.join(' / ');
      },

    addToBasket(variation) {
        alert(`Added to basket: ${this.product.title} -
${this.variantTitle(variation)}`);
      }

    }
  };
```

Note the template literals used within the alert box – this allows us to use Javascript variables without having to use string concatenation techniques. Clicking on the **Add to basket** button will now generate a popup listing of the name of the product and the variation clicked.

Displaying variations in a select box

A more common interface pattern on product pages is to have a drop-down list, or select box, with your variations displayed and available for selecting.

When using a select box, we will have a variation which has either been selected by default or that the user has interacted with and chosen specifically. Because of this, we can change the image when the user changes the select box and display other pieces of information about the variant on the product page, including price and quantity.

We won't be relying on passing through the variant to the `addToBasket` method, as it will exist as an object on the product component.

Update your `<table>` element to be a `<select>`, and the `<tr>` to an `<option>`. Move the button *outside* of this element and remove the parameter from the `click` event. Remove any HTML from the `variantTitle()` method. Because it is now inside a select box it is not required:

```
<div class="variations">
  <select>
    <option
      v-for="variation in product.variationProducts"
      :key="variation.barcode"
      v-html="variantTitle(variation)"
```

```
    ></option>
  </select>

  <button @click="addToBasket()">Add to basket</button>
</div>
```

The next step is to create a new variable available to use on the component. In a similar vein to the images, this will be completed with the first item of the `variationProducts` array and updated when the select box changes.

Create a new item in the data object, titled `variation`. Populate this variable when the data is loaded into the `product` computed variable:

```
const ProductPage = {
  name: 'ProductPage',

  template: `...`,

  components: {
    PageNotFound
  },
  data() {
    return {
      productNotFound: false,
      image: false,
      variation: false
    }
  },

  computed: {
    product() {
      let product;

      if(Object.keys(this.$store.state.products).length) {

        product = this.$store.state.products[this.$route.params.slug];

        this.image = (product.images.length) ? product.images[0] : false;
        this.variation = product.variationProducts[0];

        if(!product) {
          this.productNotFound = true;
        }
      }

      console.log(product);
      return product;
```

```
      }
    },

    methods: {
      ...
    }
};
```

Update the `addToBasket` method to use the `variation` variable of the `ProductPage` component and not rely on a parameter:

```
addToBasket() {
  alert(`Added to basket: ${this.product.title} -
${this.variantTitle(this.variation)}`);
}
```

Try clicking the **Add to basket** button – it should add the first variation, regardless of what is selected in the dropdown. To update the variable on change, we can bind the `variations` variable to the select box – in the same way, that we did our textbox filtering at the beginning of this book.

Add a `v-model` attribute to the `select` element. We will also need to tell Vue what to bind to this variable when selecting. By default, it will do the contents of the `<option>`, which is currently our custom variant title. However, we want to bind the whole `variation` object. Add a `:value` property to the `<option>` element:

```
<div class="variations">
  <select v-model="variation">
    <option
      v-for="variation in product.variationProducts"
      :key="variation.barcode"
      :value="variation"
      v-html="variantTitle(variation)"
    ></option>
  </select>

  <button @click="addToBasket()">Add to basket</button>
</div>
```

Changing the select box and clicking the **Add to basket** button will now produce the correct variation. This method gives us much more flexibility over displaying the variations in a table.

It allows us to display variation data in other places on the product. Try adding the price next to the product title and the quantity within the `meta` container:

```
template: `<div>
  <div v-if="product">
    <div class="images" v-if="image">
      <div class="main">
        <img
          :src="image.source"
          :alt="image.alt || product.title">
      </div>

      <div class="thumbnails" v-if="product.images.length > 1">
        <template v-for="img in product.images">
          <img
            :src="img.source"
            :alt="img.alt || product.title"
            width="100"
            @click="updateImage(img)">
        </template>
      </div>
    </div>

    <h1>{{ product.title }} - \${{ variation.price }}</h1>

    <div class="meta">
      <span>
        Manufacturer: <strong>{{ product.vendor.title }}</strong>
      </span>
      <span v-if="product.type">
        Category: <strong>{{ product.type }}</strong>
      </span>
      <span>
        Quantity: <strong>{{ variation.quantity }}</strong>
      </span>
    </div>

    <div class="variations">
      <select v-model="variation">
        <option
          v-for="variation in product.variationProducts"
          :key="variation.barcode"
          :value="variation"
          v-html="variantTitle(variation)"
        ></option>
      </select>
```

```
      <button @click="addToBasket()">Add to basket</button>
    </div>

    <div v-html="product.body"></div>

  </div>
  <page-not-found v-if="productNotFound"></page-not-found>
</div>`,
```

These two new attributes will update when changing the variation. We can also update the image to the selected variation if it has one. To do this, add a watch object to your component, which watches the variation variable. When updated, we can check if the variation has an image and, if so, update the image variable with this property:

```
const ProductPage = {
  name: 'ProductPage',

  template: `...`,

  components: {
    ...
  },
  data() {
    ...
  },

  computed: {
    ...
  },

  watch: {
    variation(v) {
      if(v.hasOwnProperty('image')) {
        this.updateImage(v.image);
      }
    }
  },

  methods: {
    ...
  }
};
```

When using `watch`, the function passes the new item as the first parameter. Rather than referring to the one on the component, we can use this to gather the image information.

Another enhancement we can make is to disable the **Add to basket** button and add a note in the dropdown if the variation is out of stock. This information is gathered from the variation `quantity` key.

Check the quantity and, if less than one, display an **out of stock message** in the select box and disable the **Add to basket** button using the `disabled` HTML attribute. We can also update the value of the button:

```
template: `<div>
    <div v-if="product">
      <div class="images" v-if="image">
        <div class="main">
          <img
            :src="image.source"
            :alt="image.alt || product.title">
        </div>

        <div class="thumbnails" v-if="product.images.length > 1">
          <template v-for="img in product.images">
            <img
              :src="img.source"
              :alt="img.alt || product.title"
              width="100"
              @click="updateImage(img)">
          </template>
        </div>
      </div>

      <h1>{{ product.title }} - \${{ variation.price }}</h1>

      <div class="meta">
        <span>
          Manufacturer: <strong>{{ product.vendor.title }}</strong>
        </span>
        <span v-if="product.type">
          Category: <strong>{{ product.type }}</strong>
        </span>
        <span>
          Quantity: <strong>{{ variation.quantity }}</strong>
        </span>
      </div>

      <div class="variations">
        <select v-model="variation">
```

```
            <option
              v-for="variation in product.variationProducts"
              :key="variation.barcode"
              :value="variation"
              v-html="variantTitle(variation) + ((!variation.quantity) ? ' -
      out of stock' : '')"
            ></option>
          </select>

          <button @click="addToBasket()" :disabled="!variation.quantity">
            {{ (variation.quantity) ? 'Add to basket' : 'Out of stock' }}
          </button>
        </div>

        <div v-html="product.body"></div>

      </div>
      <page-not-found v-if="productNotFound"></page-not-found>
    </div>`,
```

If using the `bicycles.csv` dataset, the Keirin Pro Track Frameset product
(`/#/product/keirin-pro-track-frame`) contains several variations, some without
stock. This allows you to test the `out of stock` functionality along with the image
changing.

Another thing we can do to the product page is only show the dropdown when there is
more than one variation. An example of a product with only one is the **15 mm Combo
Wrench** (`#/product/15mm-combo-wrench`). In this instance, it is not worth showing the
`<select>` box. As we are setting the `variation` variable on the `Product` component on
load, we are not relying on the selection to initially set the variable. Because of this, we can
completely remove the select box with a `v-if=""` when there is only one alternate product.

Like we did with the images, check if the length of the array is more than one, this time the
`variationProducts` array:

```
<div class="variations">
  <select v-model="variation" v-if="product.variationProducts.length > 1">
    <option
      v-for="variation in product.variationProducts"
      :key="variation.barcode"
      :value="variation"
      v-html="variantTitle(variation) + ((!variation.quantity) ? ' - out of
stock' : '')"
    ></option>
  </select>
```

```
<button @click="addToBasket()" :disabled="!variation.quantity">
  {{ (variation.quantity) ? 'Add to basket' : 'Out of stock' }}
</button>
</div>
```

By removing elements when they are not needed, we now have a less cluttered interface.

Updating the product details when switching URLs

While navigating through the different product URLs to check variations, you may have noticed that clicking back and forward doesn't update the product data on the page.

This is because `Vue-router` realizes the same component is being used between the pages, and so, rather than destroying and creating a new instance, it reuses the component. The downside to this is that the data does not get updated; we need to trigger a function to include the new product data. The upside is that the code is more efficient.

To tell Vue to retrieve the new data, we need to create a `watch` function; instead of watching a variable, we are going to watch the `$route` variable. When this gets updated, we can load new data.

Create a new variable in the data instance of `slug`, and set the default to be the route parameter. Update the `product` computed function to use this variable instead of the route:

```
const ProductPage = {
  name: 'ProductPage',

  template: `...`,

  components: {
    PageNotFound
  },
  data() {
    return {
      slug: this.$route.params.slug,
      productNotFound: false,
      image: false,
      variation: false
    }
  },

  computed: {
```

```
        product() {
          let product;

          if(Object.keys(this.$store.state.products).length) {

            product = this.$store.state.products[this.slug];

            this.image = (product.images.length) ? product.images[0] : false;
            this.variation = product.variationProducts[0];

            if(!product) {
              this.productNotFound = true;
            }
          }

          console.log(product);
          return product;
        }
      },

      watch: {
        ...
      },

      methods: {
        ...
      }
    };
```

We can now create a `watch` function, keeping an eye on the `$route` variable. When this changes, we can update the `slug` variable, which in turn will update the data being displayed.

When watching a route, the function has two parameters passed to it: `to` and `from`. The `to` variable contains everything about the route we are going to, including parameters and the component used. The `from` variable contains everything about the current route.

By updating the `slug` variable to the new parameter when the route changes, we are forcing the component to redraw with new data from the store:

```
const ProductPage = {
  name: 'ProductPage',

  template: `<div>
    <div v-if="product">
      <div class="images" v-if="image">
        <div class="main">
```

```
      <img
        :src="image.source"
        :alt="image.alt || product.title">
    </div>

    <div class="thumbnails" v-if="product.images.length > 1">
      <template v-for="img in product.images">
        <img
          :src="img.source"
          :alt="img.alt || product.title"
          width="100"
          @click="updateImage(img)">
      </template>
    </div>
  </div>

  <h1>{{ product.title }} - \${{ variation.price }}</h1>

  <div class="meta">
    <span>
      Manufacturer: <strong>{{ product.vendor.title }}</strong>
    </span>
    <span v-if="product.type">
      Category: <strong>{{ product.type }}</strong>
    </span>
    <span>
      Quantity: <strong>{{ variation.quantity }}</strong>
    </span>
  </div>

  <div class="variations">
    <select v-model="variation" v-if="product.variationProducts.length
> 1">
      <option
        v-for="variation in product.variationProducts"
        :key="variation.barcode"
        :value="variation"
        v-html="variantTitle(variation) + ((!variation.quantity) ? ' -
out of stock' : ''))"
      ></option>
    </select>

    <button @click="addToBasket()" :disabled="!variation.quantity">
      {{ (variation.quantity) ? 'Add to basket' : 'Out of stock' }}
    </button>
  </div>

  <div v-html="product.body"></div>
```

```
      </div>
      <page-not-found v-if="productNotFound"></page-not-found>
    </div>`,

    components: {
      PageNotFound
    },
    data() {
      return {
        slug: this.$route.params.slug,
        productNotFound: false,
        image: false,
        variation: false
      }
    },

    computed: {
      product() {
        let product;

        if(Object.keys(this.$store.state.products).length) {

          product = this.$store.state.products[this.slug];

          this.image = (product.images.length) ? product.images[0] : false;
          this.variation = product.variationProducts[0];

          if(!product) {
            this.productNotFound = true;
          }
        }

        return product;
      }
    },

    watch: {
      variation(v) {
        if(v.hasOwnProperty('image')) {
          this.updateImage(v.image);
        }
      },

      '$route'(to) {
        this.slug = to.params.slug;
      }
    },
```

```
methods: {
  updateImage(img) {
    this.image = img;
  },

  variantTitle(variation) {
    let variants = variation.variant,
      output = [];

    for(let a in variants) {
      output.push(`${variants[a].name}: ${variants[a].value}`);
    }

    return output.join(' / ');
  },

  addToBasket() {
    alert(`Added to basket: ${this.product.title} -
${this.variantTitle(this.variation)}`);
  }

}
};
```

With our product page completed, we can move on to creating a category listing for both the `type` and `vendor` variables. Remove any `console.log()` calls you have in your code, too, to keep it clean.

Summary

This chapter has covered a lot. We loaded and stored a CSV file of products into our Vuex store. From there, we created a product detail page that used a dynamic variable in the URL to load a specific product. We have created a product detail view that allows the user to look through a gallery of images and choose a variation from a drop-down list. If the variation has an associated image, the main image updates.

In `Chapter 10`, *Building an E-Commerce Store – Browsing Products*,
we will create a category page, creating filtering and ordering functions – helping the user to find the product they want.

10
Building an E-Commerce Store – Browsing Products

In *Chapter 9*, *Using Vue-Router Dynamic Routes to Load Data*, we loaded our product data into the Vuex store and created a product detail page where a user could view the product and its variations. When viewing the product detail page, a user could change the variation from the drop-down and the price and other details would update.

In this chapter, we are going to:

- Create a home page listing page with specific products
- Create a category page with a reusable component
- Create an ordering mechanism
- Create filters dynamically and allow the user to filter the products

Listing the products

Before we create any filtering, curated lists, ordering components, and functionality, we need to create a basic product list – showing all the products first, and then we can create a paginated component that we can then reuse throughout the app.

Adding a new route

Let us add a new route to our `routes` array. For now, we'll work on the `HomePage` component, which will have the / route. Make sure you add it to the top of the `routes` array, so it doesn't get overridden by any of the other components:

```
const router = new VueRouter({
  routes: [
    {
      path: '/',
      name: 'Home',
      component: HomePage
    },
    {
      path: '/product/:slug',
      component: ProductPage
    },

    {
      path: '/404',
      alias: '*',
      component: PageNotFound
    }
  ]
});
```

Within the `HomePage` component, create a new `computed` property and gather all the products from the `store`. Ensure the products have loaded before displaying anything in the template. Populate the `HomePage` component with the following code:

```
const HomePage = {
  name: 'HomePage',

  template: `<div v-if="products"></div>`,

  computed: {
    products() {
      return this.$store.state.products;
    }
  }
};
```

Looping through products

When looking at a category listing for any shop, the data displayed tends to have a recurring theme. It normally consists of an image, title, price, and manufacturer.

Add an ordered list to your template – as the products are going to have an order to them, it makes semantic sense to place them in an ordered list. Within the `<ol>`, add a `v-for` looping through the products and displaying a title for each one, as shown here. It's also good practice to ensure the `product` variable exists before proceeding with displaying it:

```
template: `<div v-if="products">
  <ol>
    <li v-for="product in products" v-if="product">
      <h3>{{ product.title }}</h3>
    </li>
  </ol>
</div>`,
```

When viewing the page in your browser, you may notice that the product list is very long. Loading images for every one of these products would be a huge load on the user's computer, along with overwhelming the user with that many products on display. Before we add more information, such as price and images, to our template, we'll look at paginating the products, allowing the data to be accessed in more manageable chunks.

Creating pagination

Creating pagination, initially, seems quite simple – as you only need to return a fixed number of products. However, if we wish to make our pagination interactive and reactive to the product list – it needs to be a bit more advanced. We need to build our pagination to be able to handle different lengths of products – in the case where our product list has been filtered into fewer products.

Calculating the values

The arithmetic behind creating a pagination component and displaying the correct products relies on four main variables:

- **Items per page**: This is usually set by the user; however, we'll use a fixed number of 12, to begin with
- **Total items**: This is the total number of products to display

- **Number of pages**: This can be calculated by dividing the number of products by the items per page
- **Current page number**: This, combined with the others, will allow us to return exactly which products we need

From these numbers, we can calculate everything needed for our pagination. This includes what products to display, whether to show next/previous links and, if desired, a component to skip to different links.

Before we proceed, we are going to convert our `products` object into an array. This allows us to use the split method on it, which will allow us to return a specific list of products. It also means we can easily count the total number of items.

Update your `products` computed function to return an `array` instead of an `object`. This is done by using the `map()` function – which is an ES2015 replacement for a simple `for` loop. This function now returns an array containing the product objects:

```
products() {
  let products = this.$store.state.products;
  return Object.keys(products).map(key => products[key]);
},
```

Create a new function in the computed object titled `pagination`. This function will return an object with various figures about our pagination, for example, the total number of pages. This will allow us to create a product list and update the navigation components. We need to only return the object if our `products` variable has data. The function is shown in the following code snippet:

```
computed: {
  products() {
    let products = this.$store.state.products;
    return Object.keys(products).map(key => products[key]);
  },

  pagination() {
    if(this.products) {
      return {
      }
    }
  }
},
```

We now need to keep track of two variables – items `perPage` and the `currentPage`. Create a `data` function on your `HomePage` component and store these two variables. We'll give the user the ability to update the `perPage` variable later on. The highlighted code portion shows our `data` function:

```
const HomePage = {
  name: 'HomePage',

  template: `...`,

  data() {
    return {
      perPage: 12,
      currentPage: 1
    }
  },

  computed: {
    ...
  }
};
```

 You may be wondering when to use local data on a component and when to store the information in the Vuex store. This all depends on where you are going to be using the data and what is going to manipulating it. As a general rule, if only one component uses the data and manipulate it, then use the local `data()` function. However, if more than one component is going to be interacting with the variable, save it in the central store.

Back to the `pagination()` computed function, store a variable with the length of the `products` array. With this as a variable, we can now calculate the total pages. To do this, we are going to do the following equation:

total number of products / items per page

Once we have this result, we need to round it up to the nearest integer. This is because if there is any hangover, we need to create a new page for it.

For example, if you were showing 12 items per page and you had 14 products, that would yield a result of 1.1666 pages – which is not a valid page number. Rounding this up ensures we have two pages to display our products. To do this, use the `Math.ceil()` JavaScript function. We can also add the total number of products to our output. Check the following code for using the `Math.ceil()` function:

```
pagination() {
  if(this.products) {
    let totalProducts = this.products.length;
    return {
      totalProducts: totalProducts,
      totalPages: Math.ceil(totalProducts / this.perPage)
    }
  }
}
```

The next calculation we need to do is work out what the current range of products for the current page is. This is a little more complicated, as not only do we need to work out what we need from the page number, but the array slicing is based on the item index – which means the first item is `0`.

To work out where to take our slice from, we can use the following calculation:

(current page number * items per page) – items per page

The final subtraction may seem odd, but it means on page `1`, the result is `0`. This allows us to work out at which index we need to slice the `products` array.

As another example, if we were on page three, the result would be 24, which is where the third page would start. The end of the slice is then this result *plus* the number of items per page. The advantage of this means we can update the items per page and all of our calculations will update.

Create an object inside the `pagination` result with these two results – this will allow us to access them later easily:

```
pagination() {
  if(this.products) {
    let totalProducts = this.products.length,
      pageFrom = (this.currentPage * this.perPage) - this.perPage;
    return {
      totalProducts: totalProducts,
      totalPages: Math.ceil(totalProducts / this.perPage),
      range: {
```

```
          from: pageFrom,
          to: pageFrom + this.perPage
        }
      }
    }
  }
```

Displaying a paginated list

With our pagination properties calculated, we are now able to manipulate our `products` array using the start and end points. Rather than use a hardcoded value, or use another computed function, we are going to use a method to truncate the product list. This has the advantage of being able to pass on any list of products while also meaning Vue does not cache the result.

Create a new method object inside your component with a new method of `paginate`. This should accept a parameter that will be the array of `products` for us to slice. Within the function, we can use the two variables we calculated previously to return the right number of products:

```
methods: {
  paginate(list) {
    return list.slice(
      this.pagination.range.from,
      this.pagination.range.to
    );
  }
}
```

Update the template to use this method when looping through the products:

```
template: `<div v-if="products">
  <ol>
    <li v-for="product in paginate(products)" v-if="product">
      <h3>{{ product.title }}</h3>
    </li>
  </ol>
</div>`,
```

We can now view this in our browser and note it returns the first 12 products from our object. Updating the `currentPage` variable within the `data` object to two or three will reveal different lists of products, depending on the number.

To continue our semantic approach to listing our products, we should update the start position of our ordered list when not on page one. This can be done using the HTML attribute of start – this allows you to specify with which number you should start an ordered list.

Use the pagination.range.from variable to set the starting point of our ordered list – remembering to add 1 as on the first page it will be 0:

```
template: `<div v-if="products">
  <ol :start="pagination.range.from + 1">
    <li v-for="product in paginate(products)" v-if="product">
      <h3>{{ product.title }}</h3>
    </li>
  </ol>
</div>`
```

When incrementing the page numbers in the code now, you will notice the ordered list starts at the appropriate place for each page.

Creating paginating buttons

Updating the page number via the code isn't user-friendly – so we should add some pages to increment and decrement the page number variable. To do this, we'll create a function that changes the currentPage variable to its value. This allows us to use it for both the **Next page** and **Previous page** buttons, plus a numbered page list if desired.

Begin by creating two buttons within your pagination container. We want to disable these buttons if we are at the extremities of the navigations – for example, you don't want to be able to go below 1 when going back, and past the maximum number of pages when going forward. We can do this by setting the disabled attribute on the button – like we did on the product detail page and comparing the current page against these limits.

Add a disabled attribute and, on the **Previous page**, the button checks if the current page is one. On the **Next page** button, compare it to the totalPages value of our pagination method. The code for implementing the previously mentioned attributes is shown here:

```
<button :disabled="currentPage == 1">Previous page</button>
<button :disabled="currentPage == pagination.totalPages">Next page</button>
```

Set the currentPage variable back to 1 and load the home page up in the browser. You should notice the Previous page button is disabled. If you change the currentPage variable, you will notice the buttons become active and inactive as desired.

We now need to create a click method for the buttons to update the currentPage. Create a new function titled toPage(). This should accept a single variable – this will directly update the currentPage variable:

```
methods: {
  toPage(page) {
    this.currentPage = page;
  },

  paginate(list) {
    return list.slice(this.pagination.range.from,
this.pagination.range.to);
  }
}
```

Add the click handlers to the buttons, passing through currentPage + 1 for the **Next page** button, and currentPage - 1 for the **Previous page button**:

```
template: `<div v-if="products">
  <button @click="toPage(currentPage - 1)" :disabled="currentPage ==
1">Previous page</button>
  <button @click="toPage(currentPage + 1)" :disabled="currentPage ==
pagination.totalPages">Next page</button>

  <ol :start="pagination.range.from + 1">
    <li v-for="product in paginate(products)" v-if="product">
      <h3>{{ product.title }}</h3>
    </li>
  </ol>
</div>`
```

We can now navigate back and forth through the products. As a nice addition to the user interface, we could give an indication of the page number and how many pages remain, using the variables available to us by using the code mentioned here:

```
template: `<div v-if="products">
  <p>
    Page {{ currentPage }} out of {{ pagination.totalPages }}
  </p>
  <button @click="toPage(currentPage - 1)" :disabled="currentPage ==
1">Previous page</button>
  <button @click="toPage(currentPage + 1)" :disabled="currentPage ==
```

```
pagination.totalPages">Next page</button>

  <ol :start="pagination.range.from + 1">
    <li v-for="product in paginate(products)" v-if="product">
      <h3>{{ product.title }}</h3>
    </li>
  </ol>
</div>`
```

Updating the URL on navigation

Another improvement to the user experience would be to update the URL on page navigation – this would allow the user to share the URL, bookmark it, and return to it later. When paginating, the pages are a *temporary* state and should not be the main endpoint of a URL. Instead, we can take advantage of the query parameters with Vue router.

Update the `toPage` method to add the parameter to the URL on page change. This can be achieved using `$router.push`, however, we need to be careful not to remove any existing parameters that may be in use for filtering in the future. This can be achieved by combining the current query object from the route with a new one containing the `page` variable:

```
toPage(page) {
  this.$router.push({
    query: Object.assign({}, this.$route.query, {
      page
    })
  });

  this.currentPage = page;
},
```

While navigating from page to page, you will notice the URL obtaining a new parameter of `?page=` equal to the current page name. However, pressing refresh will not yield the correct page results but, instead, page one again. This is because we need to pass the current `page` query parameter to the `currentPage` variable on our `HomePage` component.

This can be done using the `created()` function – updating the variables – ensuring we've checked for its existence first. The `created` function is part of the Vue life cycle and was covered in `Chapter 4`, *Getting a List of Files Using the Dropbox API*:

```
created() {
  if(this.$route.query.page) {
    this.currentPage = parseInt(this.$route.query.page);
  }
}
```

We need to ensure the `currentPage` variable is an integer, to help us with any arithmetic we need to do later on as a `string` is not a fan of calculations.

Creating pagination links

When viewing paginated products, it's often good practice to have a truncated list of page numbers, allowing the user to jump several pages. We already have the mechanism for navigating between pages – this can extend that.

As a simple entry point, we can create a link to every page by looping through until we reach the `totalPages` value. Vue allows us to do this without any JavaScript. Create a `nav` element at the bottom of the component with a list inside. Using a `v-for`, and create a variable of `page` for *every item* in the `totalPages` variable:

```
<nav>
  <ol>
    <li v-for="page in pagination.totalPages">
      <button @click="toPage(page)">{{ page }}</button>
    </li>
  </ol>
</nav>
```

This will create a button for every page – for example, if there are 24 pages in total, this will create 24 links. This is not the desired effect, as we want a few pages before and after the current page. An example of this would be, if the current page is 15, the page links should be 12, 13, 14, 15, 16, 17 and 18. This means there are fewer links and it is less overwhelming for the user.

To begin with, create a new variable in the data object, which will note how many pages to show either side of the selected page – a good value to start with is three:

```
data() {
  return {
    perPage: 12,
    currentPage: 1,
    pageLinksCount: 3
  }
},
```

Next, create a new computed function titled pageLinks. This function will need to take the current page and work out what page numbers are three less and three more than that. From there, we need to check that the lower range is not less than one, and the upper is not more than the total number of pages. Check that the products array has items before proceeding:

```
pageLinks() {
  if(this.products.length) {
    let negativePoint = parseInt(this.currentPage) - this.pageLinksCount,
      positivePoint = parseInt(this.currentPage) + this.pageLinksCount;


    if(negativePoint < 1) {
      negativePoint = 1;
    }

    if(positivePoint > this.pagination.totalPages) {
      positivePoint = this.pagination.totalPages;
    }

    return pages;
  }
}
```

The last step is to create an array and a for loop that loops from the lower range to the higher range. This will create an array containing, at most, seven numbers with the page range:

```
pageLinks() {
  if(this.products.length) {
    let negativePoint = parseInt(this.currentPage) - this.pageLinksCount,
      positivePoint = parseInt(this.currentPage) + this.pageLinksCount,
      pages = [];
```

```
    if (negativePoint < 1) {
      negativePoint = 1;
    }

    if (positivePoint > this.pagination.totalPages) {
      positivePoint = this.pagination.totalPages;
    }

    for (var i = negativePoint; i <= positivePoint; i++) {
      pages.push(i)
    }

    return pages;
  }
}
```

We can now replace the `pagination.totalPages` variable in our navigation component with the new `pageLinks` variable and the correct number of links will be created, as shown here:

```
<nav>
  <ul>
    <li v-for="page in pageLinks">
      <button @click="toPage(page)">{{ page }}</button>
    </li>
  </ul>
</nav>
```

Viewing this in the browser, however, will render some odd behavior. Although the correct number of links will be generated, clicking on them or using the next/previous buttons will cause the buttons to remain the same – even if you navigate out of the range of the buttons. This is because the computed value is cached. We can combat this in two ways – either move the function into the `method` object or, alternatively, add a `watch` function to watch the route and update the current page.

Opting for the second option means we can ensure no other results and outputs get cached and are updated accordingly. Add a `watch` object to your component and update the `currentPage` variable to that of the page query variable. Ensure it exists, otherwise default to one. The `watch` method is as shown here:

```
watch: {
  '$route' (to) {
    this.currentPage = parseInt(to.query.page) || 1;
  }
}
```

This ensures all the computed variables update when a different page is navigated to. Open your HomePage component and ensure all your pagination components work accordingly and update the list.

Updating the items per page

The last user interface addition we need to create is allowing the user to update the number of products per page. To initially set this up, we can create a <select> box with a v-model attribute that updates the value directly. This works as expected and updates the product list accordingly, as shown:

```
template: `<div v-if="products">
  <p>
    Page {{ currentPage }} out of {{ pagination.totalPages }}
  </p>
  Products per page:
  <select v-model="perPage">
    <option>12</option>
    <option>24</option>
    <option>48</option>
    <option>60</option>
  </select>

  <button @click="toPage(currentPage - 1)" :disabled="currentPage ==
1">Previous page</button>
  <button @click="toPage(currentPage + 1)" :disabled="currentPage ==
pagination.totalPages">Next page</button>

  <ol :start="pagination.range.from + 1">
    <li v-for="product in paginate(products)" v-if="product">
      <h3>{{ product.title }}</h3>
    </li>
  </ol>

  <nav>
    <ul>
      <li v-for="page in pageLinks">
        <button @click="toPage(page)">{{ page }}</button>
      </li>
    </ul>
  </nav>
</div>
```

The issue with this is if the user is on a page higher than is possible once the value has changed. For example, if there are 30 products with 12 products per page, this would create three pages. If the user navigates to page three and then selects 24 products per page, there would only be two pages needed and page three would be empty.

This can be resolved, once again, with a watch function. When the `perPage` variable updates, we can check if the current page is higher than the `totalPages` variable. If it is, we can redirect it to the last page:

```
watch: {
  '$route'(to) {
    this.currentPage = parseInt(to.query.page);
  },

  perPage() {
    if(this.currentPage > this.pagination.totalPages) {
      this.$router.push({
        query: Object.assign({}, this.$route.query, {
          page: this.pagination.totalPages
        })
      })
    }
  }
}
```

Creating the ListProducts component

Before we proceed with creating the filtering and ordering, we need to extract our product listing logic and template it into our component – allowing us to easily reuse it. This component should accept a prop of `products`, which it should be able to list and paginate.

Open up the `ListProducts.js` file and copy the code from the `HomePage.js` file into the component. Move the data object and copy the `pagination` and `pageLinks` computed functions. Move the watch and methods objects, as well as the `created()` function, from the `HomePage` to the `ListProducts` file.

Update the `HomePage` template to use the `<list-products>` components with a `products` prop, passing in the `products` computed value. In comparison, the `HomePage` component should now be significantly smaller:

```
const HomePage = {
  name: 'HomePage',
```

```
    template: `<div>
      <list-products :products="products"></list-products>
    </div>`,

    computed: {
      products() {
        let products = this.$store.state.products;
        return Object.keys(products).map(key => products[key]);
      }
    }
};
```

Within the ListProducts component, we need to add a props object, to let the component know what to expect. This component is now significant. There are a few more things we need to add to this component to make it more versatile. They include:

- Showing the next/previous links if there is more than one page
- Showing the "products per page" component if there are more than 12 products, and only showing each step if there are more products than in the preceding step
- Only showing the pageLinks component if it's more than our pageLinksCount variable

All of these additions have been added to the following component code as follows. We have also removed the unnecessary products computed value:

```
Vue.component('list-products', {
  template: `<div v-if="products">
    <p v-if="pagination.totalPages > 1">
      Page {{ currentPage }} out of {{ pagination.totalPages }}
    </p>

    <div v-if="pagination.totalProducts > 12">
      Products per page:
      <select v-model="perPage">
        <option>12</option>
        <option>24</option>
        <option v-if="pagination.totalProducts > 24">48</option>
        <option v-if="pagination.totalProducts > 48">60</option>
      </select>
    </div>

    <button
      @click="toPage(currentPage - 1)"
      :disabled="currentPage == 1"
      v-if="pagination.totalPages > 1"
    >
```

```
    Previous page
  </button>
  <button
    @click="toPage(currentPage + 1)"
    :disabled="currentPage == pagination.totalPages"
    v-if="pagination.totalPages > 1"
  >
    Next page
  </button>

  <ol :start="pagination.range.from + 1">
    <li v-for="product in paginate(products)" v-if="product">
      <h3>{{ product.title }}</h3>
    </li>
  </ol>

  <nav v-if="pagination.totalPages > pageLinksCount">
    <ul>
      <li v-for="page in pageLinks">
        <button @click="toPage(page)">{{ page }}</button>
      </li>
    </ul>
  </nav>
</div>`,

props: {
  products: Array
},

data() {
  return {
    perPage: 12,
    currentPage: 1,
    pageLinksCount: 3
  }
},

computed: {
  pagination() {
    if(this.products) {
      let totalProducts = this.products.length,
        pageFrom = (this.currentPage * this.perPage) - this.perPage,
        totalPages = Math.ceil(totalProducts / this.perPage);
      return {
        totalProducts: totalProducts,
        totalPages: Math.ceil(totalProducts / this.perPage),
        range: {
          from: pageFrom,
```

```
              to: pageFrom + this.perPage
          }
        }
      }
    },

  pageLinks() {
    if(this.products.length) {
      let negativePoint = this.currentPage - this.pageLinksCount,
        positivePoint = this.currentPage + this.pageLinksCount,
        pages = [];

      if(negativePoint < 1) {
        negativePoint = 1;
      }

      if(positivePoint > this.pagination.totalPages) {
        positivePoint = this.pagination.totalPages;
      }

      for (var i = negativePoint; i <= positivePoint; i++) {
        pages.push(i)
      }

      return pages;
    }
  }
},

watch: {
  '$route'(to) {
    this.currentPage = parseInt(to.query.page);
  },
  perPage() {
    if(this.currentPage > this.pagination.totalPages) {
      this.$router.push({
        query: Object.assign({}, this.$route.query, {
          page: this.pagination.totalPages
        })
      })
    }
  }
},

created() {
  if(this.$route.query.page) {
    this.currentPage = parseInt(this.$route.query.page);
```

```
    }
  },

  methods: {
    toPage(page) {
      this.$router.push({
        query: Object.assign({}, this.$route.query, {
          page
        })
      });

      this.currentPage = page;
    },

    paginate(list) {
      return list.slice(this.pagination.range.from,
this.pagination.range.to)
    }
  }
});
```

You can verify your conditional rendering tags are working by temporarily truncating the products array in the `HomePage` template – don't forget to remove it once you're done:

```
products() {
  let products = this.$store.state.products;
  return Object.keys(products).map(key => products[key]).slice(1, 10);
}
```

Creating a curated list for the home page

With our product listing component in place, we can proceed with making a curated list of products for our home page, and add more information to the product listing.

In this example, we are going to hardcode an array of product handles on our home page component that we want to display. If this were in development, you would expect this list to be controlled via a content management system or similar.

Create a `data` function on your `HomePage` component, that which includes an array titled `selectedProducts`:

```
data() {
  return {
    selectedProducts: []
  }
},
```

Populate the array with several `handles` from the product list. Try and get about six, but if you go over 12, remember it will paginate with our component. Add your selected handles to the `selectedProducts` array:

```
data() {
  return {
    selectedProducts: [
      'adjustable-stem',
      'colorful-fixie-lima',
      'fizik-saddle-pak',
      'kenda-tube',
      'oury-grip-set',
      'pure-fix-pedals-with-cages'
    ]
  }
},
```

With our selected handles, we can now filter the product list to only include a list of products included in our `selectedProducts` array. The initial instinct might be to use the JavaScript `filter()` function on the products array combined with `includes()`:

```
products() {
  let products = this.$store.state.products;

  products = Object.keys(products).map(key => products[key]);
  products = products.filter(product =>
this.selectedProducts.includes(product.handle));
  return products;
}
```

The issue with this is that, although it appears to work, it does not respect the ordering of the selected products. The filter function simply removes any items that do not match and leaves the remaining products in the order they are loaded.

Fortunately, our products are saved in a key/value pair with the handle as the key. Using this, we can utilize the products object and return an array using a `for` loop.

Create an empty array, output, within the computed function. Looping through the selectedProducts array, find each required product and add to the output array:

```
products() {
    let products = this.$store.state.products,
        output = [];

    if(Object.keys(products).length) {
        for(let featured of this.selectedProducts) {
            output.push(products[featured]);
        }
        return output;
    }
}
```

This creates the same product list but, this time, in the correct order. Try re-ordering, adding, and deleting items to ensure your list reacts accordingly.

Showing more information

We can now work on showing more product information in our ListProduct component. As mentioned near the beginning of the chapter, we should display:

- Image
- Title
- Price
- Manufacturer

We're already displaying the title, and the image and manufacturer can easily be pulled out from the product information. Don't forget to always retrieve the first image from the images array. Open up the ListProducts.js file and update the product to display this information – making sure you check whether the image exists before displaying it. The manufacturer title is listed under the vendor object in the product data:

```
<ol :start="pagination.range.from + 1">
    <li v-for="product in paginate(products)" v-if="product">
        <img v-if="product.images[0]" :src="product.images[0].source"
:alt="product.title" width="120">
        <h3>{{ product.title }}</h3>
        <p>Made by: {{ product.vendor.title }}</p>
    </li>
</ol>
```

The price is going to be a little more complicated to work out. This is because each variation on the product can have a different price, however, these are often the same. If there are different prices we should display the cheapest one with a *from* prepended.

We need to create a function that loops through the variations and works out the cheapest price and, if there is a price range, add the word *from*. To achieve this, we are going to loop through the variations and build up an array of unique prices – if the price does not already exist in the array. Once complete, we can check the length – if there is more than one price, we can add the prefix, if not, it means all variations are the same price.

Create a new method on the `ListProducts` component called `productPrice`. This accepts one parameter, which will be the variations. Inside, create an empty array, `prices`:

```
productPrice(variations) {
   let prices = [];
}
```

Loop through the variations and append the price to the `prices` array if it does not exist already. Create a `for` loop that uses the `includes()` function to check if the price exists in the array:

```
productPrice(variations) {
   let prices = [];

   for(let variation of variations) {
     if(!prices.includes(variation.price)) {
       prices.push(variation.price);
     }
   }
}
```

With our array of prices, we can now extract the lowest number and check whether there is more than one item.

To extract the lowest number from an array, we can use the JavaScript `Math.min()` function. Use the `.length` property to check the length of the array. Lastly, return the `price` variable:

```
productPrice(variations) {
   let prices = [];

   for(let variation of variations) {
     if(!prices.includes(variation.price)) {
       prices.push(variation.price);
     }
```

```
  }

  let price = '$' + Math.min(...prices);

  if(prices.length > 1) {
    price = 'From: ' + price;
  }

  return price;
}
```

Add your `productPrice` method to your template, remembering to
pass `product.variationProducts` into it. The last thing we need to add to our template
is a link to the product:

```
<ol :start="pagination.range.from + 1">
  <li v-for="product in paginate(products)" v-if="product">
    <router-link :to="'/product/' + product.handle">
      <img v-if="product.images[0]" :src="product.images[0].source"
:alt="product.title" width="120">
    </router-link>

    <h3>
      <router-link :to="'/product/' + product.handle">
        {{ product.title }}
      </router-link>
    </h3>

    <p>Made by: {{ product.vendor.title }}</p>
    <p>Price {{ productPrice(product.variationProducts) }}</p>
  </li>
</ol>
```

Ideally, the product links should use a named route and not a hardcoded link, in case the
route changes. Add a name to the product route and update the `to` attribute to use the
name instead:

```
{
  path: '/product/:slug',
  name: 'Product',
  component: ProductPage
}
```

Update the template to now use the route name, with the `params` object:

```
<ol :start="pagination.range.from + 1">
  <li v-for="product in paginate(products)" v-if="product">
    <router-link :to="{name: 'Product', params: {slug: product.handle}}">
      <img v-if="product.images[0]" :src="product.images[0].source"
:alt="product.title" width="120">
    </router-link>
    <h3>
      <router-link :to="{name: 'Product', params: {slug: product.handle}}">
        {{ product.title }}
      </router-link>
    </h3>
    <p>Made by: {{ product.vendor.title }}</p>
    <p>Price {{ productPrice(product.variationProducts) }}</p>
  </li>
</ol>
```

Creating categories

A shop is not really a usable shop if it does not have categories to navigate by. Fortunately, each of our products has a `type` key that indicates a category for it to be shown in. We can now create a category page that lists products from that particular category.

Creating a category list

Before we can display the products in a particular category, we first need to generate a list of available categories. To help with the performance of our app, we will also store the handles of the products in each category. The categories structure will look like the following:

```
categories = {
  tools: {
    name: 'Tools',
    handle: 'tools',
    products: ['product-handle', 'product-handle'...]
  },
  freewheels: {
    name: 'Freewheels',
    handle: 'freewheels',
    products: ['another-product-handle', 'product'...]
  }
};
```

Creating the category list like this means we readily have available the list of products within the category while being able to loop through the categories and output the `title` and `handle` to create a list of links to categories. As we already have this information, we will create the category list once we've retrieved the product list.

Open up `app.js` and navigate to the `created()` method on the `Vue` instance. Rather than creating a second `$store.commit` underneath the `products` storing method, we are going to utilize a different functionality of Vuex – `actions`.

Actions allow you to create functions in the store itself. Actions are unable to mutate the state directly – that is still down to mutations, but it allows you to group several mutations together, which in this instance, suits us perfectly. Actions are also perfect if you want to run an asynchronous operation before mutating the state – for example with a `setTimeout` JavaScript function.

Navigate to your `Vuex.Store` instance and, after the mutations, add a new object of `actions`. Inside, create a new function titled `initializeShop`:

```
const store = new Vuex.Store({
  state: {
    products: {}
  },

  mutations: {
    products(state, payload) {
      state.products = payload;
    }
  },

  actions: {
    initializeShop() {
    }
  }
});
```

With action parameters, the first parameter is the store itself, which we need to use in order to utilize the mutations. There are two ways of doing this, the first is to use a single variable and access its properties within the function. For example:

```
actions: {
  initializeShop(store) {
    store.commit('products');
  }
}
```

However, with ES2015, we are able to use argument destructuring and utilize the properties we need. For this action, we only need the `commit` function, like so:

```
actions: {
  initializeShop ({commit}) {
    commit ('products');
  }
}
```

If we wanted the state from the store as well, we could add it to the curly brackets:

```
actions: {
  initializeShop ({state, commit}) {
    commit ('products');
    // state.products
  }
}
```

Using this "exploded" method of accessing the properties makes our code cleaner and less repetitive. Remove the `state` property and add a second parameter after the curly brackets labeled `products`. This will be our formatted product's data. Pass that variable directly to the product's `commit` function:

```
initializeShop ({commit}, products) {
  commit ('products', products);
}
```

Using actions is as simple as using `mutations`, except instead of using `$store.commit`, you use `$store.dispatch`. Update your `created` method – not forgetting to change the function name too, and check your app still works:

```
created() {
  CSV.fetch({url: './data/csv-files/bicycles.csv'}).then(data => {
    this.$store.dispatch('initializeShop', this.$formatProducts(data));
  });
}
```

The next step is to create a mutation for our categories. As we may want to update our categories independently of our products – we should create a second function within the `mutations`. It should also be this function that loops through the products and creates the list of categories.

First, make a new property in the state object titled `categories`. This should be an object by default:

```
state: {
  products: {},
  categories: {}
}
```

Next, create a new mutation called `categories`. Along with the state, this should take a second parameter. To be consistent, title it `payload` – as this is what Vuex refers to it as:

```
mutations: {
  products(state, payload) {
    state.products = payload;
  },

  categories(state, payload) {
  }
},
```

Now for the functionality. This mutation needs to loop through the products. For every product, it needs to isolate the `type`. Once it has the title and slug, it needs to check if an entry exists with that slug; if it does, append the product handle to the `products` array, if not – it needs to create a new array and details.

Create an empty `categories` object and loop through the payload, setting a variable for both the product and type:

```
categories(state, payload) {
  let categories = {};

  Object.keys(payload).forEach(key => {
    let product = payload[key],
      type = product.type;
  });
}
```

We now need to check if an entry exists with the key of the current `type.handle`. If it does not, we need to create a new entry with it. The entry needs to have the title, handle, and an empty products array:

```
categories(state, payload) {
  let categories = {};

  Object.keys(payload).forEach(key => {
    let product = payload[key],
```

```
      type = product.type;

  if(!categories.hasOwnProperty(type.handle)) {
    categories[type.handle] = {
      title: type.title,
      handle: type.handle,
      products: []
    }
  }
});
}
```

Lastly, we need to append the current product handle onto the products array of the entry:

```
categories(state, payload) {
  let categories = {};

  Object.keys(payload).forEach(key => {
    let product = payload[key],
      type = product.type;

    if(!categories.hasOwnProperty(type.handle)) {
      categories[type.handle] = {
        title: type.title,
        handle: type.handle,
        products: []
      }
    }

    categories[type.handle].products.push(product.handle);
  });
}
```

You can view the categories output by adding console.log to the end of the function:

```
categories(state, payload) {
  let categories = {};

  Object.keys(payload).forEach(key => {
    ...
  });

  console.log(categories);
}
```

Add the mutation to the `initializeShop` action:

```
initializeShop({commit}, products) {
  commit('products', products);
  commit('categories', products);
}
```

Viewing the app in the browser, you will be faced with a JavaScript error. This is because some products do not contain a "type" for us to use to categorize them. Even with the JavaScript error resolved, there are still a lot of categories that get listed out.

To help with the number of categories, and to group the uncategorized products, we should make an "Miscellaneous" category. This will collate all the categories with two or fewer products and group the products into their own group.

Creating an "miscellaneous" category

The first issue we need to negate is the nameless category. When looping through our products, if no type is found, we should insert a category, so everything is categorized.

Create a new object in the `categories` method that contains the title and handle for a new category. For the handle and variable call it other. Make the title a bit more user-friendly by calling it *Miscellaneous*.

```
let categories = {},
  other = {
    title: 'Miscellaneous',
    handle: 'other'
  };
```

When looping through products, we can then check to see whether the `type` key exists, if not, create an `other` category and append to it:

```
Object.keys(payload).forEach(key => {
  let product = payload[key],
    type = product.hasOwnProperty('type') ? product.type : other;

  if(!categories.hasOwnProperty(type.handle)) {
    categories[type.handle] = {
      title: type.title,
      handle: type.handle,
      products: []
    }
  }
}
```

```
    categories[type.handle].products.push(product.handle);
});
```

Viewing the app now will reveal all the categories in the JavaScript console – allowing you to see the magnitude of how many categories there are.

Let's combine any categories with two or fewer products into the "other" category – not forgetting to remove the category afterward. After the product loop, loop through the categories, checking the count of the products available. If fewer than three, add them to the "other" category:

```
Object.keys(categories).forEach(key => {
  let category = categories[key];

  if(category.products.length < 3) {
    categories.other.products =
categories.other.products.concat(category.products);
  }
});
```

We can then delete the category we've just stolen the products from:

```
Object.keys(categories).forEach(key => {
  let category = categories[key];

  if(category.products.length < 3) {
    categories.other.products =
categories.other.products.concat(category.products);
    delete categories[key];
  }
});
```

And with that, we have a much more manageable list of categories. One more improvement we can make is to ensure the categories are in alphabetical order. This helps users find their desired category much quicker. In JavaScript, arrays can be sorted a lot more easily than objects, so once again, we need to loop through an array of the object keys and sort them. Create a new object and add the categories as they are sorted to it. Afterward, store this on the state object so we have the categories available to us:

```
categories(state, payload) {
  let categories = {},
    other = {
      title: 'Miscellaneous',
      handle: 'other'
    };
```

```
Object.keys(payload).forEach(key => {
  let product = payload[key],
    type = product.hasOwnProperty('type') ? product.type : other;

  if(!categories.hasOwnProperty(type.handle)) {
    categories[type.handle] = {
      title: type.title,
      handle: type.handle,
      products: []
    }
  }

  categories[type.handle].products.push(product.handle);
});

Object.keys(categories).forEach(key => {
  let category = categories[key];

  if(category.products.length < 3) {
    categories.other.products =
categories.other.products.concat(category.products);
    delete categories[key];
  }
});

let categoriesSorted = {}
Object.keys(categories).sort().forEach(key => {
    categoriesSorted[key] = categories[key]
});
state.categories = categoriesSorted;
}
```

With that, we can now add a list of categories to our `HomePage` template. For this, we'll create named `router-view` components – allowing us to put things in the sidebar of the shop on selected pages.

Displaying the categories

With our categories stored, we can now proceed with creating our `ListCategories` component. We want to display our category navigation in a sidebar on the home page, and also on a shop category page. As we want to show it in several places, we have a couple of options as to how we display it.

We can use the component in the template as we have with the `<list-products>` component. The issue with this is that if we want to display our list in a sidebar and our sidebar needs to be consistent across the site, we would have to copy and paste a lot of HTML between views.

A better approach would be to use named routes and set the template once in our `index.html`.

Update the app template to contain a `<main>` and an `<aside>` element. Within these, create a `router-view`, leaving the one inside `main` unnamed, while giving the one inside the `aside` element a name of `sidebar`:

```html
<div id="app">
  <main>
    <router-view></router-view>
  </main>
  <aside>
    <router-view name="sidebar"></router-view>
  </aside>
</div>
```

Within our routes object, we can now add different components to different named views. On the `Home` route, change the `component` key to `components`, and add an object - specifying each component and its view:

```js
{
  path: '/',
  name: 'Home',
  components: {
    default: HomePage,
    sidebar: ListCategories
  }
}
```

The default indicates that the component will go into the unnamed `router-view`. This allows us to still use the singular `component` key if required. For the component to be correctly loaded into the sidebar view, we need to alter how the `ListCategories` component is initialized. Instead of using `Vue.component`, initialize it as you would a `view` component:

```js
const ListCategories = {
  name: 'ListCategories'
};
```

We can now proceed with making the template for the category list. As our categories are saved in the store, loading and displaying them should be familiar by now. It is advised you load the categories from the state into a computed function - for cleaner template code and easier adaptation should you need to manipulate it in any way.

Before we create the template, we need to create a route for the category. Referring back to our plan in Chapter 9, *Using Vue-Router Dynamic Routes to Load Data*, we can see the route is going to be /category/:slug – add this route with a name and enable props, as we'll utilize them for the slug. Ensure you have made the CategoryPage file and initialized the component.

```
const router = new VueRouter({
  routes: [
    {
      path: '/',
      name: 'Home',
      components: {
        default: HomePage,
        sidebar: ListCategories
      }
    },
    {
      path: '/category/:slug',
      name: 'Category',
      component: CategoryPage,
      props: true
    },
    {
      path: '/product/:slug',
      name: 'Product',
      component: ProductPage
    },

    {
      path: '/404',
      alias: '*',
      component: PageNotFound
    }
  ]
});
```

Back to our `ListCategories` component; loop through the stored categories and create a link for each one. Show the product count in brackets after each name:

```
const ListCategories = {
  name: 'ListCategories',

  template: `<div v-if="categories">
    <ul>
      <li v-for="category in categories">
        <router-link :to="{name: 'Category', params: {slug:
category.handle}}">
          {{ category.title }} ({{ category.products.length }})
        </router-link>
      </li>
    </ul>
  </div>`,

  computed: {
    categories() {
      return this.$store.state.categories;
    }
  }
};
```

With the links to our categories now showing on the home page, we can head on to make a category page.

Displaying products in a category

Clicking one of the category links (that is, `/#/category/grips`) will navigate to a blank page – thanks to our route. We need to create a template and set up the category page to show the products. As a starting base, create the `CategoryPage` component in a similar vein to the product page.

Create a template with an empty container and the `PageNotFound` component inside. Create a data variable titled `categoryNotFound`, and ensure the `PageNotFound` component displays if this is set to `true`. Create a `props` object, which allows the `slug` property to be passed and, lastly, create a `category` computed function.

The `CategoryPage` component should look like the following:

```
const CategoryPage = {
  name: 'CategoryPage',
```

```
template: `<div>
  <div v-if="category"></div>
  <page-not-found v-if="categoryNotFound"></page-not-found>
</div>`,

components: {
  PageNotFound
},

props: {
  slug: String
},
data() {
  return {
    categoryNotFound: false,
  }
},

computed: {
  category() {
  }
}
};
```

Inside the `category` computed function, load the correct category from the store based on the slug. If it is not on the list, mark the `categoryNotFound` variable to true - similar to what we did in the `ProductPage` component:

```
computed: {
  category() {
    let category;

    if(Object.keys(this.$store.state.categories).length) {
      category = this.$store.state.categories[this.slug];

      if(!category) {
        this.categoryNotFound = true;
      }
    }

    return category;
  }
}
```

With our category loaded, we can output the title in the template:

```
template: `<div>
  <div v-if="category">
    <h1>{{ category.title }}</h1>
  </div>
  <page-not-found v-if="categoryNotFound"></page-not-found>
</div>`,
```

We can now proceed with displaying the products on our category page. To do this, we can use the code from the HomePage component as we have exactly the same scenario – an array of product handles.

Create a new computed function that takes the current category products and processes them as we did on the home page:

```
computed: {
  category() {
    ...
  },

  products() {
    if(this.category) {
      let products = this.$store.state.products,
        output = [];

      for(let featured of this.category.products) {
        output.push(products[featured]);
      }

      return output;
    }
  }
}
```

We don't need to check whether the products exist in this function as we are checking whether the category exists, and that would only return true if the data had been loaded. Add the component to the HTML and pass in the products variable:

```
template: `<div>
  <div v-if="category">
    <h1>{{ category.title }}</h1>
    <list-products :products="products"></list-products>
  </div>
  <page-not-found v-if="categoryNotFound"></page-not-found>
</div>`
```

With that, we have our category products listed out for each category.

Code optimization

With our `CategoryPage` component complete, we can see a lot of similarities between that and the home page – the only difference being the home page has a fixed product array. To save repetition, we can combine these two components – meaning we only have to ever update one if we need to.

We can address the fixed array issue by displaying it when we identify that we are on the home page. The way of doing that is to check if the slug prop has a value. If not, we can assume we are on the home page.

First, update the `Home` route to point to the `CategoryPage` component and enable props. When using named views, you have to enable props for each of the views. Update the props value to be an object with each of the named views, enabling the props for each:

```
{
  path: '/',
  name: 'Home',
  components: {
    default: CategoryPage,
    sidebar: ListCategories
  },
  props: {
    default: true,
    sidebar: true
  }
}
```

Next, create a new variable in the `data` function of the `CategoryPage`, titled `categoryHome`. This is going to be an object that follows the same structure as the category objects, containing a `products` array, title, and handle. Although the handle won't be used, it is good practice to follow conventions:

```
data() {
  return {
    categoryNotFound: false,
    categoryHome: {
      title: 'Welcome to the Shop',
      handle: 'home',
      products: [
        'adjustable-stem',
        'fizik-saddle-pak',
```

```
      'kenda-tube',
      'colorful-fixie-lima',
      'oury-grip-set',
      'pure-fix-pedals-with-cages'
    ]
  }
 }
}
```

The last thing we need to do is check whether the slug exists. If not, assign our new object to the category variable within the computed function:

```
category() {
  let category;

  if(Object.keys(this.$store.state.categories).length) {
    if(this.slug) {
      category = this.$store.state.categories[this.slug];
    } else {
      category = this.categoryHome;
    }

    if(!category) {
      this.categoryNotFound = true;
    }
  }

  return category;
}
```

Head to the home page and verify your new component is working. If it is, you can delete `HomePage.js` and remove it from `index.html`. Update the category route to also include the category list in the sidebar and use the `props` object:

```
{
  path: '/category/:slug',
  name: 'Category',
  components: {
    default: CategoryPage,
    sidebar: ListCategories
  },
  props: {
    default: true,
    sidebar: true
  }
},
```

Ordering products in a category

With our category pages displaying the right products, it's time to add some ordering options within our `ListProducts` component. When viewing a shop online, you can normally order the products by the following:

- Title: Ascending (A - Z)
- Title: Descending (Z - A)
- Price: Ascending ($1 - $999)
- Price: Descending ($999 - $1)

However, once we have the mechanism in place, you can add any ordering criteria you want.

Start off by creating a select box in your `ListProducts` component with each of the preceding values. Add an extra first one of **Sort products by...**:

```
<div class="ordering">
  <select>
    <option>Order products</option>
    <option>Title - ascending (A - Z)</option>
    <option>Title - descending (Z - A)</option>
    <option>Price - ascending ($1 - $999)</option>
    <option>Price - descending ($999 - $1)</option>
  </select>
</div>
```

We now need to create a variable for the select box to update in the `data` function. Add a new key titled `ordering` and add a value to each option, so interpreting the value is easier. Construct the value by using the field and order, separated by a hyphen. For example, `Title - ascending (A - Z)` would become `title-asc`:

```
<div class="ordering">
  <select v-model="ordering">
    <option value="">Order products</option>
    <option value="title-asc">Title - ascending (A - Z)</option>
    <option value="title-desc">Title - descending (Z - A)</option>
    <option value="price-asc">Price - ascending ($1 - $999)</option>
    <option value="price-desc">Price - descending ($999 - $1)</option>
  </select>
</div>
```

And the updated `data` function becomes:

```
data() {
  return {
    perPage: 12,
    currentPage: 1,
    pageLinksCount: 3,

    ordering: ''
  }
}
```

To update the order of the products we now need to manipulate the product list. This needs to be done before the list gets split for pagination - as the user would expect the whole list to be sorted, not just the current page.

Store the product price

Before we proceed, there is an issue we need to address. To sort by price, the price needs to ideally be available on the product itself, not calculated specifically for the template, which it currently is. To combat this, we are going to calculate the price before the products get added to the store. This means it will be available as a property on the product itself, rather than being dynamically created.

The details we need to know are the cheapest price and whether the product has many prices within its variations. The latter means we know whether we need to display the `"From: "` when listing the products out. We will create two new properties for each product: `price` and `hasManyPrices`.

Navigate to the `products` mutation in the store and create a new object and a loop of the products:

```
products(state, payload) {
  let products = {};

  Object.keys(payload).forEach(key => {
    let product = payload[key];

    products[key] = product;
  });
  state.products = payload;
}
```

Copy the code from the `productPrice` method on the `ListProducts` component and place it within the loop. Update the second `for` loop so it loops through `product.variationProducts`. Once this `for` loop has completed, we can add the new properties to the product. Lastly, update the state with the new products object:

```
products(state, payload) {
  let products = {};

  Object.keys(payload).forEach(key => {
    let product = payload[key];

    let prices = [];
    for(let variation of product.variationProducts) {
      if(!prices.includes(variation.price)) {
        prices.push(variation.price);
      }
    }

    product.price = Math.min(...prices);
    product.hasManyPrices = prices.length > 1;

    products[key] = product;
  });

  state.products = products;
}
```

We can now update the `productPrice` method on the `ListProducts` component. Update the function so it accepts the product, instead of variations. Remove the `for` loop from the function, and update the variables so they use the `price` and `hasManyPrices` properties of the product instead:

```
productPrice(product) {
  let price = '$' + product.price;

  if(product.hasManyPrices) {
    price = 'From: ' + price;
  }

  return price;
}
```

Update the template so the product is passed to the function:

```
<p>Price {{ productPrice(product) }}</p>
```

Wiring up the ordering

With our price readily available, we can proceed with wiring up the ordering. Create a new computed function titled `orderProducts` that returns `this.products`. We want to ensure we are always sorting from the source and not ordering something that has previously been ordered. Call this new function from within the `paginate` function and remove the parameter from this method and from the template:

```
computed: {
  ...

  orderProducts() {
    return this.products;
  },
},

methods: {
  paginate() {
    return this.orderProducts.slice(
      this.pagination.range.from,
      this.pagination.range.to
    );
  },
}
```

To determine how we need to sort the products, we can use the `this.ordering` value. If it exists, we can split the string on the hyphen, meaning we have an array containing the field and order type. If it does not exist, we need to simply return the existing product array:

```
orderProducts() {
  let output;

  if(this.ordering.length) {
    let orders = this.ordering.split('-');
  } else {
    output = this.products;
  }
  return output;
}
```

Sort the `products` array based on the value of the first item of the ordering array. If it is a string, we will use `localCompare`, which ignores cases when comparing. Otherwise, we will simply subtract one value from the other – this is what the `sort` function expects:

```
orderProducts() {
  let output;
```

```
        if(this.ordering.length) {
          let orders = this.ordering.split('-');
          output = this.products.sort(function(a, b) {
            if(typeof a[orders[0]] == 'string') {
              return a[orders[0]].localeCompare(b[orders[0]]);
            } else {
              return a[orders[0]] - b[orders[0]];
            }
          });

        } else {
          output = this.products;
        }
        return output;
      }
```

Lastly, we need to check if the second item in the `orders` array is `asc` or `desc`. By default, the current sort function will return the items sorted in an `ascending` order, so if the value is `desc`, we can reverse the array:

```
      orderProducts() {
        let output;

        if(this.ordering.length) {
          let orders = this.ordering.split('-');
          output = this.products.sort(function(a, b) {
            if(typeof a[orders[0]] == 'string') {
              return a[orders[0]].localeCompare(b[orders[0]]);
            } else {
              return a[orders[0]] - b[orders[0]];
            }
          });

          if(orders[1] == 'desc') {
            output.reverse();
          }
        } else {
          output = this.products;
        }
        return output;
      }
```

Head to your browser and check out the ordering of products!

Creating Vuex getters

The last step to making our category page just like any other shop is the introduction of filtering. Filtering allows you to find products that have particular sizes, colors, tags, or manufacturers. Our filtering options are going to be built from the products on the page. For example, if none of the products have an XL size or a blue color, there is no point showing that as a filter.

To achieve this, we are going to need to pass the products of the current category to the filtering component as well. However, the products get processed on the `CategoryPage` component. Instead of repeating this processing, we can move the functionality to a Vuex store `getter`. Getters allow you to retrieve data from the store and manipulate it like you would in a function on a component. Because it is a central place, however, it means several components can benefit from the processing.

Getters are the Vuex equivalent of computed functions. They are declared as functions but called as variables. However, they can be manipulated to accept parameters by returning a function inside them.

We are going to move both the `category` and `products` functions from the `CategoryPage` component into the getter. The `getter` function will then return an object with the category and products.

Create a new object in your store titled `getters`. Inside, create a new function called `categoryProducts`:

```
getters: {
  categoryProducts: () => {
  }
}
```

Getters themselves receive two parameters, the state as the first, and any other getters as the second. To pass a parameter to a getter, you have to return a function inside of the getter that receives the parameter. Fortunately, in ES2015, this can be achieved with the double arrow (=>) syntax. As we are not going to be using any other getters in this function, we do not need to call the second parameter.

As we are abstracting all of the logic out, pass in the `slug` variable as the parameter of the second function:

```
categoryProducts: (state) => (slug) => {

}
```

As we are transferring the logic for selecting and retrieving the categories and products into the store, it makes sense to store the `HomePage` category content in the `state` itself:

```
state: {
  products: {},
  categories: {},

  categoryHome: {
    title: 'Welcome to the Shop',
    handle: 'home',
    products: [
      'adjustable-stem',
      'fizik-saddle-pak',
      'kenda-tube',
      'colorful-fixie-lima',
      'oury-grip-set',
      'pure-fix-pedals-with-cages'
    ]
  }
}
```

Move category-selecting logic from the `category` computed function in the `CategoryPage` component into the getter. Update the `slug` and `categoryHome` variables to use the content from the relevant places:

```
categoryProducts: (state) => (slug) => {
  if(Object.keys(state.categories).length) {
    let category = false;
    if(slug) {
      category = this.$store.state.categories[this.slug];
    } else {
      category = state.categoryHome;
    }
  }
}
```

With a category assigned, we can now load the products based on the handles stored in the category. Move the code from the `products` computed function into the getter. Combine the variable assignments together and remove the store product retrieval variable, as we have the state readily available. Ensure the code that checks to see whether the category exists is still in place:

```
categoryProducts: (state) => (slug) => {
  if(Object.keys(state.categories).length) {
    let category = false,
      products = [];

    if(slug) {
      category = this.$store.state.categories[this.slug];
    } else {
      category = state.categoryHome;
    }

    if(category) {
      for(let featured of category.products) {
        products.push(state.products[featured]);
      }
    }
  }
}
```

Lastly, we can add a new `productDetails` array on the `category` with the fleshed-out product data. Return the `category` at the end of the function. If the `slug` variable input exists as a category, we will get all of the data back. If not, it will return `false` – from which we can display our `PageNotFound` component:

```
categoryProducts: (state) => (slug) => {
  if(Object.keys(state.categories).length) {
    let category = false,
      products = [];

    if(slug) {
      category = state.categories[slug];
    } else {
      category = state.categoryHome;
    }

    if(category) {
      for(let featured of category.products) {
        products.push(state.products[featured]);
      }
```

```
        category.productDetails = products;
    }

    return category;
  }
}
```

In our `CategoryPage` component, we can remove the `products()` computed function and update the `category()` function. To call a `getter` function, you refer to `this.$store.getters`:

```
computed: {
  category() {
    if(Object.keys(this.$store.state.categories).length) {
      let category = this.$store.getters.categoryProducts(this.slug);

      if(!category) {
        this.categoryNotFound = true;
      }
      return category;
    }
  }
}
```

Unfortunately, we are still having to check whether the categories exist before proceeding. This is so we can tell that there is no category with the name, rather than an unloaded one.

To make this neater, we can extract this check into another getter and utilize it in both our other getter and the component.

Create a new getter titled `categoriesExist`, and return the contents of the `if` statement:

```
categoriesExist: (state) => {
  return Object.keys(state.categories).length;
},
```

Update the `categoryProducts` getter to accept getters in the arguments of the first function and to use this new getter to indicate its output:

```
categoryProducts: (state, getters) => (slug) => {
  if(getters.categoriesExist) {
    ...
  }
}
```

In our `CategoryPage` component, we can now call on the new getter with `this.$store.getters.categoriesExist()`. To save having `this.$store.getters` repeated twice in this function, we can map the getters to be locally accessed. This allows us to call `this.categoriesExist()` as a more readable function name.

At the beginning of the `computed` object, add a new function titled `...Vuex.mapGetters()`. This function accepts an array or an object as a parameter and the three dots at the beginning ensure the contents are expanded to be merged with the `computed` object.

Pass in an array containing the names of the two getters:

```
computed: {
  ...Vuex.mapGetters([
    'categoryProducts',
    'categoriesExist'
  ]),
  category() {
    ...
  }
}
```

This now means we have `this.categoriesExist` and `this.categoryProducts` at our disposal. Update the category function to use these new functions:

```
computed: {
  ...Vuex.mapGetters([
    'categoriesExist',
    'categoryProducts'
  ]),

  category() {
    if(this.categoriesExist) {
      let category = this.categoryProducts(this.slug);

      if(!category) {
        this.categoryNotFound = true;
      }
      return category;
    }
  }
}
```

Update the template to reflect the changes in the computed data:

```
template: `<div>
  <div v-if="category">
    <h1>{{ category.title }}</h1>
    <list-products :products="category.productDetails"></list-products>
  </div>
  <page-not-found v-if="categoryNotFound"></page-not-found>
</div>`,
```

Building the filtering component based on products

As mentioned, all our filters are going to be created from the products in the current category. This means if there are no products made by *IceToolz*, it won't appear as an available filter.

To begin with, open the `ProductFiltering.js` component file. Our product filtering is going to go in our sidebar, so change the component definition from `Vue.component` to an object. We still want our categories to display after the filtering, so add the `ListCategories` component as a declared component within `ProductFiltering`. Add a template key and include the `<list-categories>` component:

```
const ProductFiltering = {
  name: 'ProductFiltering',

  template: `<div>
    <list-categories />
  </div>`,

  components: {
    ListCategories
  }
}
```

Update the category route to include the `ProductFiltering` component in the sidebar instead of `ListCategories`:

```
{
  path: '/category/:slug',
  name: 'Category',
  components: {
    default: CategoryPage,
```

```
        sidebar: ProductFiltering
    },
    props: {
        default: true,
        sidebar: true
    }
}
```

You should now have the `Home` route, which includes the `CategoryPage` and `ListCategories` components, and the `Category` route, which includes the `ProductFiltering` component instead.

From the `CategoryPage` component, copy the props and computed objects - as we are going to be utilizing a lot of the existing code. Rename the `category` computed function to `filters`. Remove both the return and the `componentNotFound` if statement. Your component should now look like the following:

```
const ProductFiltering = {
    name: 'ProductFiltering',

    template: `<div>
        <list-categories />
    </div>`,

    components: {
        ListCategories
    },

    props: {
        slug: String
    },

    computed: {
        ...Vuex.mapGetters([
            'categoriesExist',
            'categoryProducts'
        ]),

        filters() {
            if(this.categoriesExist) {
                let category = this.categoryProducts(this.slug);

            }
        }
    }
}
```

We now need to construct our filters, based on the products in the category. We will be doing this by looping through the products, collecting information from preselected values, and displaying them.

Create a `data` object that contains a key of `topics`. This will be an object containing child objects with a, now familiar, pattern of `'handle': {}` for each of the properties we want to filter on.

Each child object will contain a `handle`, which is the value of the product of which to filter (for example, vendor), a `title`, which is the user-friendly version of the key, and an array of values, which will be populated.

We'll start off with two, `vendor` and `tags`; however, more will be dynamically added as we process the products:

```
data() {
  return {
    topics: {
      vendor: {
        title: 'Manufacturer',
        handle: 'vendor',
        values: {}
      },
      tags: {
        title: 'Tags',
        handle: 'tags',
        values: {}
      }
    }
  }
},
```

We will now begin looping through the products. Along with the values, we are going to keep track of how many products have the same value, allowing us to indicate to the user how many products will be revealed.

Loop through the `products` on the category within the `filters` method and, to begin with, find the `vendor` of each product. For every one encountered, check whether it exists within the `values` array.

If it does not, add a new object with the `name`, `handle`, and a `count`, which is an array of product handles. We store an array of handles so that we can verify that the product has already been seen. If we were keeping a raw numerical count, we could encounter a scenario where the filters get triggered twice, doubling the count. By checking whether the product handle exists already, we can check it's only been seen once.

If a filter of that name does exist, add the handle to the array after checking it does not exist:

```
filters() {
  if(this.categoriesExist) {
    let category = this.categoryProducts(this.slug),
      vendors = this.topics.vendor;

    for(let product of category.productDetails) {

      if(product.hasOwnProperty('vendor')) {
        let vendor = product.vendor;

        if(vendor.handle) {
          if(!vendor.handle.count.includes(product.handle)) {
            category.values[item.handle].count.push(product.handle);
          }
        } else {
          vendors.values[vendor.handle] = {
            ...vendor,
            count: [product.handle]
          }
        }
      }

    }

  }
 }
}
```

This utilizes the previously-used object-expanding ellipsis (. . .), which saves us from having to write:

```
vendors.values[product.vendor.handle] = {
  title: vendor.title,
  handle: vendor.handle,
  count: [product.handle]
}
```

Although, feel free to use this if you are more comfortable with it.

Duplicate the code to work with `tags`, however as `tags` are an array themselves, we need to loop through each tag and add accordingly:

```
for(let product of category.productDetails) {

  if(product.hasOwnProperty('vendor')) {
    let vendor = product.vendor;

    if(vendor.handle) {
      if(!vendor.handle.count.includes(product.handle)) {
        category.values[item.handle].count.push(product.handle);
      }
    } else {
      vendors.values[vendor.handle] = {
        ...vendor,
        count: [product.handle]
      }
    }
  }

  if(product.hasOwnProperty('tags')) {
    for(let tag of product.tags) {
      if(tag.handle) {
        if(topicTags.values[tag.handle]) {
          if(!topicTags.values[tag.handle].count.includes(product.handle))
{
            topicTags.values[tag.handle].count.push(product.handle);
          }
        } else {
          topicTags.values[tag.handle] = {
            ...tag,
            count: [product.handle]
          }
        }
      }
    }
  }

}
```

Our code is already getting repetitive and complex, let's simplify it by creating a method to handle the repetitive code.

Create a `methods` object with a function of `addTopic`. This will take two parameters: the object to append to and the singular item. For example, its usage would be:

```
if(product.hasOwnProperty('vendor')) {
    this.addTopic(this.topics.vendor, product.vendor, product.handle);
}
```

Create the function and abstract out the logic from inside the `hasOwnProperty` if declaration. Name the two parameters `category` and `item`, and update the code accordingly:

```
methods: {
    addTopic(category, item, handle) {
        if(item.handle) {

            if(category.values[item.handle]) {
                if(!category.values[item.handle].count.includes(handle)) {
                    category.values[item.handle].count.push(handle);
                }

            } else {

                category.values[item.handle] = {
                    ...item,
                    count: [handle]
                }
            }
        }
    }
}
```

Update the `filters` computed function to use the new `addTopic` method. Remove the variable declarations at the top of the function, as they are being passed directly into the method:

```
filters() {
    if(this.categoriesExist) {

        let category = this.categoryProducts(this.slug);

        for(let product of category.productDetails) {

            if(product.hasOwnProperty('vendor')) {
                this.addTopic(this.topics.vendor, product.vendor, product.handle);
            }

            if(product.hasOwnProperty('tags')) {
```

```
        for(let tag of product.tags) {
          this.addTopic(this.topics.tags, tag, product.handle);
        }
      }

    }
  }
}
```

At the end of this function, return `this.topics`. Although we could reference `topics` directly in the template, we need to ensure the `filters` computed property gets triggered:

```
filters() {
  if(this.categoriesExist) {

    ...
  }

  return this.topics;
}
```

Before we proceed to create our dynamic filters based on the various types, let's display the current filters.

Due to how the `topics` object is set up, we can loop through each of the child objects and then through the `values` of each one. We are going to make our filters out of checkboxes, with the value of the input being the handle of each of the filters:

```
template: `<div>
  <div class="filters">
    <div class="filterGroup" v-for="filter in filters">
      <h3>{{ filter.title }}</h3>
      <label class="filter" v-for="value in filter.values">
        <input type="checkbox" :value="value.handle">
        {{ value.title }} ({{ value.count }})
      </label>
    </div>
  </div>

  <list-categories />
</div>`,
```

In order to keep track of what is checked, we can use a `v-model` attribute. If there are checkboxes with the same `v-model`, Vue creates an array with each item.

Add an array of `checked` to each of the `topic` objects in the data object:

```
data() {
  return {
    topics: {
      vendor: {
        title: 'Manufacturer',
        handle: 'vendor',
        checked: [],
        values: {}
      },
      tags: {
        title: 'Tags',
        handle: 'tags',
        checked: [],
        values: {}
      }
    }
  }
}
```

Next, add a `v-model` attribute to each checkbox, referencing this array on the `filter` object along with a click binder, referencing an `updateFilters` method:

```
<div class="filters">
  <div class="filterGroup" v-for="filter in filters">
    <h3>{{ filter.title }}</h3>

    <label class="filter" v-for="value in filter.values">
      <input type="checkbox" :value="value.handle" v-model="filter.checked"
@click="updateFilters">
        {{ value.title }} ({{ value.count }})
    </label>
  </div>
</div>
```

Create an empty method for now - we'll configure it later:

```
methods: {
  addTopic(category, item) {
    ...
  },

  updateFilters() {
  }
}
```

Dynamically creating filters

With our fixed filters created and being watched, we can take the opportunity to create dynamic filters. These filters will observe the `variationTypes` on the products (for example, color, and size) and list out the options – again with the count of each one.

To achieve this, we need to first loop through the `variationTypes` on the products. Before adding anything, we need to check to see if that variation type exists on the `topics` object, if not – we need to add a skeleton object. This expands the variation (which contains the `title` and `handle`) and also includes empty `checked` and `value` properties:

```
filters() {
  if(this.categoriesExist) {

    let category = this.categoryProducts(this.slug);

    for(let product of category.productDetails) {

      if(product.hasOwnProperty('vendor')) {
        this.addTopic(this.topics.vendor, product.vendor);
      }

      if(product.hasOwnProperty('tags')) {
        for(let tag of product.tags) {
          this.addTopic(this.topics.tags, tag);
        }
      }

      Object.keys(product.variationTypes).forEach(vkey => {
        let variation = product.variationTypes[vkey];

        if(!this.topics.hasOwnProperty(variation.handle)) {
          this.topics[variation.handle] = {
            ...variation,
            checked: [],
            values: {}
          }
        }
      });

    }
  }

  return this.topics;
}
```

With our empty object created, we can now loop through the `variationProducts` on the product object. For each one, we can access the variant with the handle of the current variation. From there, we can use our `addTopic` method to include the value (for example, Blue or XL) within the filters:

```
Object.keys(product.variationTypes).forEach(vkey => {
  let variation = product.variationTypes[vkey];

  if(!this.topics.hasOwnProperty(variation.handle)) {
    this.topics[variation.handle] = {
      ...variation,
      checked: [],
      values: {}
    }
  }
}

  Object.keys(product.variationProducts).forEach(pkey => {
    let variationProduct = product.variationProducts[pkey];

    this.addTopic(
      this.topics[variation.handle],
      variationProduct.variant[variation.handle],
      product.handle
    );
  });

});
```

We do need to update our `addTopic` method, however. This is because the dynamic properties have a `value`, instead of a title.

Add an `if` statement to your `addTopic` method to check whether a `value` exists, if it does – set it to the `title`:

```
addTopic(category, item, handle) {
  if(item.handle) {

    if(category.values[item.handle]) {
      if(!category.values[item.handle].count.includes(handle)) {
        category.values[item.handle].count.push(handle);
      }
    } else {

      if(item.hasOwnProperty('value')) {
        item.title = item.value;
      }
```

```
      category.values[item.handle] = {
         ...item,
         count: [handle]
      }
    }
  }
}
```

Viewing the app in the browser should reveal your dynamically-added filters, along with the original ones we had added.

Resetting filters

When navigating between categories you will notice that, currently, the filters do not reset. This is because we are not clearing the filters between each navigation, and the arrays are persisting. This is not ideal, as it means they get longer as you navigate around and do not apply to the products listed.

To remedy this, we can create a method that returns our default topic object and, when the slug updates, call the method to reset the topics object. Move the topics object to a new method titled defaultTopics:

```
methods: {
  defaultTopics() {
    return {
      vendor: {
        title: 'Manufacturer',
        handle: 'vendor',
        checked: [],
        values: {}
      },
      tags: {
        title: 'Tags',
        handle: 'tags',
        checked: [],
        values: {}
      }
    }
  },

  addTopic(category, item) {
    ...
  }

  updateFilters() {
```

```
    }
  }
```

Within the `data` function, change the value of topics to be `this.defaultTopics()` to call the method:

```
data() {
  return {
    topics: this.defaultTopics()
  }
},
```

Lastly, add a watch function to reset the topics key when the `slug` gets updated:

```
watch: {
  slug() {
    this.topics = this.defaultTopics();
  }
}
```

Updating the URL on checkbox filter change

Our filtering component, when interacted with, is going to update the URL query parameters. This allows the user to see the filters in effect, bookmark them, and share the URL if needed. We already used query parameters for our pagination, and it makes sense to put the user back on page one when filtering – as there may only be one page.

To construct our query parameters of filters, we need to loop through each filter type and add a new parameter for each one that has items in the `checked` array. We can then call a `router.push()` to update the URL and, in turn, change the products displayed.

Create an empty object in your `updateFilters` method. Loop through the topics and populate the `filters` object with the items checked. Set the `query` parameters in the router to the `filters` object:

```
updateFilters() {
  let filters = {};

  Object.keys(this.topics).forEach(key => {
    let topic = this.topics[key];
    if(topic.checked.length) {
      filters[key] = topic.checked;
    }
  });
```

```
    this.$router.push({query: filters});
}
```

Checking and unchecking the filters on the right should update the URL with the items checked.

Preselecting filters on page load

When loading a category with filters already in the URL, we need to ensure the checkboxes are checked on the right-hand side. This can be done by looping through the existing query parameters and adding any matching keys and arrays to the topics parameter. As the `query` can either be an array or a string, we need to ensure the checked property is an array no matter what. We also need to ensure the query key is, indeed, a filter and not a page parameter:

```
filters() {
  if(this.categoriesExist) {

    let category = this.categoryProducts(this.slug);

    for(let product of category.productDetails) {
      ...
    }

    Object.keys(this.$route.query).forEach(key => {
      if(Object.keys(this.topics).includes(key)) {
        let query = this.$route.query[key];
        this.topics[key].checked = Array.isArray(query) ? query : [query];
      }
    });
  }


  return this.topics;
}
```

On page load, the filters in the URL will be checked.

Filtering the products

Our filters are now being created and appended to dynamically, and activating a filter updates the query parameter in the URL. We can now proceed with showing and hiding products based on the URL parameters. We are going to be doing this by filtering the products before being passed into the `ListProducts` component. This ensures the pagination works correctly.

As we are filtering, open up `ListProducts.js` and add a `:key` attribute to each list item, with the value of the `handle`:

```
<ol :start="pagination.range.from + 1">
  <li v-for="product in paginate(products)" :key="product.handle">
    ...
  </li>
</ol>
```

Open up the `CategoryPage` view and create a method within the `methods` object titled `filtering()` and add a `return true` to begin with. The method should accept two parameters, a `product` and `query` object:

```
methods: {
  filtering(product, query) {

    return true;
  }
}
```

Next, within the `category` computed function, we need to filter the products if there is a query parameter. However, we need to be careful that we don't trigger the filters if the page number is present – as that is also a query.

Create a new variable called `filters`, which is a copy of the query object from the route. Next, if the page parameter is present, `delete` it from our new object. From there, we can check whether the query object has any other contents and if so, run the native JavaScript `filter()` function on our product array – passing in the product and new query/filters object to our method:

```
category() {
  if(this.categoriesExist) {
    let category = this.categoryProducts(this.slug),
      filters = Object.assign({}, this.$route.query);

    if(Object.keys(filters).length && filters.hasProperty('page')) {
```

```
      delete filters.page;
    }
    if(Object.keys(filters).length) {
      category.productDetails = category.productDetails.filter(
        p => this.filtering(p, filters)
      );
    }

    if(!category) {
      this.categoryNotFound = true;
    }
    return category;
  }
}
```

Refresh your app to ensure the products still show.

To filter products, there is quite a complex process involved. We want to check whether an attribute is in the query parameters; if it is, we set a placeholder value of false. If the attribute on the product matches that of the query parameter, we set the placeholder to true. We then repeat this for each of the query parameters. Once complete, we then only show products that have all of the criteria.

The way we are going to construct this allows products to be OR within the categories, but AND with different sections. For example, if the user were to pick many colors (red and green) and one tag (accessories), it will show all products that are red or green accessories.

Our filtering is created with the tags, vendor, and then dynamic filters. As two of the properties are fixed, we will have to check these first. The dynamic filters will be verified by reconstructing the way they were built.

Create a hasProperty object, which will be our placeholder object for keeping track of the query parameters the product has. We'll begin with the vendor – as this is the simplest property.

We start by looping through the query attributes – in case there is more than one (for example, red and green). Next, we need to confirm that the vendor exists in the query – if it does, we then set a vendor attribute in the hasProperty object to false. We then check whether the vendor handle is the same as the query attribute. If this matches, we change our hasProperty.vendor property to true:

```
filtering(product, query) {
  let display = false,
    hasProperty = {};
```

```
Object.keys(query).forEach(key => {
  let filter = Array.isArray(query[key]) ? query[key] : [query[key]];

  for(attribute of filter) {
    if(key == 'vendor') {

      hasProperty.vendor = false;
      if(product.vendor.handle == attribute) {
        hasProperty.vendor = true;
      }

    }
  }
});

return display;
}
```

This will update the hasProperty object with whether the vendor matches the selected filter. We can row replicate the functionality with the tags – remembering that tags on a product are an object we need to filter.

The dynamic properties constructed by the filters will also need to be checked. This is done by checking the variant object on each variationProduct, and updating the hasProperty object if it matches:

```
filtering(product, query) {
  let display = false,
    hasProperty = {};

  Object.keys(query).forEach(key => {
    let filter = Array.isArray(query[key]) ? query[key] : [query[key]];

    for(attribute of filter) {
      if(key == 'vendor') {

        hasProperty.vendor = false;
        if(product.vendor.handle == attribute) {
          hasProperty.vendor = true;
        }

      } else if(key == 'tags') {
        hasProperty.tags = false;

        product[key].map(key => {
          if(key.handle == attribute) {
            hasProperty.tags = true;
```

```
          }
        });

      } else {
        hasProperty[key] = false;

        let variant = product.variationProducts.map(v => {
          if(v.variant[key] && v.variant[key].handle == attribute) {
            hasProperty[key] = true;
          }
        });
      }
    }
  });

  return display;
}
```

Lastly, we need to check each of the properties of the `hasProperty` object. If all the values are set to `true`, we can set the display of the product to `true` – meaning it will show. If one of them is `false`, the product will not show as it does not match all of the criteria:

```
filtering(product, query) {
  let display = false,
    hasProperty = {};

  Object.keys(query).forEach(key => {
    let filter = Array.isArray(query[key]) ? query[key] : [query[key]];

    for(attribute of filter) {
      if(key == 'vendor') {

        hasProperty.vendor = false;
        if(product.vendor.handle == attribute) {
          hasProperty.vendor = true;
        }

      } else if(key == 'tags') {
        hasProperty.tags = false;

        product[key].map(key => {
          if(key.handle == attribute) {
            hasProperty.tags = true;
          }
        });

      } else {
```

```
            hasProperty[key] = false;

            let variant = product.variationProducts.map(v => {
              if(v.variant[key] && v.variant[key].handle == attribute) {
                hasProperty[key] = true;
              }
            });
          }
        }

        if(Object.keys(hasProperty).every(key => hasProperty[key])) {
          display = true;
        }

    });

  return display;
}
```

We now have a successful filtering product list. View your app in the browser and update the filters – noting how products show and hide with each click. Note how even when you press refresh, only the filtered products display.

Summary

In this chapter, we created a category listing page, allowing the user the view all the products in a category. This list is able to be paginated, along with the order changing. We also created a filtering component, allowing the user to narrow down the results.

With our products now browseable, filterable, and viewable, we can proceed on to making a Cart and Checkout page.

11
Building an E-Commerce Store – Adding a Checkout

Over the last couple of chapters, we have been creating an e-commerce store. So far, we have created a product page that allows us to view the images and product variations, which may be size or style. We have also created a category page with filters and pagination—including a homepage category page that features specific, selected products.

Our users can browse and filter products and view more information about a specific product. We are now going to:

- Build the functionality to allow the user to add and remove products to their basket
- Allow a user to **Checkout**
- Add an **Order Confirmation** page

As a reminder—we won't be taking any billing details but we will make an Order Confirmation screen.

Creating the basket array placeholder

To help us persist the products in the basket throughout the app, we are going to be storing the user's selected products in the Vuex store. This will be in the form of an array of objects. Each object will contain several key pieces of information that will allow us to display the products in the basket without having to query the Vuex store each time. It also allows us to store details about the current state of the product page—remembering the image updates when a variant is selected.

The details we're going to store for each product added to the basket are as follows:

- Product title
- Product handle, so we can link back to the product
- Selected variation title (as it appears in the select box)
- Currently selected image, so we can show an appropriate image in the Checkout
- Variation details, this contains price and weight along with other details
- Variation SKU, this will help us identify whether the product has already been added
- Quantity, how many items the user has added to their basket

As we will be storing all this information within an object, contained in an array, we need to create a placeholder array within the store. Add a new key to the `state` object within the store titled `basket` and make it a blank array:

```
const store = new Vuex.Store({
  state: {
    products: {},
    categories: {},

    categoryHome: {
      title: 'Welcome to the Shop',
      handle: 'home',
      products: [
        ...
      ]
    },

    basket: []

  },

  mutations: {
    ...
  },

  actions: {
    ...
  },

  getters: {
    ...
  }
});
```

Adding product information to the store

With our `basket` array ready to receive data, we can now create a mutation to add the product object. Open the `ProductPage.js` file and update the `addToBasket` method to call a `$store` commit function, instead of the `alert` we put in place.

All of the information we require for products to be added to the basket is stored on the `ProductPage` component—so we can pass the component instance through to the `commit()` function using the `this` keyword. This will become clear when we build the mutation.

Add the function call to the `ProductPage` method:

```
methods: {
  ...

  addToBasket() {
    this.$store.commit('addToBasket', this);
  }
}
```

Creating the store mutation to add products to the basket

Navigate to the Vuex store and create a new mutation titled `addToBasket`. This will accept the `state` as the first parameter and the component instance as the second. Passing the instance through allows us to access the variables, methods, and computed values on the component:

```
mutations: {
  products(state, payload) {
    ...
  },

  categories(state, payload) {
    ...
  },

  addToBasket(state, item) {
  }
}
```

We can now proceed with adding the products to the `basket` array. The first step is to add the product object with the mentioned properties. As it's an array, we can use the `push()` function to add the object.

Next, add an object to the array, using the `item` and its properties to build the object. With access to the `ProductPage` component, we can construct the variant title as it appears in the select box, using the `variantTitle` method. Set the quantity to 1 by default:

```
addToBasket(state, item) {
  state.basket.push({
    sku: item.variation.sku,
    title: item.product.title,
    handle: item.slug,
    image: item.image,
    variationTitle: item.variantTitle(item.variation),
    variation: item.variation,
    quantity: 1
  });
}
```

This now adds the product to the `basket` array. An issue appears, however, when you add two of the same item to the basket. Rather than increasing the `quantity`, it simply adds a second product.

This can be remedied by checking if the `sku` exists within the array already. If it does, we can increment the quantity on that item, if not we can add a new item to the `basket` array. The `sku` is unique for each variation of each product. Alternatively, we could use the barcode property.

Using the native `find` JavaScript function, we can identify any products that have an SKU matching that of the one being passed in:

```
addToBasket(state, item) {
  let product = state.basket.find(p => {
    if(p.sku == item.variation.sku) {
    }
  });

  state.basket.push({
    sku: item.variation.sku,
    title: item.product.title,
    handle: item.slug,
    image: item.image,
    variationTitle: item.variantTitle(item.variation),
    variation: item.variation,
```

```
      quantity: 1
    });
  }
```

If it matches, we can increment the quantity by one on that object, using the ++ notation in JavaScript. If not, we can add the new object to the basket array. When using the find function, we can return the product if it exists. If not, we can add a new item:

```
addToBasket(state, item) {
  let product = state.basket.find(p => {
    if(p.sku == item.variation.sku) {
      p.quantity++;

      return p;
    }
  });

  if(!product) {
    state.basket.push({
      sku: item.variation.sku,
      title: item.product.title,
      handle: item.slug,
      image: item.image,
      variationTitle: item.variantTitle(item.variation),
      variation: item.variation,
      quantity: 1
    });
  }
}
```

We now have a basket being populated as the item is added to the basket, and incrementing when it exists already.

To improve the usability of the app, we should give the user some feedback when they have added an item to the basket. This can be done by updating the "Add to Basket" button briefly and showing a product count with a link to the basket in the header of the site.

Updating the Add to basket button when adding an item

As a usability improvement to our shop, we are going to update the **Add to basket** button when a user clicks it. This will change to **Added to your basket** and apply a class for a set period of time, for example, two seconds, before returning to its previous state. The CSS class will allow you to style the button differently—for example, changing the background to green or transforming it slightly.

This will be achieved by using a data property on the component—setting it to `true` and `false` as the item gets added. The CSS class and text will use this property to determine what to show and a `setTimeout` JavaScript function will change the state of the property.

Open the `ProductPage` component and add a new key to the data object titled `addedToBasket`. Set this to `false` by default:

```
data() {
  return {
    slug: this.$route.params.slug,
    productNotFound: false,
    image: false,
    variation: false,
    addedToBasket: false
  }
}
```

Update the button text to allow for this variation. As there is already a ternary `if` within this, we are going to nest them with another one. This could be abstracted into a method if desired.

Replace the `Add to basket` condition in your button with an additional ternary operator, dependent on whether the `addedToBasket` variable is true. We can also add a conditional class based on this property:

```
<button
  @click="addToBasket()"
  :class="(addedToBasket) ? 'isAdded' : ''"
  :disabled="!variation.quantity"
>
  {{
    (variation.quantity) ?
    ((addedToBasket) ? 'Added to your basket' : 'Add to basket') :
    'Out of stock'
  }}
```

```
</button>
```

Refresh the app and navigate to a product to ensure the correct text is being shown. Update the addedToBasket variable to true to make sure everything is displaying as it should. Set it back to false.

Next, within the addToBasket() method, set the property to true. This should update the text when the item is added to the basket:

```
addToBasket() {
  this.$store.commit('addToBasket', this);

  this.addedToBasket = true;
}
```

When you click the button, the text will now update, however it will never reset. Add a setTimeout JavaScript function afterward, which sets it back to false after a certain period of time:

```
addToBasket() {
  this.$store.commit('addToBasket', this);

  this.addedToBasket = true;
  setTimeout(() => this.addedToBasket = false, 2000);
}
```

The timing for setTimeout is in milliseconds, so 2000 is equal to two seconds. Feel free to tweak and play with this figure as much as you see fit.

One last addition would be to reset this value back to false if the variation is updated or the product is changed. Add the statement to both watch functions:

```
watch: {
  variation(v) {
    if(v.hasOwnProperty('image')) {
      this.updateImage(v.image);
    }
    this.addedToBasket = false;
  },

  '$route'(to) {
    this.slug = to.params.slug;
    this.addedToBasket = false;
  }
}
```

Showing the product count in the header of the app

It's common practice for a shop to show a link to the cart in the site's header—along with the number of items in the cart next to it. To achieve this, we'll use a Vuex getter to calculate and return the number of items in the basket.

Open the `index.html` file and add a `<header>` element to the app HTML and insert a placeholder, `span`—we'll convert this to a link once we've set up the routes. Within the span, output a `cartQuantity` variable:

```
<div id="app">
  <header>
    <span>Cart {{ cartQuantity }}</span>
  </header>
  <main>
    <router-view></router-view>
  </main>
  <aside>
    <router-view name="sidebar"></router-view>
  </aside>
</div>
```

Navigate to your `Vue` instance and create a `computed` object containing a `cartQuantity` function:

```
new Vue({
    el: '#app',

    store,
    router,

    computed: {
      cartQuantity() {
      }
    },

    created() {
      CSV.fetch({url: './data/csv-files/bicycles.csv'}).then(data => {
        this.$store.dispatch('initializeShop', this.$formatProducts(data));
      });
    }
});
```

If our header were to feature more items than our cart link, it would be advisable to abstract it out into a separate component to keep the methods, layout, and functions contained. However, as it is only going to feature this one link in our example app, adding the function to the `Vue` instance will suffice.

Create a new getter in the store titled `cartQuantity`. As a placeholder, return `1`. The `state` will be required to calculate the quantity, so ensure that is passed into the function for now:

```
getters: {
  ...

  cartQuantity: (state) => {
    return 1;
  }
}
```

Head back to your `Vue` instance and return the result of the getter. Ideally, we want to show the count of the `basket` in brackets, but we only want to show the brackets if there are items. Within the computed function, check the result of this getter and output the result with brackets if the result exists:

```
cartQuantity() {
  const quantity = this.$store.getters.cartQuantity;
  return quantity ? `(${quantity})` : '';
}
```

Changing the result within the Vuex getter should reveal either the number in brackets or nothing at all.

Calculating the basket quantity

With the display logic in place, we can now proceed with calculating how many items are in the basket. We could count the number of items in the `basket` array, however, this will only tell us how many different products are there now and not if the same product was added many times.

Instead, we need to loop through each product in the basket and add the quantities together. Create a variable called `quantity` and set it to `0`. Loop through the basket items and add the `item.quantity` variable to the `quantity` variable. Lastly, return our variable with the right sum:

```
cartQuantity: (state) => {
  let quantity = 0;
  for(let item of state.basket) {
    quantity += item.quantity;
  }
  return quantity;
}
```

Navigate to the app and add some items to your basket to verify the basket count is being calculated correctly.

Finalizing the Shop Vue-router URLs

We're now at a stage where we can finalize the URLs for our shop - including creating the redirects and Checkout links. Referring back to `Chapter 8`, *Introducing Vue-Router and Loading URL-Based Components*, we can see which ones we are missing. These are:

- `/category` -redirect to `/`
- `/product` - redirect to `/`
- `/basket` - load `OrderBasket` component
- `/checkout`- load `OrderCheckout` component
- `/complete`- load `OrderConfirmation` component

Create the redirects in the appropriate places within the routes array. At the bottom of the routes array, create three new routes for the `Order` components:

```
routes: [
  {
    path: '/',
    name: 'Home',
    ...
  },
  {
    path: '/category',
    redirect: {name: 'Home'}
  },
  {
```

```
    path: '/category/:slug',
    name: 'Category',
    ...
  },
  {
    path: '/product',
    redirect: {name: 'Home'}
  },
  {
    path: '/product/:slug',
    name: 'Product',
    component: ProductPage
  },
  {
    path: '/basket',
    name: 'Basket',
    component: OrderBasket
  },
  {
    path: '/checkout',
    name: 'Checkout',
    component: OrderCheckout
  },
  {
    path: '/complete',
    name: 'Confirmation',
    component: OrderConfirmation
  },

  {
    path: '/404',
    alias: '*',
    component: PageNotFound
  }
]
```

We can now update the placeholder <span> in the header of our app with a router-link:

```
<header>
  <router-link :to="{name: 'Basket'}">Cart {{ cartQuantity }}</router-link>
</header>
```

Building the Order process and ListProducts component

For the three steps of the Checkout, we are going to be utilizing the same component in all three: the `ListProducts` component. In the `OrderCheckout`, and `OrderConfirmation` components, it will be in a fixed, uneditable state, whereas when it is in the `OrderBasket` component, the user needs to be able to update quantities and remove items if desired.

As we're going to be working at the Checkout, we need products to exist in the `basket` array. To save us having to find products and add them to the basket every time we refresh the app, we can ensure there are some products in the `basket` array by hardcoding an array in the store.

To achieve this, navigate to a few products and add them to your basket. Ensure there is a good selection of products and quantities for testing. Next, open your JavaScript console in the browser and enter the following command:

```
console.log(JSON.stringify(store.state.basket));
```

This will output a string of your products array. Copy this and paste it into your store—replacing the `basket` array:

```
state: {
  products: {},
  categories: {},

  categoryHome: {
    title: 'Welcome to the Shop',
    handle: 'home',
    products: [
      ...
    ]
  },

  basket: [{"sku":...}]
},
```

On page load, your **Cart** count in the header should update to be the correct number of items you added.

We can now proceed with building our Checkout process. The product display in the basket is more complicated than the **Checkout** and **Order Confirmation** screens so, unusually, we'll work backward. Starting with the **Order Confirmation** page and moving to the **Checkout** page, adding more complexity before we head to the basket, adding the ability to exit the products.

Order Confirmation screen

The Order Confirmation screen is one that is shown once the order is complete. This confirms the items purchased and may include the expected delivery date.

Create a template within the `OrderConfirmation.js` file with a `<h1>` and some relevant content relating to the order being complete:

```
const OrderConfirmation = {
  name: 'OrderConfirmation',

  template: `<div>
    <h1>Order Complete!</h1>
    <p>Thanks for shopping with us - you can expect your products within 2
- 3 working days</p>
  </div>`
};
```

Open up the application in your browser, add a product to your basket and complete an order to confirm it's working. The next step is to include the `ListProducts` component. First, ensure the `ListProducts` component is correctly initialized and features an initial template:

```
const ListPurchases = {
  name: 'ListPurchases',

  template: `<table></table>`
};
```

Add the `components` object to the `OrderConfirmation` component and include the `ListProducts` component. Next, include it in the template:

```
const OrderConfirmation = {
  name: 'OrderConfirmation',

  template: `<div>
    <h1>Order Complete!</h1>
    <p>Thanks for shopping with us - you can expect your products within 2
```

```
  - 3 working days</p>
    <list-purchases />
  </div>`,

  components: {
    ListPurchases
  }
};
```

Open the `ListPurchases` component once more to start displaying the products. The default state of this component will be to list the products in the basket, along with the variation selected. The price for each product will be displayed, along with the price if the quantity is more than one. Lastly, a grand total will be shown.

The first step is to get the basket list into our component. Create a `computed` object with a `products` function. This should return the basket products:

```
const ListPurchases = {
  name: 'ListPurchases',

  template: `<table></table>`,

  computed: {
    products() {
      return this.$store.state.basket;
    }
  }
};
```

With the products in the basket now available to us, we can loop through them in the table displaying the information required. This includes a thumbnail image, the product and variation title, price, quantity, and the total price of the item. Add a header row to the table too, so the user knows what the column is:

```
template: `<table>
  <thead>
    <tr>
      <th></th>
      <th>Title</th>
      <th>Unit price</th>
      <th>Quantity</th>
      <th>Price</th>
    </tr>
  </thead>
  <tbody>
    <tr v-for="product in products">
      <td>
```

```
            <img
              :src="product.image.source"
              :alt="product.image.alt || product.variationTitle"
              width="80"
            >
          </td>
          <td>
            <router-link :to="{name: 'Product', params: {slug:
product.handle}}">
                {{ product.title }}
            </router-link><br>
            {{ product.variationTitle }}
          </td>
          <td>{{ product.variation.price }}</td>
          <td>{{ product.quantity }}</td>
          <td>{{ product.variation.price * product.quantity }}</td>
        </tr>
      </tbody>
    </table>`,
```

Note that the price for each row is simply the unit price multiplied by the quantity. We now have a standard product list of the items the user has purchased.

Using Vue filters to format the price

The price is currently an integer, as that it is in the data. On the product page, we just prepended a $ sign to represent a price, however, this is now the perfect opportunity to utilize Vue filters. Filters allow you to manipulate the data in the template without using a method. Filters can be chained and are used to carry out, generally, a single modification—for example converting a string to lowercase or formatting a number to be a currency.

Filters are used with the pipe (|) operator. If, for example, we had a filter to lowercase text, it would be used like the following:

```
{{ product.title | lowercase }}
```

Filters are declared within a `filters` object on the component and accept a single parameter of the output preceding it.

Create a `filters` object within the `ListPurchases` component and create a function inside titled `currency()`. This function accepts a single parameter of `val` and should return the variable inside:

```
filters: {
  currency(val) {
    return val;
  }
},
```

We can now use this function to manipulate the price integers. Add the filter to both the unit and total price within the template:

```
<td>{{ product.variation.price | currency }}</td>
<td>{{ product.quantity }}</td>
<td>{{ product.variation.price * product.quantity | currency }}</td>
```

You won't notice anything in the browser, as we have yet to manipulate the value. Update the function to ensure the number is fixed to two decimal places and has a $ preceding it:

```
filters: {
  currency(val) {
    return ' + val.toFixed(2);
  }
},
```

Our prices are now nicely formatted and displaying correctly.

Calculating a total price

The next addition to our purchase list is a total value of the basket. This will need to be calculated in a similar way to the basket count we did earlier.

Create a new `computed` function title: `totalPrice`. This function should loop through the products and add the price up, taking into consideration any multiple quantities:

```
totalPrice() {
  let total = 0;

  for(let p of this.products) {
    total += (p.variation.price * p.quantity);
  }

  return total;
}
```

We can now update our template to include the total price—ensuring we pass it through the `currency` filter:

```
template: `<table>
  <thead>
    <tr>
      <th></th>
      <th>Title</th>
      <th>Unit price</th>
      <th>Quantity</th>
      <th>Price</th>
    </tr>
  </thead>
  <tbody>
    <tr v-for="product in products">
      <td>
        <img
          :src="product.image.source"
          :alt="product.image.alt || product.variationTitle"
          width="80"
        >
      </td>
      <td>
        <router-link :to="{name: 'Product', params: {slug:
product.handle}}">
          {{ product.title }}
        </router-link><br>
        {{ product.variationTitle }}
      </td>
      <td>{{ product.variation.price | currency }}</td>
      <td>{{ product.quantity }}</td>
      <td>{{ product.variation.price * product.quantity | currency }}</td>
    </tr>
  </tbody>
  <tfoot>
    <td colspan="4">
      <strong>Total:</strong>
    </td>
    <td>{{ totalPrice | currency }}</td>
  </tfoot>
</table>`,
```

Creating an Order Checkout page

Our `OrderCheckout` page will have a similar makeup to the `OrderConfirmation` page -
however, in a real shop, this would be the page before payment. This page would allow the
user to fill in their billing and delivery details before navigating to the payment page. Copy
the `OrderConfirmation` page and update the title and info text:

```
const OrderCheckout = {
  name: 'OrderCheckout',

  template: '<div>;
    <h1>Order Confirmation</h1>
    <p>Please check the items below and fill in your details to complete
your order</p>
    <list-purchases />
  </div>',

  components: {
    ListPurchases
  }
};
```

Below the `<list-purchases />` component, create a form with several fields so we can
collect the billing and delivery name and addresses. For this example, just collect the name,
first line of the address, and ZIP code:

```
template: '<div>
  <h1>Order Confirmation</h1>
  <p>Please check the items below and fill in your details to complete your
order</p>
  <list-purchases />

  <form>
    <fieldset>
      <h2>Billing Details</h2>
      <label for="billingName">Name:</label>
      <input type="text" id="billingName">
      <label for="billingAddress">Address:</label>
      <input type="text" id="billingAddress">
      <label for="billingZipcode">Post code/Zip code:</label>
      <input type="text" id="billingZipcode">
    </fieldset>
    <fieldset>
      <h2>Delivery Details</h2>
      <label for="deliveryName">Name:</label>
      <input type="text" id="deliveryName">
```

```
        <label for="deliveryAddress">Address:</label>
        <input type="text" id="deliveryAddress">
        <label for="deliveryZipcode">Post code/Zip code:</label>
        <input type="text" id="deliveryZipcode">
      </fieldset>
    </form>
  </div>',
```

We now need to create a data object and bind each field to a key. To help group each set, create an object for both `delivery` and `billing` and create the fields inside with the correct names:

```
data() {
  return {
    billing: {
      name: '',
      address: '',
      zipcode: ''
    },
    delivery: {
      name: '',
      address: '',
      zipcode: ''
    }
  }
}
```

Add a `v-model` to each input, linking it to the appropriate data key:

```
<form>
  <fieldset>
    <h2>Billing Details</h2>
    <label for="billingName">Name:</label>
    <input type="text" id="billingName" v-model="billing.name">
    <label for="billingAddress">Address:</label>
    <input type="text" id="billingAddress" v-model="billing.address">
    <label for="billingZipcode">Post code/Zip code:</label>
    <input type="text" id="billingZipcode" v-model="billing.zipcode">
  </fieldset>
  <fieldset>
    <h2>Delivery Details</h2>
    <label for="deliveryName">Name:</label>
    <input type="text" id="deliveryName" v-model="delivery.name">
    <label for="deliveryAddress">Address:</label>
    <input type="text" id="deliveryAddress" v-model="delivery.address">
    <label for="deliveryZipcode">Post code/Zip code:</label>
    <input type="text" id="deliveryZipcode" v-model="delivery.zipcode">
```

```
    </fieldset>
  </form>
```

The next step is to create a `submit` method and collate the data to be able to pass it on to the next screen. Create a new method titled `submitForm()`. As we are not handling payment in this example, we can route to the confirmation page in the method:

```
methods: {
  submitForm() {
    // this.billing = billing details
    // this.delivery = delivery details
    this.$router.push({name: 'Confirmation'});
  }
}
```

We can now bind a `submit` event to the form and add a submit button. Like the `v-bind:click` attribute (or `@click`), Vue allows you to bind a `submit` event to a method using a `@submit=""` attribute.

Add the declaration to the `<form>` element and create a submit button in your form:

```
<form @submit="submitForm()">
  <fieldset>
    ...
  </fieldset>

  <fieldset>
    ...
  </fieldset>

  <input type="submit" value="Purchase items">
</form>
```

On submitting your form, the app should redirect you to our Confirmation page.

Copying details between addresses

One feature that several shops have is the ability to mark the delivery address to be the same as the billing address. There are several ways we could approach this, and how you choose to do it is up to you. The immediate options are:

- Have a "copy details" button—this copies the details from billing to delivery but does not keep them in sync

- Have a checkbox that keeps the two in sync—checking the box disables the delivery box fields but populates them with the billing details

For this example, we are going to code the second option.

Create a checkbox between the two fieldsets that is bound to a property in the data object via v-model called sameAddress:

```
<form @submit="submitForm()">
  <fieldset>
    ...
  </fieldset>
  <label for="sameAddress">
    <input type="checkbox" id="sameAddress" v-model ="sameAddress">
    Delivery address is the same as billing
  </label>
  <fieldset>
    ...
  </fieldset>

  <input type="submit" value="Purchase items">
</form>
```

Create a new key in the data object and set it to false by default:

```
data() {
  return {
    sameAddress: false,
    billing: {
      name: '',
      address: '',
      zipcode: ''
    },
    delivery: {
      name: '',
      address: '',
      zipcode: ''
    }
  }
},
```

The next step is to disable the delivery fields if the checkbox is checked. This can be done by activating the `disabled` HTML attribute based on the checkbox result. In a similar way to how we disabled the "Add to cart" button on the product page, bind the disabled attribute on the delivery fields to the `sameAddress` variable:

```
<fieldset>
  <h2>Delivery Details</h2>
  <label for="deliveryName">Name:</label>
  <input type="text" id="deliveryName" v-model="delivery.name"
:disabled="sameAddress">
  <label for="deliveryAddress">Address:</label>
  <input type="text" id="deliveryAddress" v-model="delivery.address"
:disabled="sameAddress">
  <label for="deliveryZipcode">Post code/Zip code:</label>
  <input type="text" id="deliveryZipcode" v-model="delivery.zipcode"
:disabled="sameAddress">
</fieldset>
```

Checking the box will now deactivate the fields - making the user unable to enter any data. The next step is to replicate the data across the two sections. As our data objects are the same structure, we can create a `watch` function to set the `delivery` object to the same as the `billing` object when the checkbox is checked.

Create a new `watch` object and function for the `sameAddress` variable. If it is `true`, set the delivery object to the same as the billing one:

```
watch: {
  sameAddress() {
    if(this.sameAddress) {
      this.delivery = this.billing;
    }
  }
}
```

With the `watch` function added, we can enter data into the billing address, check the box, and the delivery address gets populated. The best thing about this is that they now stay in sync, so if you update the billing address, the delivery address updates on the fly. The problem arises when you uncheck the box and edit the billing address—the delivery address still updates. This is because we have bound the objects together.

Add an `else` statement to make a *copy* of the billing address when the box is unchecked:

```
watch: {
  sameAddress() {
    if(this.sameAddress) {
      this.delivery = this.billing;
    } else {
      this.delivery = Object.assign({}, this.billing);
    }
  }
}
```

We now have a functioning Order Confirmation page, which collects billing and delivery details.

Creating an editable basket

We now need to create our basket. This needs to show the products in a similar fashion to the Checkout and Confirmation, but it needs to give the user the ability to edit the basket contents—either to delete an item or update the quantity.

As a starting point, open `OrderBasket.js` and include the `list-purchases` component, as we did on the confirmation page:

```
const OrderBasket = {
  name: 'OrderBasket',

  template: `<div>
    <h1>Basket</h1>
    <list-purchases />
  </div>`,

  components: {
    ListPurchases
  }
};
```

The next thing we need to do is edit the `list-purchases` component. To ensure we can differentiate between the views, we are going to add an `editable` prop. This will be set to `false` by default and `true` in the basket. Add the `prop` to the component in the basket:

```
template: `<div>
  <h1>Basket</h1>
  <list-purchases :editable="true" />
</div>`,
```

We now need to tell the `ListPurchases` component to accept this parameter so we can do something with it within the component:

```
props: {
  editable: {
    type: Boolean,
    default: false
  }
},
```

Creating editable fields

We now have a prop determining if our basket should be editable or not. This allows us to show the delete links and make the quantity an editable box.

Create a new table cell next to the quantity one in the `ListPurchases` component and make it visible only when the purchases are visible. Make the static quantity hidden in this state too. In the new cell, add an input box with the value set to the quantity. We are also going to bind a `blur` event to the box. The `blur` event is a native JavaScript event that triggers when the input is unfocused. On blur, trigger an `updateQuantity` method. This method should accept two arguments; the event, which will contain the new quantity, and the SKU for that particular product:

```
<tbody>
  <tr v-for="product in products">
    <td>
      <img
        :src="product.image.source"
        :alt="product.image.alt || product.variationTitle"
        width="80"
      >
    </td>
    <td>
      <router-link :to="{name: 'Product', params: {slug: product.handle}}">
        {{ product.title }}
```

```
      </router-link><br>
      {{ product.variationTitle }}
    </td>
    <td>{{ product.variation.price | currency }}</td>
    <td v-if="!editable">{{ product.quantity }}</td>
    <td v-if="editable">
      <input
        type="text"
        :value="product.quantity"
        @blur="updateQuantity($event, product.sku)"
      >
    </td>
    <td>{{ product.variation.price * product.quantity | currency }}</td>
  </tr>
</tbody>
```

Create the new method on the component. This method should loop through the products, locating the one with a matching SKU and updating the quantity to an integer. We also need to update the store with the result - so that the quantity can be updated at the top of the page. We'll create a general mutation that accepts the full `basket` array back with new values to allow the same one to be used for the product deletion.

Create the mutation that updates the quantity and commits a mutation titled `updatePurchases`:

```
methods: {
  updateQuantity(e, sku) {
    let products = this.products.map(p => {
      if(p.sku == sku) {
        p.quantity = parseInt(e.target.value);
      }
      return p;
    });

    this.$store.commit('updatePurchases', products);
  }
}
```

In the store, create the mutation that sets the `state.basket` equal to the payload:

```
updatePurchases(state, payload) {
  state.basket = payload;
}
```

Updating the quantity should now update the total price of the item and the basket count at the top of the page.

Removing items from your cart

The next step is to give the user the ability to remove items from their cart. Create a button in the `ListPurchases` component with a click binding. This button can go anywhere you want - our example shows it as an extra cell at the end of the row. Bind the click action to a method titled `removeItem`. This just needs to accept a single parameter of the SKU. Add the following to the `ListPurchases` component:

```
<tbody>
  <tr v-for="product in products">
    <td>
      <img
        :src="product.image.source"
        :alt="product.image.alt || product.variationTitle"
        width="80"
      >
    </td>
    <td>
      <router-link :to="{name: 'Product', params: {slug: product.handle}}">
        {{ product.title }}
      </router-link><br>
      {{ product.variationTitle }}
    </td>
    <td>{{ product.variation.price | currency }}</td>
    <td v-if="!editable">{{ product.quantity }}</td>
    <td v-if="editable"><input
      type="text"
      :value="product.quantity"
      @blur="updateQuantity($event, product.sku)"
    ></td>
    <td>{{ product.variation.price * product.quantity | currency }}</td>
    <td v-if="editable">
      <button @click="removeItem(product.sku)">Remove item</button>
    </td>
  </tr>
</tbody>
```

Create the `removeItem` method. This method should filter the `basket` array, only returning the objects that *don't* match the SKU passed in. Once the result is filtered, pass the result to the same mutation we used in the `updateQuantity()` method:

```
removeItem(sku) {
  let products = this.products.filter(p => {
    if(p.sku != sku) {
      return p;
    }
  });
  this.$store.commit('updatePurchases', products);
}
```

One last enhancement we can make is to trigger the `removeItem` method if the quantity is set to 0. Within the `updateQuantity` method, check the value before looping through the products. If it is 0, or doesn't exist, run the `removeItem` method - passing the SKU through:

```
updateQuantity(e, sku) {
  if(!parseInt(e.target.value)) {
    this.removeItem(sku);
  } else {
    let products = this.products.map(p => {
      if(p.sku == sku) {
        p.quantity = parseInt(e.target.value);
      }
      return p;
    });

    this.$store.commit('updatePurchases', products);
  }
},
```

Completing the shop SPA

The last step is to add a link from the `OrderBasket` component to the `OrderCheckout` page. This can be done by linking to the `Checkout` route. With that, your checkout is complete, along with your shop! Add the following link to the basket:

```
template: `<div>
  <h1>Basket</h1>
  <list-purchases :editable="true" />
  <router-link :to="{name: 'Checkout'}">Proceed to Checkout</router-link>
</div>`,
```

Summary

Well done! You have created a full shop single-page application using Vue.js. You have learned how to list products and their variations, along with adding specific variations to the basket. You've learned how to create shop filters and category links, along with creating an editable shopping basket.

As with everything, there are always improvements to be made. Why don't you give some of these ideas a go?

- Persisting the basket using localStorage—so products added to the basket are retained between visits and the user pressing refresh
- Calculating shipping based on the weight attribute of the products in the basket—use a switch statement to create bands
- Allowing products without variations to be added to the basket from the category listing page
- Indicating which products have items out of stock when filtered on that variation on the category page
- Any ideas of your own!

12
Using Vue Dev Tools and Testing Your SPA

Over the last 11 chapters, we've been developing several **Single-Page Applications (SPAs)** using Vue.js. Although development is a big chunk of creating an SPA, testing also forms a significant part of creating any JavaScript web app.

The Vue developer tools, available in Chrome and Firefox, provide great insights into the components being used within a certain view or the current state of the Vuex store – along with any events being emitted from the JavaScript. These tools allow you to check and validate the data within your app while developing to ensure everything is as it should be.

The other side of SPA testing is with automated tests. Conditions, rules, and routes you write to automate tasks within your app, allow you to then specify what the output should be and the test runs the conditions to verify whether the results match.

In this chapter, we will:

- Cover the usage of the Vue developer tools with the applications we've developed
- Have an overview of testing tools and applications

Using the Vue.js developer tools

The Vue developer tools are available for Chrome and Firefox and can be downloaded from GitHub (`https://github.com/vuejs/vue-devtools`). Once installed, they become an extension of the browser developer tools. For example, in Chrome, they appear after the **Audits** tab.

The Vue developer tools will only work when you are using Vue in development mode. By default, the unminified version of Vue has the development mode enabled. However, if you are using the production version of the code, the development tools can be enabled by setting the `devtools` variable to `true` in your code:

```
Vue.config.devtools = true
```

Throughout the book, we've been using the development version of Vue, so the dev tools should work with all three of the SPAs we have developed. Open the Dropbox example and open the Vue developer tools.

Inspecting Vue components data and computed values

The Vue developer tools give a great overview of the components in use on the page. You can also drill down into the components and preview the data in use on that particular instance. This is perfect for inspecting the properties of each component on the page at any given time.

For example, if we inspect the Dropbox app and navigate to the **Components** tab, we can see the **<Root>** Vue instance and we can see the **<DropboxViewer>** component. Clicking this will reveal all of the data properties of the component – along with any computed properties. This lets us validate whether the structure is constructed correctly, along with the computed path property:

Drilling down into each component, we can access individual data objects and computed properties.

Using the Vue developer tools for inspecting your application is a much more efficient way of validating data while creating your app, as it saves having to place several `console.log()` statements.

Viewing Vuex mutations and time-travel

Navigating to the next tab, **Vuex**, allows us to watch store mutations taking place in real time. Every time a mutation is fired, a new line is created in the left-hand panel. This element allows us to view what data is being sent, and what the Vuex store looked like before and after the data had been committed.

It also gives you several options to revert, commit, and time-travel to any point. Loading the Dropbox app, several structure mutations immediately populate within the left-hand panel, listing the mutation name and the time they occurred. This is the code pre-caching the folders in action. Clicking on each one will reveal the Vuex store state – along with a mutation containing the payload sent. The state display is *after* the payload has been sent and the mutation committed. To preview what the state looked like *before* that mutation, select the preceding option:

On each entry, next to the mutation name, you will notice three symbols that allow you to carry out several actions and directly mutate the store in your browser:

- **Commit this mutation**: This allows you to commit all the data up to that point. This will *remove* all of the mutations from the dev tools and update the **Base State** to this point. This is handy if there are several mutations occurring that you wish to keep track of.

- **Revert this mutation**: This will undo the mutation and all mutations after this point. This allows you to carry out the same actions again and again without pressing refresh or losing your current place. For example, when adding a product to the basket in our shop app, a mutation occurs. Using this would allow you to remove the product from the basket and undo any following mutations without navigating away from the product page.
- **Time-travel to this state**: This allows you to preview the app and state at that particular mutation, without reverting any mutations that occur after the selected point.

The mutations tab also allows you to commit or revert all mutations at the top of the left-hand panel. Within the right-hand panel, you can also import and export a JSON encoded version of the store's state. This is particularly handy when you want to re-test several circumstances and instances without having to reproduce several steps.

Previewing event data

The **Events** tab of the Vue developer tools works in a similar way to the Vuex tab, allowing you to inspect any events emitted throughout your app. Our Dropbox app doesn't use events, so open up the people-filtering app we created in `Chapter 2`, *Displaying, Looping, Searching, and Filtering Data*, and `Chapter 3`, *Optimizing our App and Using Components to Display Data*, of this book.

Changing the filters in this app emits an event each time the filter type is updated, along with the filter query:

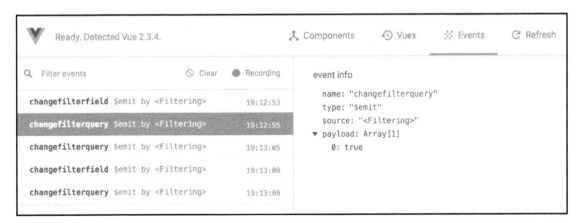

The left-hand panel again lists the name of the event and the time it occurred. The right panel contains information about the event, including its component origin and payload. This data allows you to ensure the event data is as you expected it to be and, if not, helps you locate where the event is being triggered.

The Vue dev tools are invaluable, especially as your JavaScript application gets bigger and more complex. Open the shop SPA we developed and inspect the various components and Vuex data to get an idea of how this tool can help you create applications that only commit mutations they need to and emit the events they have to.

Testing your SPA

The majority of Vue testing suites revolve around having command-line knowledge and creating a Vue application using the **CLI** (**command-line interface**). Along with creating applications in frontend-compatible JavaScript, Vue also has a CLI that allows you to create applications using component-based files. These are files with a `.vue` extension and contain the template HTML along with the JavaScript required for the component. They also allow you to create scoped CSS – styles that only apply to that component. If you chose to create your app using the CLI, all of the theory and a lot of the practical knowledge you have learned in this book can easily be ported across.

Command-line unit testing

Along with component files, the Vue CLI allows you to integrate with command-line unit tests easier, such as Jest, Mocha, Chai, and TestCafe (`https://testcafe.devexpress.com/`). For example, TestCafe allows you to specify several different tests, including checking whether content exists, to clicking buttons to test functionality. An example of a TestCafe test checking to see if our filtering component in our first app contains the work *Field* would be:

```
test('The filtering contains the word "filter"', async testController => {
  const filterSelector = await new Selector('body > #app > form >
label:nth-child(1)');

  await testController.expect(paragraphSelector.innerText).eql('Filter');
});
```

This test would then equate to `true` or `false`. Unit tests are generally written in conjunction with components themselves, allowing components to be reused and tested in isolation. This allows you to check that external factors have no bearing on the output of your tests.

Most command-line JavaScript testing libraries will integrate with Vue.js; there is a great list available in the awesome Vue GitHub repository (`https://github.com/vuejs/awesome-vue#test`).

Browser automation

The alternative to using command-line unit testing is to automate your browser with a testing suite. This kind of testing is still triggered via the command line, but rather than integrating directly with your Vue application, it opens the page in the browser and interacts with it like a user would. A popular tool for doing this is `Nightwatch.js` (`http://nightwatchjs.org/`).

You may use this suite for opening your shop and interacting with the filtering component or product list ordering and comparing the result. The tests are written in very colloquial English and are not restricted to being on the same domain name or file network as the site to be tested. The library is also language agnostic – working for any website regardless of what it is built with.

The example `Nightwatch.js` gives on their website is for opening Google and ensuring the first result of a Google search for `rembrandt van rijn` is the Wikipedia entry:

```
module.exports = {
  'Demo test Google' : function (client) {
    client
      .url('http://www.google.com')
      .waitForElementVisible('body', 1000)
      .assert.title('Google')
      .assert.visible('input[type=text]')
      .setValue('input[type=text]', 'rembrandt van rijn')
      .waitForElementVisible('button[name=btnG]', 1000)
      .click('button[name=btnG]')
      .pause(1000)
      .assert.containsText('ol#rso li:first-child',
        'Rembrandt - Wikipedia')
      .end();
  }
};
```

An alternative to Nightwatch is Selenium (`http://www.seleniumhq.org/`). Selenium has the advantage of having a Firefox extension that allows you to visually create tests and commands.

Testing, especially for big applications, is paramount – especially when deploying your application to a development environment. Whether you choose unit testing or browser automation, there is a host of articles and books available on the subject.

Summary

Throughout this book, we have covered several techniques, and learned how to use Vue and official Vue plugins. We covered how to build three single-page applications, covering different methodologies and approaches while doing so.

In the first section of the book, we covered how to initialize a Vue instance. We explored looping through data and how to create a user interface to filter the data displayed. We also looked at how to conditionally render CSS classes on each row.

We then moved on to integrating Vuex into our applications and communicating with an API, with Dropbox being the example. We looked at accessing data and storing it locally. This helped to improve the performance of the app and speed it up, improving the user experience.

Lastly, we created a mock shop. Using real data from Shopify CSV files, we created an application that allowed products to be viewed individually. We also created a category listing page that could be filtered and ordered, allowing the user to find specifically the products they wanted. To complete the experience, we built an editable **Basket**, **Checkout**, and **Order Confirmation** screen.

In this chapter, we covered the use of the Vue dev tools, followed by how to build tests. This completed the process of building single-page applications with `Vue.js`.

Index

filtering 36, 37, 38, 39, 40
CSS classes
  modifying 42, 44, 45, 46
CSV
  loading 243, 244
  loading, with CSV Parser 246
  loading, with d3 library 244, 246
  products, storing 248, 249, 250
curated list
  creating, for home page 305
current path
  breadcrumb, creating from 123, 124, 125, 126,
    127, 128
custom classes 46

D

data
  displaying 27, 100
  filtering 31
  loading, from store 162, 163
  passing, to components 67, 69, 73
  storing 163, 164
declarative rendering 23
DocBlock 193
download links
  caching, on files 190, 191
Dropbox app
  creating 99, 100
Dropbox data
  displaying 104, 106
  retrieving 101, 102
dropbox-viewer component
  updating, to work with Vuex 155, 156
dynamic routes, with parameters
  about 211, 213, 214, 215
  GET parameters 216
  props, using 216, 217

E

editable basket
  creating 375, 376
  editable fields, creating 376
  items, removing from cart 378
event data

previewing 385

F

file components
  making 118
file download ability
  adding 130
file meta information 106
file size
  formatting 107
files
  download links, caching on 190, 191
  separating 116
  storing 241, 242
filter variables
  grouping, logically 53
  replacing 53
filtering 46
filtering component
  building, based on products 335, 336, 338, 340,
    341
filters, making component
  about 87
  component, creating 87
  custom events, used for modifying filter field 89,
    90
  filter query, updating 91, 92
  JavaScript errors, resolving 89
filters
  creating, dynamically 343, 344
  filtering 41
  preselecting, on page load 347
  resetting 345
folder components
  making 118
folder contents
  caching 158, 160, 161
folder structure
  updating 119, 120, 121
folders
  displaying, based on URL 134
  linking 119, 120, 121
  modifying, for Vue-router 208
  separating 116
form